From Jerusalem to Delhi, through Persia

From Jerusalem to Delhi, through Persia

Susan Adelman

GORGIAS PRESS

2022

Gorgias Press LLC, 954 River Road, Piscataway, NJ, 08854, USA

www.gorgiaspress.com

2022 Copyright © by Gorgias Press LLC

2022　　　ܪ

ISBN 978-1-4632-4406-4

Library of Congress Cataloging-in-Publication Data

A Cataloging-in-Publication Record is available at the Library of Congress.

Printed in the United States of America

TABLE OF CONTENTS

CONTENTS

ACKNOWLEDGEMENTS

Many people, over many years, made this book possible. In the last fifty years, my husband and I have made twenty trips to India, and we had the pleasure of spending much of that time with our life-long friend, Ram Jethmalani. Ram was a legendary lawyer, a remarkable friend, and an endless fount of stories. Not only that, he and his family introduced us to countless other people who taught us even more. But before I even met him, his daughter, my friend and colleague, Shobha Gehani M.D., was the one who originally connected us with her father on our second trip to India. Since then, Shobha traveled with us several times in India, encouraged me to write her father's biography when he reached ninety, and brought us right into the heart of the Jethmalani family, who deserve our sincere thanks for their many courtesies. I remember Shobha's sister Rani Jethmalani for her charm and dignity, and for providing us with opportunities and experiences that we could never have had otherwise. Both Ram and Rani are sorely missed.

Drs. Kanta Bhambani and Ravi Yeddanapudi, also friends for almost 50 years, have traveled with us in India, but, most important, they have taught us an incomparable amount about Indian culture during our friendship here at home, a friendship that has lasted almost for a lifetime.

Mrs. Shehernaz Joshi, the Director of Graduate and International Programs at George Washington University Law School, and a Parsi from Bombay, has been my best source for Zoroastrian information, sending me to the top literature, although any mistakes that I have made in the material are mine alone.

My husband's colleague Raj Dave played a critical role in organizing the George Washington University India Project, which took us to India seven years in a row, and he too introduced us to numerous fascinating people across India. Through that project we met an eminent Israeli scientist, Eliora Ron, now a close friend who – before Covid – we met regularly in Tel Aviv for many years, and through Eliora we met her daughter, Michal Ron. Michal introduced me to the Buddhist scene in Israel, and she has been helpful in assisting me when I wrote about it. To be clear, all errors that may remain are mine.

For listening to the entire manuscript, offering critiques, and supplementing the Jewish history, I must thank David and Sara Waldshan, friends for many years.

My Hebrew teacher, Maayan Sharet, critiqued and added to this story, as a result of her unique experience with Buddhist practice in Israel. And I would like to thank Yael Landman, Tuomas Rasimus, and Melissa Sung of Gorgias Press for all that they have done to make this book a reality. It would not have happened without them.

Throughout it all, I owe my most special thanks to my husband, Prof. Martin Adelman, who has encouraged me, whose India Project took me to India seven times, and whose conversations with Ram about legal matters were the cement in our relationship with him. In addition to Marty's teaching in India, he has taught for many years at major law schools in Israel, which has led to many friendships there and has given us deep roots in the country. Marty has added his ideas and memories to this book, critiqued it, encouraged me when I was down during the Covid epidemic, and made it all possible.

INTRODUCTION

What is it with Jews and India? Why are so many Jews drawn to a country that looks so different from theirs? Why am I so attracted to India? Could it have something to do with random memories, a fan-cooled evening on a porch in Delhi when the conversation turned to whether, after death, our spirits will be reincarnated as individuals or as part of a cloud-like, combined spirit? Are the warm miasmas of India an ideal setting for a group of strangers to slip quite naturally from casual social chatter to the deepest of spiritual questions? Would complete strangers in New York or Tel Aviv find it normal to suddenly begin discussing their deepest mystical beliefs?

In part my own mystical experiences started me on the long road that led to this book. This was not a direct road, nor did I realize I was traveling it, but the route is apparent in retrospect. And since I see it all now, I will freely admit that this book is both a personal chronicle and a product of considerable historical research. In part, I want the reader to see India through my eyes, to see why I feel such an attachment to it, and to understand why I am attracted by its philosophies. Yet I also want to explain to the reader the reason why I believe that so many Jews throughout the ages have felt this same attachment. First, allow me to begin with my story.

One day when I was a teenage summer camp counselor in New Hampshire, I took a day off to explore some narrow roads that crisscrossed the thick forest. I walked without any plan in mind, until I spotted a particularly inviting view that pulled me like a magnet. Alone and mesmerized by the beauty around me, I wandered through acres of white birch trees, marveling at the great oaks that still survived from the original virgin forest. I smelled the evergreens. Last autumn's leaves and pine needles crunched beneath my feet. Later in the afternoon, I began to think about returning to my camp, and I realized that I had no idea where the road back would be. Serenely confident in my forestry skills, I simply had walked heedlessly, assuming that I would find it. Moss always grows on the north side of the tree, doesn't it?

As the sun sank, I began looking for a landmark that I might have seen earlier in the day. The duskier the woods became, the faster I walked. What if I had to spend the night in the forest? There were no cell phones then. Would there be bears? I did not know. Were there snakes? Yes. Would I be able to see poison ivy at night without a flashlight? No. Would they be worried about me at camp? Yes.

After choosing a direction and picking up the pace, I recognized a distinctive-looking tree stump, and I realized that I had passed it at least a half hour before. I was walking in circles. Was I lost? If I continued walking, would I just keep circling? In a growing panic, I felt my breathing quicken, my face tense up. My throat constricted. I fought off the urge to cry, or to scream. After all, I could not be childish. I was 16, and I knew what I was doing, right? It was getting darker.

I sat down on a stump and prayed as I had never prayed before. I had never been a real believer. I had little interest in religious services or formal prayer. Eyes squeezed closed, fists balled up, fingernails pressed into my palms, I just begged God not to let me be lost. Afterwards, I opened my eyes. Oddly, I saw what seemed to be a pasture in front of me, and cutting through it, then vanishing into the distance, was a narrow trail, maybe an animal path. Do rabbits make paths? I had not seen this path before.

I knew I had to get up and follow the path, so I did. Soon the path became wider, and in minutes it led me to a road, the road to my camp.

This was the moment when my young self believed that there is a God. I knew little or nothing yet of war, of genocides, of

international affairs or of great national tragedies. All I had
was this, my own experience. And I never forgot.

Surely any self-respecting skeptic would take apart my story, question my observations, complain that I had not looked carefully enough before my prayer, or argue that I could not prove cause and effect. Still, none of this will ever take away the sense of awe that I felt at that time, or the prickly feeling I have now in the skin of my arms when I look back at the experience.

Without knowing it, that was when I first became a believer. In something. I called it God.

While an inexplicable spiritual experience does not prove the existence of God, it does not vanish from memory either. Behind a rational facade, many of us harbor a secret belief in God. Many of us cannot help but believe, whether it be in a mighty force that fills the universe, or in a spark of the divine nestled deep within ourselves. Some seek the answers over a lifetime. Some, probably most, do not even articulate the questions. Some find the answers within their own culture or religion, but others only find them in countries and cultures that an outsider would consider to be completely foreign.

My first trip to India just was to see textiles, vibrant colors and art. My childhood story did not come back to me right away, but it was there, under the surface, waiting for me. Somehow though, I felt an eerie sense of familiarity – with something I could not name – in India.

After my first trip, I immersed myself in Hindu and Buddhist literature. In time I began to feel guilty, as if I were a secret traitor to my religion. Still, I found this literature strangely compelling. Only when I traveled to Israel for the first time did I discover that almost everyone I met had visited India at least once, many becoming so smitten that they stayed for months. Some had taken up Buddhism or Hinduism quite seriously. In short, I was not a traitor or an outlier. To my shock, I was a typical Israeli.

It turns out that, when Israelis finish their mandatory stint in the army, they normally take off a year for travel. One favorite destination is India, and once there, many feel unaccountably drawn to the country, as if something beckons them. Conversely, increasing numbers of Indian students come to Israel to study, and they feel at home in Israel. Is there a reason?

Soon I discovered that numerous Hindu ashrams and Buddhist meditation centers in America and India have Jewish leaders, and many still identify as Jews. What has drawn them to Hinduism or Buddhism? Do these faiths resemble Judaism in some way? Or are they interesting because they are so different? If so, in what way? Are these travelers just attracted to India because many people speak English, or the living is cheap, drugs are plentiful, and it is safe? Is there more to the story?

It turns out that a whole series of interrelated religious traditions once stretched between the Mediterranean and India. In memory of that, do Jews sense an atavistic connection with India still today? Does this ancient history remain in the collective consciousness?

In today's interconnected world, India has become a popular travel destination for American Jews as well as Israelis, and once there, they often find themselves awakened in a strange way. Some of them grew up in secular environments devoid of the rich rituals that have sustained and nourished Jews for centuries. Others grew up in Orthodox religious communities that maintained their traditions, but whose rituals felt like meaningless rote exercises to their children. As a result, these children grew up spiritually thirsty.

In India, Jews find rituals aplenty, pageantry, a profusion of colors, exotic temples, holy men, spicy food, and a whole country full of people who live in an environment that supports their religious beliefs. And Jews who choose to put a toe into the waters of Hinduism or Buddhism are able to explore a whole range of spiritual possibilities, without guilt, not constricted by rules, and, with a little luck, guided by experienced spiritual advisors. In the end, they may adopt elements that are meaningful to them without giving up their own religion or formally converting.

When they return home, some may continue at least one new practice, perhaps meditation or yoga. Some shrug it all off. For others, India is a life-changing experience – a great 'aha moment.'

The combined history is important. Jews and Indians have been connected for millennia. Massive empires stretched in ancient times between the Mediterranean and India. Within these empires, languages spread, bureaucracies ruled, and religious beliefs merged, one into another, between the two poles of this vast expanse. And in the middle always was Persia.

The largest of the ancient empires were Persian. Their culture was Persian, and their dominant religion was Zoro-astrianism, a Persian faith that resembled both Judaism and Hinduism more than most of us ever realized. Jews in a Persian empire were exposed to Zoroastrian ideas, and Zoroastrians in Persia shared ideas, myths and gods with Hindus in India, thus, Jews indirectly shared with Hindus. This spectrum of religious beliefs spread organically from village to village, city to city. Meanwhile in Persia, new religions continually bubbled up for many centuries, and they flowed outwards into the neighborhood.

This discovery struck me as I wrote the book, *After Saturday Comes Sunday*.[1] While doing my research, I was amazed at the number of religions that had started in Persia, religions I had never heard of, and I decided to learn more. And it turns out that they still matter. Now I invite the reader to join me in these explorations.

We will study why India, Hinduism and Buddhism attract so many Jews, and we will discover the many links – both ancient and modern – between Israel and India. We will study how far-flung empires of the past connected the people of Israel with the people of India over thousands of years. We will learn about the spiritual connections between Judaism, Zoroastrianism, and Hinduism, and we will be on alert to see how these religions influenced each other. Throughout, we will try to understand how Persia served as the bridge between east and west, how the traditional religions of Persia contributed concepts to Judaism as it developed, and how the Zoroastrianism of Persia grew up in concert with Hinduism in India. In short, we will see that the Holy Land and India were never far apart, even though they may seem to be on the map.

Finally, we will try to answer these questions: "What are the Jews looking for in Hinduism? In Buddhism? Or in India itself?"

---

[1] Adelman, Susan, *After Saturday Comes Sunday*, (New Jersey: Gorgias Press, 2018). This book examines the last living people to still speak Aramaic – the Chaldean and Assyrian Christians and the Kurdish Jews. It also gives the history of their churches, communities and their persecutions.

CHAPTER ONE.
MY INDIA

When people hear about this book, their usual question is, "What is it about India that you like so much?"

Anyone who has never been to India might have trouble understanding the attraction. It is overcrowded with masses of people, right? You get sick there, do you not? It is strangely different from the United States, is it not? Yet there is so much to marvel at. In this chapter, I would like to start by taking you on a trip around the India that has never failed to surprise and delight me, my India.

KASHMIR

Kashmir is one of the most magnificent parts of India, surely one of the most beautiful places in the world. The Vale of Kashmir is surrounded by foothills of the Himalayas, with views of high mountains all around. In the vale is a wide lake, where magnificently carved houseboats are available to rent for short stays. The craftsmanship displayed in the markets of Kashmir is amazing – intricately carved wood furniture, fabulous carpets, richly embroidered clothes, and miniature paintings on all manner of wares. With all that beauty, Kashmir also has been the site of multiple wars between India and Pakistan because, today, most of the population is Muslim, but the rulers remain Hindu, just as they were in pre-Islamic times.

In 1981, we stayed there in a British era houseboat on Dal Lake, just outside of the capital, Srinagar. Made entirely of Kashmiri walnut, the houseboat was carved inside and out in impossibly lacey patterns, polished to a glassy surface, and completely kitted out with walnut furniture that also was carved with incredible delicacy. A cook prepared our meals; a houseman cleaned every day and helped us with our travel plans. Between excursions, we would sit on the deck, looking out at shimmering waters dotted with flowers and bordered by more houseboats. Around us we could feel the looming presence of the Himalayas. Even hidden by clouds, we knew they were there.

Boatmen would paddle by in shikaras, the characteristic small vessels of Kashmir, hawking "fil-lim, choc-o-lat," or anything else that they could bring by boat, much as traders must have done for thousands of years. One day a man pulled up and offered to sell me emeralds. Intrigued, I let him come aboard. Opening his suitcase, he showed me numerous small cloudy stones the pale yellow-green color of dying seaweed. After looking patiently through them and under considerable pressure from the salesman, I finally told him that I am an expert on stones, and I knew that these were not good specimens.

Indignantly he pulled himself up and said, "Madam. Do you think that I would come out in the middle of a lake with *good* emeralds?"

One day the cook and houseman asked permission to visit a woman from their village who was in the hospital after delivering a baby. When they returned, I asked how the mother and baby were. They answered that they had been asked to go to the pharmacy to buy medicine for the baby because he was sick. I forgot about the baby between our fabulous sightseeing trips. When I asked again a couple of days later, they shrugged, "Oh, he died."

I was a pediatric surgeon. I was horrified, thinking that I should have gone to see the baby, and I should have asked them if the situation was critical. But this was oriental fatalism, which could lead to inaction, or to wisdom. The opposite of Jewish activism, it shocked me. Did our cultures have anything in common?

Kashmir is divided between India and Pakistan. A piece of it was snatched by China in 1962, and periodically China flexes its muscles, trying to grab another bite. Meanwhile, the conflict between India and Pakistan waxes and wanes, with every threat by a prime minister or an election a potential provocation. While we were there, there was impending war in Kashmir. The people seemed perfectly happy to take our tourist dollars, but an almost palpable hostility was in the air.

Before we left home, a Kashmiri colleague in Detroit had urged us to call her family once we arrived. We called, and they instantly invited us over. It turns out that this family had been the ruling family until recently. Now they were out of power. Not surprisingly, they had a huge family compound full of elaborate dwellings, clearly once richly appointed, now run-down. It looked like all the swag now must be going to their successors, and they no longer could keep up as munificently as they did during their glory days.

They asked us what we wanted to do first, and I said I wanted to shop. They offered to take us to merchants who they knew, and they ushered us into a caravan of large black cars. At each shop, all the cars stopped, all the doors opened, and out of each door came men in black. We felt like we were in a Mafia movie. Not surprisingly, without our Mafiosa saying much, all the merchants showed us their best wares, and we received excellent discounts.

That evening we were invited to the family compound, where we entered a building that was supposed to have been the home of the former prime minister. In fact, his actual home was closed and boarded up. We sat in one room of a dark, dank building with low light, only one visible servant and little food on the table. The room was dingy, the furniture old, the carpet worn. Our host was not accompanied by other family members, and he explained that the family fortunes had fallen. This was obvious. The atmosphere was oppressive. This was not my India.

But we did shop. We were floored by the elegance of the crafts, the woodcarving, woven rugs, and the paper-mache. Even my husband, who normally loathes shopping, became a shopping fool. We bought a coffee table that surely was created by a master carver. The top is very deeply carved with a Chinese dragon, executed with skill and elegance. It was large though, and we had to ship it. Later in our trip we met someone who told us about buying Kashmiri furniture that never arrived.

At the airport we talked with an American expatriate living in Bangkok, and she told us that she had ordered a set of furniture from Kashmir before moving into a new apartment. Once installed, she began hearing a 'ping' every night. She searched the apartment. She called the landlord. Nothing explained it. At last she inspected her beautiful new Kashmiri furniture, and she saw that it was made of unseasoned wood that was progressively splitting in her centrally heated apartment. Fortunately, our table came safely; it has never gone ping, and we love it.

Oh, and did I mention that we came home with six hand-woven rugs that my husband bought – the husband who hates shopping – in Kashmir, in a frenzy of enthusiasm?

Before we get too serious, I must admit that a part of the magic of India, a part that books on philosophy and sociology omit, is the shopping. There is something unique about the crafts, textiles, embroidering, prints and wood carving that is unparalleled almost anywhere. The silk is incomparable. The color combinations are ones that nobody else would ever even imagine, but, surprisingly, they are just perfect. The workmanship itself is not perfect. You can see flaws. You can see the artist striving, maybe producing something that looks a bit primitive, yet it is intensely sophisticated. The needlecraft is done with great skill, but not with the soulless perfection of the embroidery in many East Asian countries, where the stitches can barely be seen with the naked eye. Indian work has a soul, and that soul is the essence of its magic.

PAST LIVES AND OTHER MYSTICISM

When we first traveled to south India, my husband and I visited Madras and Mahabalipuram in Tamil Nadu, a southeast Indian coastal state punctuated by dramatic temples topped by massive *gopuram* towers. Years later, we returned to India with a group of lawyers. This time, our friends arranged for us to fly to Madras (now Chennai), and from there to take a bus to a fabulous pilgrimage temple in Andra Pradesh, Tirupati. On the way they told us that this one temple hosts more pilgrims a year than Mecca. As I followed the map, I realized that our route passed by a famous temple city, Kanchipuram. In great excitement, I asked if we could stop in Kanchipuram, because a temple there had made a powerful impression on me on our previous visit, and I wanted to see it again. My husband objected, insisting we had never been to Kanchipuram. I answered that we had, on our first trip to Madras. "No, we have never been to Kanchipuram," he asserted, with the firm certainty of a lawyer.

With equal confidence, I insisted that we had. No we had not, pressed my husband. I convinced our hosts to stop in Kanchipuram though. Upon arrival, they asked me which temple I wanted to see. I did not know the name, but I remembered exactly what it looked like. I was sure I would recognize it. We asked around in the city, and we were sent to two or three temples. The first two were not what I remembered. The third one was.

The moment I saw it, I knew. It was just as I remembered it. Most distinctive were the rows and rows of columns marching down long shadowy corridors in a wide hall. I learned later that it is called the Temple of 1000 Pillars, though the formal name is Ekambareswarar Temple, one of the largest in India. Anyhow it was clear to me that this was the temple, even if my husband was sure we never had seen it, and we had never been to Kanchipuram. Even today, as I write, I see it in my mind, with absolute specificity.

On our second trip to India, in 1971, my husband and I met the famed senior Indian lawyer, Ram Jethmalani. He already was Chairman of the Bar Council of India, and he was one of the most renowned lawyers in the country. Later he became Law Minister and a member of Parliament for some 40 years. A major figure in our lives, he was our dear friend for over 45 years, until his death at almost 95. I have written of his life in *The Rebel: A biography of Ram Jethmalani*. One year, I told Ram my story of the temple of 1000 pillars. He listened, and he declared immediately that I had been a South Indian in a previous life.

My husband and I had first gone to India as tourists in 1971, but the vagaries of Indian air travel confined us to northern India. On our return in 1973, we were able to visit Trivandrum, the capital of Kerala, a tropical southwestern coastal state graced by peaceful, palm-shaded backwaters. On the shore of the Arabian

Sea, the pure white sand of Kovalam Beach stretches north from the city of Trivandrum for hundreds of miles, traditionally considered the most beautiful beach in India. Though now the tourist industry has sullied it, then it was pristine. Palm trees fringed the beach, and just beyond them were the backwaters, long lazy streams of water thick with tropical vegetation. A boat trip along them passed tiny villages with women squatting on the ground, pounding coconuts. Along the way we saw little artificial islands made of coconut husks, and on these islands the villagers had planted crops.

On our first morning walk along the beach, not far from Trivandrum, we saw two hippies rouse themselves from their overnight sleep, stretch, and get ready for the day, the girl industriously picking sand out of her blond pubic hair as the local men peeped out from behind the palm trees.

The villagers of Kerala are fishermen. We remember the crew that hauled their old wooden boat to shore with heavy hemp ropes, pulling in rhythm with a fisherman's chant that they sang in deep men's voices, a haunting melody they surely learned from their fathers, who learned it from their fathers. That was my India.

We also explored the city, where we passed by a small temple that had particularly beautiful carvings covering the *gopuram*. It was not a temple that was featured in any tourist book, and – not knowing its name – the next time we visited we could not find it, but the sculpture was exceptionally fine. Next to the temple sat a mammoth wooden wagon, also covered with carving. I pointed out the chariot to my husband.

I explained that this was a temple chariot, called a *juggernaut*, and that on festival days they hoist the temple god up onto it for a processional parade around the city. My husband nodded. At the end of the day when we returned to the hotel, I reviewed in my mind all the sights we had seen, and I began to think about the temple chariot. With a start, I realized that I never had read anything about any temple chariot, anywhere, and that I never had heard the name *juggernaut* applied to such a thing. Had I made it all up? Yet it seemed so real, so obvious to me.

I told that story to Ram Jethmalani. He confirmed that a *juggernaut* was a temple chariot, and it was used exactly in the way that I had described. Later, I remembered the word juggernaut, and a bit of research revealed that this is the name of a huge chariot belonging to the Jagannatha Temple in Puri, the capital of the state of Orissa (Odisha). This chariot does go out on procession, and one of the gods it carries is called Jagannatha, an alternate name for the god Krishna, the Lord of the World. Ram repeated that I surely had been a South Indian in a past life.

Some Indians have records of past lives, or at least of their own family's past. In Detroit one of my fellow surgical residents told me that he once had visited a wise man who kept a book that recorded his family history, going back a thousand years. I tried to research this remarkable tale. It seems that Brahmin pandits in the Hindu holy city of Haridwar do keep such genealogy records, some dating back more than 20 generations. No wonder. Haridwar is quite special, the location of the Kumbh Mela. Ram's daughter Rani visited it in 2010, returning to tell us ecstatically about the millions – rich, poor, holy and less holy – who gather every 12 years for ritual bathing in the Ganges at this very spot, for this is the place where pious Hindus believe that the elixir of immortality spilled when the celestial bird Garuda carried it over the Ganges in a pitcher.

This kind of mysticism feels perfectly believable in India, entirely normal. Could millions of Indians all be wrong? And could millions of Indians be wrong about their other practices, about meditation, for instance? I knew they could not be, so after years of hearing about it, I thought that it would be possible for me just to sit down and meditate. But then again, as I was to find, maybe not.

MY MEDITATION

Let me tell a more recent personal story. In between my many trips to India, I read copiously about Hinduism and Buddhism, and I practiced a bit of yoga; I had never attempted any serious meditation. One day I learned why you do not do deep meditation without knowing what you are doing.

After many years as a surgeon, I became involved in national medical politics, moving up the political ladder until I was elected to the Board of Trustees of the American Medical Association. Finally, I needed to be reelected to the Board in order to progress further. That last election did not go well, and suddenly I was off the board. Moreover, I had retired in anticipation of my election. I suddenly went from being unbelievably busy to even more unbelievably unemployed. The shock to my system was stunning.

It took me some time to reconstitute myself. I continued to attend a few medical meetings though, and at a dinner one evening I began talking with a medical society executive, who asked me what had happened with my election and how I was doing. I told him that I was not doing very well. I probably needed to do something like meditation. In truth I never had been instructed or guided in meditative techniques, but I could not help thinking that all these years of exposure to the culture, religion, philosophy and general gestalt of meditation might be enough background for me. Desperate to calm my anxieties, but loathe to actually engage in the meditation practices of another religion, I said that I felt meditation might help, but Hindu or Buddhist meditation, the only forms I knew anything about, seemed wrong for me.

He said, "But there is such a thing as Jewish meditation." He and his wife even held Jewish meditation sessions in their home in another city. He offered me a book to guide me in Jewish meditation. I took him up on it.

One day when I was alone in the house, I put the book on my easel, opened it to a centerfold that depicted the four-letter Hebrew name of God, turned down the lights and sat down to meditate. After a while, the four letters appeared to lift off the pages and sort of dance, or at least wobble. I sensed that they would move if asked, and I knew immediately what I wanted to ask them to do.

I knew of the work of Dr. Elisabeth Kubler-Ross, a Swiss-American psychiatrist who wrote a book called On Death and Dying. In her book, Dr. Kubler-Ross described patients who had died but who came back to life. And when they returned, they reported that they had seen a great light. As they moved toward it, someone they knew had come to greet them. It might have been their spouse, a parent, or even Jesus, but someone did arrive to show them the way. That light was what I wanted to see.

Now the letters began to move, and I followed them. I was not asleep, but awake, as if in a trance. And I saw that light, distant, but not that far. Soon, my father came to greet me, looking as he had when he was middle-aged. He was tender, but not overly emotional, much as he always had been. After we greeted one another, he began to walk next to me, and we walked side by side, toward the light. Suddenly I looked over at him, and I could see him becoming transparent. At that moment I realized that I too was about to become transparent. Then I knew that, if we continued in that direction, I would die.

With all the strength I could muster, I tried to pull myself out of the vision, gritting my teeth, straining, fighting to wrestle myself free. At last I came out of it, thankfully alive, my father presumably gone back to meet me another day. Long afterward, I worked up the courage to ask an Indian colleague whether anyone had ever died in the course of that sort of meditation. "Oh yes," he answered, "it has happened. That is why we wear a copper bracelet when we know we are going to do deep meditation. It anchors us here." I was not sure about all that, but I knew that I had been completely unprepared for deep meditation. I was quite sure that I almost died that day.

It took me two years before I could paint that vision on canvas, and that was the beginning of my cure. I returned to painting, which I had stopped for several years. I became a full-time artist, starting with family paintings based on old sepia-colored photos, and then I moved on to portraits, landscapes, a variety of themes. I did not meet that medical executive again. Even the book I had meditated on seems to have vanished.

Despite my once reaching into spiritual realms for which I was unprepared, my attachment to India deepened over time, the most important connections becoming those with the Jethmalani family. Not only did we see Ram when he came to Michigan to visit his daughter Shobha once or twice a year, but we also saw him on our trips to India, some with Shobha. On those trips, I found my India.

MUMBAI, DELHI AND JETHMALANIS

It was my India the day that I walked out of the elegant Jehangir Art Gallery in the most fashionable, artsy part of Mumbai only to see an itinerant holy man walking calmly by on the crowded sidewalk, absolutely naked, a blanket slung over one shoulder, absentmindedly scratching his behind, seemingly unnoticed by anybody but me.

These are the contrasts. In 2014, I released my biography of Ram. It was my immense good fortune to have it published by Penguin Random House under the personal mark of Shobhaa De, an uber-glamorous author, a former model and a figure widely known in India for her risqué books. My book launch was elegant, as befits high society in India. Held in the vast yard of Ram's government house in Delhi, they had built a stage for the occasion, the drapes color-coordinated with my pink dress. Several hundred seats were set out for the audience, all decorated with white cloth and adorned with bows of the same pink. The guest speaker was the Chief Justice of India. Ram spoke, and, to the delight of the audience, so did Shobhaa De.

The event was attended by judges, members of the government and invitees from India's intelligentsia. One notable attendee was L.K. Advani, a former Prime Minister originally from Sindh with whom Ram recently had a public falling-out. Pictures of him sitting next to Ram at the event were all over the papers the next day. I do not remember seeing any pictures of me, but we all were thrilled, nonetheless.

Another year, Ram's daughter Shobha flew with us from Delhi up to the Punjabi city of Amritsar, the home of the Sikh Golden Temple. The plan was to stop there, then to drive to Dharamshala, where the Dalai Lama makes his home. When we arrived at the Amritsar airport, five huge turbaned policemen welcomed us and escorted us to our hotel. This was to show their respect for Ram, who had represented Punjabi interests in the past. They were in a hurry, and we realized we were being rushed to the Golden Temple, urged past a long crowd of people all along the bridge that leads to the temple. Our policemen were some of the largest men we had ever seen, and they packed guns. The crowd let us go by. Then the policemen pushed us through the door of the temple, just as it closed.

We squeezed into whatever sitting room we could find on the floor, and soon one woman plopped herself firmly on one of my feet. As the Sikh service started, our companions made sure we noticed that there were no graven images in the temple. The service started with preliminaries, and then it moved to the centerpiece, a ceremonial reading from the *Granth*, the Sikh holy book. After the service ended, they took us on a tour through the temple, where we saw the Sikhs treat their holy book with the same reverence that Jews show to the Torah. In fact, we learned that at their services they regularly read portions of the Granth, just as Jews read a *parsha* of the Torah at their services.

Shobha told us that her mother – even though she was not Sikh – used to read a portion of the Granth every morning, as religious Jews will study a portion of Torah every day. We further discovered that Sikhs reject the polytheism of Hinduism, and they believe in one God. In fact, it was difficult to find any significant conflict between these Sikh beliefs and practices and our own Jewish practices, except that they use a different book. Now this truly was my India, and even my husband's.

It was clear that I needed to study more about this. Fortunately, our police presented us with six small books that outlined the history and beliefs of the Sikh religion. We will return to this later.

But now before we leave, we should mention former U.S. Ambassador Nikki Haley here, an outspoken advocate for Israel during her tenure at the UN. Notably, while today she is a Christian, she comes from a Sikh background. People have wondered why she was such a staunch defender of Israel, but it is not hard to figure out. Her family values must have resembled those of the Jewish community, and her family must have had first-hand knowledge of the trials the Sikhs endured during the partition of India.

On that same trip, our Sikh policemen escorted us to Dharamshala, the home of the Dalai Lama. Of course, they really came with us just as a courtesy, but they came in handy during a traffic jam along the way. After what seemed like an interminable wait, they left their car, cocked their rifles and went to the front of the line. Miraculously, traffic resumed immediately. Then when we reached the hotel, the former palace of the maharaja, the clerk asked for our passports. My husband said, "You better return them. See those big guys out there?" He returned them promptly.

Typical of India, we were installed ceremoniously in the maharaja's suite and Shobha in the maharani's suite, amid great faded opulence. This was wintertime in the Himalayas, and it was freezing. In our suites we luxuriated with space heaters and with hot water bottles under the covers, but the bathrooms had no such amenities. In the next few days, we met the Karmapa, and toured the Tibetan Buddhist monasteries there in fascination, my husband with a very luxurious cold.

In 1992 we traveled to Hampi at a time of violent unrest in the north, though Hampi was unaffected down in south India. We traveled there by overnight train from Bangalore with Ram, a companion of his, and our friends from home, Kanta and Ravi. Along the way we munched on Indian train snacks. When we toured the 16 square mile archeological site at Hampi, a guide explained that it was the ancient capital of the 14th century Vigayanagara Empire, a Hindu kingdom that had covered south India until the 16th century. After that, the jungle reclaimed the site.

Archaeologists had unearthed examples of monumental architecture, and we saw elaborately carved scenes of the Ramayana covering the magnificent Vittala Temple. Still, most of the monuments were still slumbering quietly beneath tropical vegetation. Villagers had built little houses among the ruins, and we would see a dwelling here, a shop there, built into the old stone walls. These old stone piles and the town of Hampi were cozily nestled together, comfortable, not showy, unchanged for tourists or anyone else. At each turn of the road, one saw a fragment of a wall, or perhaps an arch, through the vines and trees. We simply noticed, and drove on. Since then, Hampi has been discovered by the tourism industry, but what we saw was my India.

All this archeology was comfortably distant; it was history, just romantic artifacts. In my mind, none of it related to anything religious. As an artist and sculptor, I loved the art, the workmanship, but nothing more. Right?

THERE WERE TIMES WHEN I FELT LIKE A TRAITOR TO MY OWN RELIGION.

At first, I saw no relationship between intricately carved Indian temples and any beliefs of mine. Their religion was theirs. Art was art. Craft was craft. Obviously, I did not worship images of anyone's gods. There was no reason to feel any conflict. Yet occasionally this blithe assumption was tested.

On a trip to Nepal in 1981, I bought a simple ring that had a blue ceramic disc with a molded image of an Indian god. The ring was not expensive, just a souvenir. The idea of it being an idol barely entered my mind. I obviously did not believe in the god; I just liked the ring. When I returned home, one day I wore the ring while working in the kitchen. Suddenly, as I scraped food off a plate into the disposal, the ring fell off my finger right into the running disposal, and it was ground up. Never had I had a ring fall off in my life. The band had not been loose.

All I could do was look up toward the sky and complain: 'Now what was that all about? You know perfectly well that I did not believe in that god; I only wore the ring as an ornament. That was absolutely unnecessary.' Nevertheless, I still am afraid to wear the other piece of jewelry that I bought at the same time, a beautiful necklace that also features an Indian god. I know in my heart that I do not worship it as an idol, but, then again...

Is it superstition? Yes, in part. Was my reaction a relic of beliefs from my own upbringing? I was brought up as far from Orthodox as possible. Nobody in my family ever would have noticed this ring. Did it reflect my knowledge of the Ten Commandments? As it says in Exodus 20:3–6, "You shall not make for yourself any graven image, nor any manner of likeness, of anything that is heaven above, or that is in the earth beneath, or that is in the water under the earth. You shall not bow down to them, nor serve them." Most likely. The bible itself says that God is a jealous God. I feared retribution.

I might have been reassured had I known about a passage in the Talmud, Avodah Zara 3:4, in which a rabbi teaches that someone who goes naked or performs unclean actions in front of an image clearly does not regard this image as a god. The teaching is: "what is treated as a god is prohibited, what is not treated as a deity is permitted." Then again, there is much I did not know.

When I first traveled in India, not only did I not know much about the Sikh religion, I had never heard of the Jain religion. Soon though, I saw their work. We will save a discussion of the religion for later, but my first impression was of their pristine temples.

JAIN TEMPLES

Jain temples are among the most spectacular that we have seen in India. We have seen several, but one of the finest is at Mt. Abu, and we were lucky enough to see it on a trip through the Rajasthan Desert. It was intricately carved inside and out of pure white marble; the lacey interior of the dome was an experience in beauty. Another Jain site was in the southern state of Karnataka. There, young enough not to worry about our feet, we hiked barefoot up the 500 steps to the massive Jain Gomateshwara statue. Carved in the image of a man 42 feet high out of a solid block of granite, it is the largest monolithic statue in the world. Said to be over a thousand years old, it is situated in the middle of a large temple complex. The dominant impression it made was that it was the most absolutely naked, exposed, figure we have ever seen, and it loomed up toward the sky like an Art Nouveau giant.

Hinduism, Buddhism, Sikhism and Jainism all are important religions of India, but so is Islam. Of all the countries in the world, the one with the largest Muslim population is Indonesia; the second is Pakistan, and the third is India. Despite the partition into Muslim Pakistan and Hindu India, India remains 13% Muslim, and that means 195 million people.

MUSLIM INDIA

In 1973, a Detroit colleague suggested that on a coming trip to India we should call on his relatives, who lived in Kerala, a southwest Indian state that had a mixture of Hindus, Christians and Muslims. Our hosts turned out to be Muslim. They invited us for dinner, but I felt them hesitate briefly before asking. That evening, to our discomfort, the men were ushered in to dine first, the women later. We found out later that even some conservative Hindu homes followed this custom, but it was our first exposure to it. We felt uncomfortable. The conversation did not flow well. The atmosphere seemed a bit reserved. It was just a feeling we had.

That was completely different from our encounter in 1973 with a young Hindu couple at a New Year's Eve buffet in the newly opened Taj Mahal Coromandel Hotel in Madras. When we met them, we began talking, and they told us that her mother was a retired obstetrician. Once they knew I was a doctor, the invitation came immediately to come to their house for dinner and to meet her mother. At dinner, the mother invited me to come with her the next day to the local women's hospital where she was invited to demonstrate a surgical procedure.

After the operation, we gathered in the surgical lounge with the young residents, all wearing their white operating room saris, to talk about health care in their institution. By the by, when I asked whether they had the capability to do blood transfusions, they answered that their patients were wives, and the husbands were likely to refuse transfusions, saying that it would be cheaper to just get another wife. The following day, before we went off on a scheduled weekend side trip, the same young couple offered to let us leave our extra suitcase with them until we came back, and it was there, safe and sound, when we came back. We felt exactly like part of the family. That was my India, not the dinner in Kerala.

The same year that we visited Hampi, we traveled with Kanta and Ravi to south India at a time when north India had just erupted with a sudden sectarian conflict between Muslims and Hindus. Trains were attacked in Bombay. Air traffic was in complete disarray. Kanta's family warned her not to get on the train she used to take when she was a schoolgirl in Bombay, and Ravi was not able to travel from Bombay to the conference in Calcutta that he had come to attend. We went down south, but none of us were sure how we were going to get back to Bombay and connect with our flights home. Meanwhile, when we arrived in Hyderabad, Ravi proposed a walk through the city center, where he would show us his old medical school and the area where he used to live.

Hyderabad has the highest percentage of Muslims of any large city in south India, and this was a time of violent sectarian conflict in northern India. We set out on a walk toward the market, and Ravi pointed out the *Charminar*, the landmark mosque with four minarets that is the symbol of the city. The market was quiet, not bustling with the riotous colors and noise of the Indian cities we were used to seeing. The air felt fraught, presumably a reflection of the tension up north. People on the streets seemed drawn into themselves, walking by quickly with a purpose. They were not standing about and chatting in groups as is usual in India. We upped our pace unconsciously, looking in all directions, uncomfortable. We had the same feeling my husband and I once had in Morocco at a time when everyone wore a hooded wool djellaba and floated silently along nameless alleys in the medina, not even nodding to a passerby. So it was here. This was not my India.

All that notwithstanding, I must talk about the first time I saw the Taj Mahal, an Islamic marvel. From across the broad lawn it looked like an exquisite music box, small, perfect. As we approached, we saw that it was huge, but the proportions were so ideal that it did not seem large until one came right up to it. The entire building was pure white marble, and inside were lace-like screens lavishly set with precious stones. Then, as we looked more closely, we realized that the screens too were of white marble, carved into impossibly delicate filigree patterns. This Islamic architecture is the apogee of all the monumental buildings in northern India.

Friends have asked us if India is too dirty to visit. A Japanese judge on our India Project trip for law professors and judges was frightened to pieces by his doctor in Japan before he left. The doctor told him that he probably would get deathly sick in India. Well, he did not. In fact, the judge had the time of his life, loved the trip and returned to join us on our next trip the following year.

That is the same judge who was sitting in a conference room while Indian panelists with very thick accents were speaking, when I slipped into a seat next to him. "Can you understand them?" I asked quietly. With a beautiful, gentle smile, he answered, "Not a single word."

AND RATS

When we went to Nepal and its capital, Katmandu, even our Bombay friends warned us that those places would be dirty! We knew it was a bad sign if the Bombay people called them dirty. It became clear on our first visit to a temple. As usual, we took off our shoes before entering, walked in barefoot, and proceeded to the middle of the courtyard where an idol sat on the floor surrounded by offerings of food and flowers. And at its feet, gobbling down the offerings were rats, large, black, and jostling for the best treats. The local worshippers seemed lost in contemplation of the idol. We were lost in contemplation of the rats.

On one trip we stayed in a former palace, its regal restaurant decorated in white stucco carved into elaborate patterns, carefully painted gold and white. As we were eating, I noticed something black scurry across the floor. Calling over the waiter, I told him I had seen a rat. He appeared not to understand. With my hand I mimed a critter running across the table. "Oh, mouse," he said.

"No," I said. "Not mouse. Rat."

UNTOUCHABLES AND CAVE MASTERPIECES

On our second visit to India, when we met Ram, he reviewed our travel plans and rerouted us so that we would visit friends and colleagues of his in every city we were planning to visit. In Aurangabad, the jumping off place for visits to the wondrous cave temples at Ajanta and Ellora, he sent us to meet a law school dean. When we met the dean, he told us that it was a law school for untouchables, and that they were going to dedicate a new law school building the next day. We spent a very enjoyable evening that night at his home, where he showed us pictures and proudly told us about the untouchable jurist, Bhimrao Ramj Ambedkar, who was famous for writing the Indian constitution. He also told us that the law school is named in honor of Ambedkar. Thrilled that a keynote speaker seemingly had dropped down from heaven, the dean insisted that my husband be the featured speaker the next day. The topic he requested was the American civil rights law. My husband was an expert on patent law. He said yes.

The next morning, we arrived at the dedication site in time to see a newly painted sign at the entrance, announcing the keynote speaker: Eminent Personality, Prof. Martin J Adelman, Wayne State University Law School. To begin the ceremony, my husband was told to follow the dean and to put rose petals in basins of water placed in front of two statues. The audience humbly squatted on the floor in front of us. In his booming voice, my husband asked, "I recognize Ambedkar, but who is the other one?" Very courteously, the dean said, "Lord Buddha." Nobody even tittered. At lunch, when I made a joke about my husband not recognizing Lord Buddha, they roared with laughter.

Just a note of explanation. Ambedkar himself converted to Buddhism, as did many from the untouchable caste, so they would no longer carry the stigma of that word. The Ambedkar Law School now has nothing about untouchables on its website, nor do any of the several other law schools that carry his name in India. In many cases, members of this community have converted to other religions, especially to Christianity, but this entire movement to reject the caste system in India is beyond our purview.

That evening we were invited for dinner at the apartment of another faculty member, where we were discomfited to see a huge beehive hanging in front of the door leading from the dining room to the balcony. The family told us it is considered a sign of good luck, and they just shrugged it off. "Just don't bump into it, because they know us, but they do not know you," they said.

The caves we visited over the next two days were among the most memorable sights we have ever seen. The Ajanta caves are one of the oldest Buddhist sites in the world, commenced between the first and second centuries BCE, and finished in the fifth century CE. Over the centuries, Buddhist monks carved some 30 caves into a basalt hillside, covering the interiors with paintings of gods and divine legends. While much paint has chipped off, the combination of man-made cave and multicolor murals, lit briefly by a flashlight, is brilliant.

At Ellora, another UNESCO World Heritage site, from 600 to 1000 CE, Hindu, Jain and Buddhist monks carved more than 100 caves into another hill, creating temples that look just they had been built out of individual blocks of stone. The masterpiece is cave number 16, the Kailasanatha Cave, though it is not a cave. Here, the monks started from the top of the cliff and chiseled down, leaving in place a large, heavily ornamented temple, a towering gopuram, a rococo stone pillar and numerous statues of elephants, all carved from a single cliff.

GODMEN, PERHAPS GURUS

Ram once told us he had four gods as clients. In fact, they were what Indians call godmen, by which they usually mean sketchy characters who profess holiness but show a decidedly unholy interest in young nubile followers and in collecting money. The more highly respected of these men are more commonly called gurus. The youngest of the gods who Ram represented was to give a lecture one evening, and Ram suggested we come with him to listen. The entire area must have been the size of several football fields, and the audience sat hip to hip on the ground as far as we could see. The godman was enthroned several stories high on an elaborate, brightly lit dais larger than the screen of a drive-in theater. We were ushered to the front into an area that had sofas and carpets for westerners. The godman began to speak, in Hindi. His cadence was hypnotic. Next to me was a rapt young western man, eyes closed, apparently lost in the flow of words. I asked if he understood. Yes, he sighed. Did he speak Hindi? Well, he admitted, maybe he understood 10%, maybe less. But he was mesmerized.

A MIRACLE

Then there was the miracle. My friend's sister contracted Hepatitis C while at home in India and, many years later, went into liver failure. In the last stages, close to death, she came to the U.S., then went to London to say goodbye to a friend before returning to Bombay to die. In London, her friend took one look at her and asked what happened. Once she heard the diagnosis, she said she was friends with the best liver surgeon in the U.K, and she called him on her cell phone. My friend's sister was in his office the next day.

He hospitalized her immediately, gave her the nutritional support, vitamins and everything else she needed, to prepare her for a liver transplant. The problem was that, since she was not a British national, she had no priority in the queue for a transplant, but they continued hoping. My friend went to London once she knew her sister's situation. Her sister had brought a servant with her, and the servant stayed at her side in the hospital. Time passed, but no liver. She rapidly was approaching the point of no return.

One day the servant called from the hospital, "Madam, they have just taken her away." My friend was almost, but not quite, prepared. "What time did she die?" she asked. "No," replied the servant. "They have taken her away for surgery."

Right outside the hospital there had been an auto accident, and the victim's blood type would only match the blood of an Indian. This was the liver she was about to receive. And it gave her fifteen more years of life. Those of us who lived this story believe in miracles to this day.

These stories are of my India, beautiful, wondrous, funny, disquieting, poor, lavish, exotic, mystic, and occasionally miraculous. These marvels, and my friends, have drawn me back to India, again and again. But so many other Jews have felt the same pull. Why? Many Jews initially travel from America and Israel simply to visit India; then they stay, leave, return, study an Indian religion, and visit again. What is the attraction? Moreover, many have studied the wisdom of India without ever leaving their home countries, and some of these studies have become life changing. Besides the visitors and besides the seekers of spiritual knowledge though, there are Jews who simply have lived in India for generations. What brought them to India? What has held them? We will meet many Jews from all the groups above, but, first, let us start now by meeting the Indian Jews.

Chapter Two.
The Jews of India

When I began writing this book, I was thinking primarily about American Jews and Israelis who are attracted to India, to Hinduism, or to Buddhism, people like me. What are they looking for? Why India? Then, I remembered that Jews have lived in India for centuries. Long before any of us in the west ever knew anything about India, they were there. Eventually most of them left, many for Israel. What about them? What can they tell us? Soon I realized that, before we meet a whole succession of Jewish travelers, we should meet the Indian Jews.

Recently I told an Israeli Hebrew teacher that I was writing this book. Oh yes, she said, her mother is from Calcutta. We will learn more now about Jews like her mother.

It should not be surprising that Jews have been coming to India for centuries. Historically Israel and India have been joined by many links from the time of the Old Testament, of Darius the Great of Persia, and of the early Hindu Vedas. Of great relevance, in ancient days, these lands lay within enormous, sprawling Persian Empires; the Silk Road connected Mediterranean lands to China; the Royal Road connected Persia with India, and the folk tales of each of these contiguous lands passed imperceptibly into the myths of the next.

In the chapters that follow, we will study these empires and their religions, but first we should learn how Jews could have lived in India for millennia, experiencing no prejudice apart from the brief period when the Portuguese imported the Inquisition to Goa. But then it left. India was not hospitable to an Inquisition.

She just swallowed it up, leaving no vestige behind, and the Jews of India remained, continuing to live undisturbed.

The first that my husband and I heard of this community was in 1994 when Ram told us about the White Jews of Cochin. He explained that they are called White Jews because they never intermarried. In contrast, he said, other Jews had fully assimilated, becoming the color of the other Indians around them. It was not until many years later that we asked any questions about this.

Jews came to India from many places, for many reasons, long before any backpacking Israelis or venturesome Americans ever showed up. They came for refuge, and they came for commerce. The first Jews came to India in the tenth century BCE, in the time of King Solomon, as traders, and some may have stayed, although we know little about them. The next group came seeking safety after the destruction of the Jewish Second Temple in 70 CE, and they followed traditional trade routes to the western Indian coast; this is the Malabar Coast of the Arabian Sea, facing toward the Middle East. The trip took forty days, if they took advantage of the monsoon winds. Next, Jews came in the Middle Ages as spice traders. Others may have come through Yemen during the Persian persecutions of the fifth century. In the ninth century and later, Jewish traders traveled between Cairo and South Asia, by way of Arabia, north Africa, and the Nile River. This trade has been called the backbone of medieval international commerce, and evidence of all this commercial activity piled up in the form of letters, bills of lading, and other business records in the Genizah of the Ben Ezra Synagogue in Cairo.[1]

In the 14th through 16th centuries, Jews came to India from Spain, Portugal, the Middle East and the Ottoman Empire. Some were Portuguese Jews who escaped the Inquisition, fled to Amsterdam, and then traveled to India. They built their first synagogues in India in the 1500s, ironically, just as the Portuguese arrived in Goa. Some Jews came from Majorca. The Sephardic (Spanish and Portuguese) Jews who came after the

---

[1] Hoffman, Adina and Cole, Peter, *Sacred Trash: The lost and found world of the Cairo Geniza,* (New York: Schocken Books, 2011).

expeditions of Vasco da Gama in the sixteenth century were called Paradesi Jews.[2] These became the so-called White Jews of Cochin. Their Sanskrit name, Paradesi, comes from the local word for foreigner. Another group went to Madras, where they formed a merchant community that dealt in diamonds and precious stones. By the seventeenth century, Jewish mercantile centers were established in Madras, Calicut, and many other ports.[3]

COCHIN

According to their story, the Cochin Jews are descended from the tribe of Manasseh, one of the original 12 Tribes of Israel. They first disembarked in India at the port of Cranganore on the Malabar Coast, but later they moved 35 km south to Cochin, in the state of Kerala.

Ram told us a story that he had heard about the first Jews to arrive in Cochin. When the Jews explained to the maharaja who they were and what they believed, the maharaja said, "This sounds like a good religion indeed. Please, feel welcome. I invite you to put your god up right here on this shelf, next to ours." In their explanations, the Jews may have omitted the part about not being allowed to worship graven images.

Apparently, they made a good impression, because the maharaja granted the Jewish community broad property rights, the right to build synagogues, and the right to live in freedom. These rights were commemorated on historic copper plates, dated 1000 CE, long displayed in a synagogue on an island off the shore of Cochin.

The truth is that we really are not sure when the Cochin Jews came to India. More recent discoveries suggest that this entire origin story is more legend than verified fact. More likely,

---

[2] Blady, Ken, *Jewish Communities in Exotic Places*, (North Bergen, Jason Aronson, Inc., 2000), pp. 230–45.

[3] Weil, Shalva, 'Where are Cochin Jews Today?',
http://cochinsyn.com/page-cultural-
where.html#:~:text=The%20interior%20of%20the%20Kadavumbagam
%20synagogue%20from%20Cochin,were%20originally%20from%20the
%20Parur%20synagogue%20in%20Kerala.'
The introduction to her book discusses much of this material.

different populations of Jews came at differing times, either fleeing from danger, or just settling in convenient trading outposts for business reasons. Western visitors usually are told that there were two populations, as we were told, the so-called White Jews, or Paradesi, and the so-called Black Jews, the Malabari Jews of Cochin. A more recent theory is that they arrived in different eras, with different histories, and Indian culture promptly fit each new set of arrivals into different categories within the traditional caste system, with predictable results on Jewish willingness to marry between castes.

In the state of Kerala, the Jews established themselves in two cities and three villages, where they observed the Sabbath, celebrated the Jewish holidays and followed the rules of Kashrut. Today they credit their continued survival as Jews to the religious commitment of those tight-knit communities.

Barbara Johnson adds[4] a remarkable detail to the story of Cochin Jews. When the Portuguese came to Goa, some "New Christians" came with them. These were Conversos, Jews who were converted forcibly during the Inquisition. She writes that some of them established social and economic relationships with the Jews of Cochin, and, as a result, some of these were caught by the Portuguese, deported to Portugal and put to death in the Inquisition. Others were undetected, and they even contributed money secretly to the building fund for the Kadavumbhagam Synagogue, now in the Israel Museum.

We visited the main Jewish colony, called Jew Town, on one of the islands of Cochin. By that time, almost all the Jews had left for Israel, but the town still was there. One rather pale man was sitting in front of a shop. To look at him, he easily could have been a Jew sitting in front of a store on the lower east side of New York. On the facade of the shop, a sign announced that the proprietor was Mr. Cohen. We asked the man whether the proprietor, Mr. Cohen, was in. He told us that he was not. He had left for Israel. Then we asked him his name. It too was Mr. Cohen.

---

[4] Johnson, Barbara C., 'New Research, Discoveries and Paradigms: A Report on the Current Study of Kerala Jews,' Chap. 7 in Katz, Nathan et al ed, *Indo-Judaic Studies in the Twenty-first Century: A view from the Margin*, (New York: Palgrave MacMillan, 2007).

Some 2,800 Cochin Jews moved to Israel in the 1950s and 60s, first to *moshavim*, farming cooperatives. From there they spread out, building synagogues in the Cochin style wherever possible. Now they are scattered throughout the country, notably to Benyamina and Petah Tikvah.[5]

Near Nevatim is a Cochin Jewish Heritage Museum, built to preserve their unique culture, and it mounts rotating exhibitions of the dress and traditions of their life in India. But their memories are not restricted to Nevatim. In Cochin, we had visited a beautiful synagogue, whose most dramatic feature was the ceiling, tinkling with countless delicate glass lamps hanging down everywhere. At one time there were many such synagogues, but as the community emptied out, so did they. Going through the Israel Museum in Jerusalem one day, I saw the beautiful Kadavumbhagam Synagogue that had been disassembled, moved from India, and reassembled inside the museum. It was a bit of a shock to see it there. I felt transported right back to Cochin.

Today in Cochin, only eight Jews remain. Over, 8,000 live in Israel.

Shalva Weil from the Hebrew University has published a lifetime's worth of research on all the Indian Jewish communities, including the Jews of Cochin. Several other researchers and members of the Cochin community who now live in Israel also have published books with fine pictures of their remarkable synagogues, ritual objects and culture. One unique effort to preserve this heritage was a compilation of Jewish folksongs in the language of Kerala – Malayalam – all sung by women.

The Cochin Jews were not the only ones who came by the old trade routes. From the first century on, several groups of early Christians also left the land of Israel for India. Today they are called St. Thomas Christians. One group came from Persia, coming sometime between the first and eighth century CE, and organizing their community as part of the outreach of the Church

---

[5] Weil, Shalva, 'Where are Cochin Jews Today?',
http://cochinsyn.com/page-cultural-
where.html#:~:text=The%20interior%20of%20the%20Kadavumbagam
%20synagogue%20from%20Cochin,were%20originally%20from%20the
%20Parur%20synagogue%20in%20Kerala.

of the East. They landed first at Surat, Gujarat, and from there they moved to Kerala.

This community believes that St. Thomas himself came to India, and that he made many local conversions that enlarged their community. Additional Christian migrations came when their homes in the Middle East were threatened by Islam, by Genghis Khan, or by any of a multitude of others.

Another wave of migration landed in India between the fourth and eighth century CE, the Kananaya. This group held themselves apart from the others, because they believed that they were descended from Jewish royalty, the House of David. Though they are loyal Christians, some have called them Jewish-Christians, in part because many of their practices resemble those of Cochin Jews.

The various churches of St. Thomas Christians form a community of almost four million today, most of them living in Kerala.

BAGHDADI JEWS

During the seventeenth and eighteenth centuries, the Mughal Empire drew adventurous Jewish merchants to India from Baghdad, Aleppo, Syria and Yemen. Though they come from several different countries, by custom they all were called Baghdadi Jews. Some came to India and stayed, others kept moving east. A friend of ours comes from a Shanghai Jewish family that the Sassoons brought from Iraq. This was typical. When possible, the Sassoon family preferred to bring Jews from home to manage their far-flung businesses. In all probability, our friend's family moved to India first, then went to Shanghai, which at that time was the eastern outpost of a vast Sassoon trading network stretching from Bombay through Calcutta, Burma, Singapore, Hong Kong and Shanghai, not unlike an empire of old.

In India, the Baghdadis came first to the port city of Surat. This was a major Mughal trading center in the north that attracted both Portuguese-Dutch Jews from Amsterdam and Arabic speaking Jews from the Middle East.[6] From there, they fanned out to Bombay, Calcutta and Pune. Using India as a base, Arabic-speaking merchants sailed to the Middle East, trading in cotton, spices, nuts and coffee. Later, in the mid-nineteenth century, Persian Jews came to India to buy the luxurious textiles of Kashmir and Bukhara.

Jews came again in the nineteenth century from Aleppo, Yemen, Baghdad and Basra, where they had been subject to harsh persecution. This Diaspora split families between India, Burma, Singapore, Java, Hong Kong and Shanghai. The reader will notice that almost all these were British colonies, and indeed the community prided itself in identifying with the British in their dress and manners. According to expert observers, above all, they wanted to be seen as European.

This community was not particularly Zionist, and their religious observance often was quite relaxed. Even in Baghdad and Calcutta the synagogues did not necessarily have rabbis, though there were many learned men who were more than qualified to lead their communities in prayer. The Baghdadis preferred a secular education for their children, who were expected to join largely successful family businesses, especially in Bombay. Religious or not, the community always took responsibility for their poor, through trust funds, charities and other forms of social assistance. Baghdadi Jews have described the community as like a family, very tightly knit and close, though they did not lack outside ties, especially in Bombay with the Parsis and in Calcutta with the Armenians, both similarly successful minority communities.

The most prominent figure in the Jewish community of Bombay was David Sassoon, who came from Iraq in 1832. One photograph shows him resplendent in a massive turban and flowing robes. Over the next decade he developed trade networks from the Persian Gulf to China, which became the basis of the family's huge commercial network. His textile mills alone

---

[6] Manasseh, Rachel, *Baghdadian Jews of Bombay – Their life and achievements, a personal and historical account,* (Great Neck: Midrash Ben Ish Hai, 2013), p. 36.

generated huge profits when American cotton exports diminished during the American Civil War. With the fortune he accumulated, in Bombay alone he and his sons established synagogues, the Sassoon Docks, the magnificent Elphinstone High School, and the showy Flora Fountain, prominently located in the middle of Bombay and purportedly named after his daughter-in-law. He also built the ornate David Sassoon Library, the entrance foyer dominated by a marble bust of, surprise, David Sassoon.

The Sassoons also built a synagogue in the hill town of Pune, a synagogue in Byculla (a suburb of Bombay), enormous hospitals in both Byculla and Pune, and much more. They even contributed financially to both the Gateway of India and the grand Victoria and Albert Museum. Anyone who has spent any time in Bombay (Mumbai) will realize how major these Sassoon contributions were. The Sassoons, along with the British, built many of the most memorable buildings in the city.

On one trip to Mumbai, at a Jethmalani event we met a man who introduced himself to us as one of the last Baghdadis remaining in Mumbai. Because of that good fortune, we had a Jewish tour of many of the splendid Sassoon buildings of Mumbai, several of them ones I had driven past many times, and admired, but had no idea there was a Jewish connection. On another trip, I happened to visit the Sassoon-built Keneseth Eliahoo synagogue in Mumbai on a day when a Bar Mitzvah was being celebrated, and I saw the Bar Mitzvah boy read from a Torah scroll mounted inside a rich silver Iraqi case.

There never were very many Baghdadi Jews in India. Rachel Manasseh, a Baghdadi Jew herself, writes that there were 5–6,000 Baghdadi Jews in Bombay in the mid-twentieth century. Roland[7] cites an estimate of 3,800 in Calcutta in 1942, fewer than 7,000 in the whole country, a miniscule percentage of India's population.

Why are almost no Baghdadi Jews left in Bombay? When the state of Israel was formed and the British left India, the Baghdadi Jews left for Israel, England, Canada and the U.S. They were not

---

[7] Roland, Joan, 'The Baghdadi Jews of India: Perspectives on the Study and Portrayal of a Community,' Chap. 9, in Katz et al.

fleeing persecution. They were regarded by the Indians as high caste, and they were held in high esteem. It is just that during the early days of Indian independence the government became increasingly socialist; the Indian government put currency restrictions in place, and the community feared that they would not be able to get their money out of the country if the big Jewish companies were to be shuttered. Zionism may have been a factor, but it was not the main reason.

Luckily, once as I started out on a trip through Calcutta (Kolkata) we found out that our guide was Jewish. Since several members of our group were too, we asked her to show us a synagogue. That was how I came to see the three immaculate, elegant Baghdadi synagogues of Calcutta, one of which was said to be the largest synagogue in Asia. At least one of them was almost hidden by shops and small market stalls in front of it, and all the synagogues were locked. Our guide was a member of the community though, and she knew how to get the keys. Despite the noisy marketplace just outside, inside the synagogues were pristine.

By that time, they had too few people left in any one congregation to maintain regular services, so they were rotating services among all three throughout the year, to make sure that they all were kept in use. Now that almost the entire Jewish population of Kolkata has left, all three are locked. The synagogues have ample endowments, but they sit empty, noble monuments to a community that has moved on.

BENE ISRAEL

The oldest and largest community of Jews in India is the Bene Israel. One version of the story says that they came to India in the time of King Solomon. Another has them descended from Ten Lost Tribes who were deported from Israel by the Assyrians in 722 BCE. Theories abound. They may have escaped Nebuchadnezzar and the Babylonians in 586 BCE. Maybe once they were Persian Jews. According to their own history, they arrived between 300 and 100 BCE, because the Greeks and Romans were harassing them in Jerusalem. Whatever the threat may have been, they may be the earliest example of Jews running to India for safety.

The Bene Israel landed first on the shores of Maharashtra, and according to legend, they all are the descendants of seven Jewish couples who were shipwrecked on the coast. They settled on the Konkan Coast, about twenty miles south of Bombay (Mumbai), adopted Indian ways, clothing and food, and became assimilated into Indian culture. Many took up the occupation of pressing seeds for oil, and they became known as the Oil Presser Caste[8] in the Indian social order. The British also called them the Native Jew Caste. In the eighteenth century they moved to Bombay (Mumbai), Pune, Delhi, Calcutta and even Aden, which was part of the British Empire at that time.

Shalva Weil writes[9] that they kept the Sabbath, recited the Hebrew prayer Sh'ma Yisroel, circumcised their sons, observed some but not all the major Jewish holidays and added a few local holidays of their own invention. They adopted the popular Indian henna ceremony before weddings, but they remained staunchly monotheistic despite all the Hindu deities all around them. DNA tests have shown that a small number of them carry the genetic marker for Cohanim, the Jewish hereditary priests.

Bene Israel had their own social and charitable organizations, sports clubs, Zionist organizations, newspapers and credit organizations. At the height of their population, they maintained more than 20 synagogues in the state of Maharashtra (the state of Bombay) alone. Still, when they arrived in Israel, they were suspected of not being proper Jews, and they had to fight for recognition.

Certainly, when the wealthy Baghdadi Jews came to India and found them, they regarded the Bene Israel as barely Jewish. Nevertheless, we were told that, when they left for Israel, the Baghdadi Jews were so keen to have daily prayers continue in the synagogues they were leaving behind, especially in Calcutta, that they reached out to the Bene Israel – the same Jews they never used to associate with – even paying them to pray in these synagogues. The Baghdadi Jew who we met in Mumbai told us

---

[8] Blady, Ken, *Jewish Communities in Exotic Places*, (Northvale, Jason Aronson, 2000), pp. 215–229.
[9] Weil, Shalva, 'On Origins, the Arts, and Transformed Identities: Foci of Research into the Bene Israel,' Chap. 8, in Katz et al.

proudly that his synagogue never had a "paid" minyan. (the quorum of ten men needed for community prayer.)

Eventually most of the Bene Israel moved to Israel after 1947–48. There were several reasons – Zionist, social, political, religious and economic – but they had not faced hostility or discrimination. The Bene Israel, Cochinis and Baghdadis each had their own place in the Indian caste system, and they remained in those places. They did not intermarry with other Jewish "castes" any more than members of different Hindu castes would intermarry. Gandhi however attacked the entire caste system with the intention of abolishing it, and now the Jewish leaders knew it would be hard for their small communities to preserve their identities in India.[10]

In Israel they moved first to development towns – Beersheba, Dimona, Lod and Kiryat Shemoneh. Even though many of them moved out of pure Zionistic fervor, once they arrived, they were met by doubts about whether they really were Jews, and they had to present proof to a skeptical rabbinate before they were permitted to marry under Jewish law. Ultimately the battle for recognition was resolved by an act of the Knesset, and now they have taken their rightful place in the Jewish community. There are approximately 40–50,000 living in Israel now,[11] with 5,000 still in India and 5,000 in other countries. Altogether, with 5,000–8,000 Jews from Cochin and some Baghdadis, there may be 85,000 Jews of Indian origin living in Israel today.

TRIBAL JEWS

One more community has been in the news recently, the Bene Menashe, a name signifying that they consider themselves to be descendants of one of the 10 Lost Tribes of the northern Kingdom of Israel, the tribe of Menassah (Menashe). Living in northeast India and Burma, they come from several small central Asian tribes. Those who identify with Judaism call themselves Shinlung,

---

[10] The Jewish People Policy Institute, The Jews of India: A Long-Lasting Symbiosis | The Jewish People Policy Institute (jppi.org.il)

[11] 'India', *Jewish Virtual Library*, 1998–2020, a project of AICE, https://www.jewishvirtuallibrary.org/india

though they also are referred to as Mizos. It appears that this Jewish identification results from the efforts of Christian missionaries, who first came there to convert Assamese to Christianity. When these tribes read the Bible though, they also learned about Judaism, and they discovered aspects that sounded familiar. Encouraged by Christian missionaries who saw parallels between their customs and Jewish customs, their legends and Jewish legends, many of them made the next step to adopt Jewish practices and a Jewish identity.

Now this community keeps the Sabbath and observes some Jewish practices, but the breadth of their Jewish knowledge is limited. Several years ago, a group came to Israel, only to find out that they were required to undergo a formal conversion. Immigration stopped at that point, though at the end of 2020, a special project brought 250 Bene Menashe to Israel, where their status as Jews was to be confirmed by a formal conversion. Currently, 3,000 have come to Israel,[12] over 5,000 Bene Menashe are still in India, possibly 10,000, and they too hope to come to Israel.

Other small groups aspire to be Jewish, such as the Benai Ephraim in Andra Pradesh. Setting aside the question of whether these really are Jewish lost tribes, it is interesting to see how many communities in India seek a Jewish identity in order to leave poverty, or perhaps to stop being treated as untouchables, who are outside the caste system. But more to the point, why do they want to be Jewish?

Talking about lost tribes and their possible kin, we also could mention the Pathans (Pashtuns).[13] Formidable Muslim fighters, they have a strong presence in Afghanistan, Pakistan and northern India, and nobody would ever say that they are Jewish. However, the claim has been made for their ancestry. According to the Museum of the Jewish People (Beit Hatfutsot), in Israel, they too could have been descended from the Ten Lost Tribes of Israel. Well maybe. We do know that Jewish communities existed

---

[12] 'Ten Indian-Jewish 'lost tribe' couples remarried in Israel,' *The Times of Israel*, April 5, 2017.

[13] Foltz, Richard, *Religions of Iran – from prehistory to the present* (London: Oneworld Publications, 2013), p. 2134 in the Kindle edition.

in Afghanistan and Pakistan until the 1990s. And I have found the jewelry to prove it.

A Jewish friend from the Afghani portion of Baluchistan once showed me the elegant, and precious, family jewelry that she was about to donate to the Israel Museum. As I salivated over the tourmalines and other gemstones, it never occurred to me to visualize another jeweler, perhaps right across the street from the man who set these stones, a humble Jewish jeweler sitting cross-legged on the floor of his little shop in Kabul, making folkloric Jewish jewelry out of the deep blue lapis lazuli of Afghanistan. Yet, one day while riffling around jewelry trays in an Afghani shop in Seattle, I was stunned to find a large lapis lazuli and silver pendant in the shape of a six-pointed Jewish star, the workmanship of an Afghani jeweler, almost certainly Jewish. Obviously, I bought the pendant.

The Bene Israel, the Cochin Jews and the Baghdadi Jews all moved originally from the Middle East to India, and some migrated back centuries later, many of them for better economic opportunities, some for religious reasons, some for Zionism, but they were not running away from India. They simply were running back home, to the land of Israel.

But what about the Jews from Israel who run, or just wander, back to India? Who are they? Where do they go? And why?

CHAPTER THREE.
THE MODERN WANDERING JEW

Jews have always traveled, either to escape persecution, for commerce, or just for adventure – the proverbial "wandering Jew." There even is a houseplant of that name. Young Israeli backpackers trek all over Asia and South America, but one of their most enduring and endearing destinations is India.

Who are these wandering Jews of today? Are they American Jews who suddenly feel moved to have a new experience? Are they restless Jews who feel the need to meditate in an ashram somewhere? Are they Israelis who just want to party in Goa? Are they Jews who go to India on vacation and then just stay? Are they serious students of Hinduism or Buddhism? Maybe they truly seek spiritual enlightenment. Or not.

Since their first experience with India, some have taken on Hindu or Buddhist names, and they have made new lives for themselves. Some simply attend one meditation session a week, near their homes. Some have become eminent authors and academics who specialize in East Asian, Hindu or Buddhist studies. Some have founded ashrams or Buddhist study institutes, either at home or abroad, and some were given the honor of leading the programs that were founded by their teachers. Many an ashram or Buddhist zendo today flourishes under an inspired leader, here or abroad, who was born a Jew.

Alon Goshen-Gottstein divides these Jews into three categories: those who have enriched their lives through an experience with Hinduism, then returned to Judaism; those who have become Hindu, most of them without giving up their ethnic

41

identification with Judaism, and those who have sought to maintain multiple identities at the same time.[1] One could parse these distinctions and split them further, but the essential truth is that they travel the same roads.

In this and the next chapters we will meet people who are serious and some who are not so serious. We will learn about JuBus and HinJews in Israel, America and India, and we will meet the occasional European Jew who happens to find her way into our story. We will catch a glimpse of Jews who live in other countries, but we will not seek them there. That would be another book.

We will look at the directions these Jewish seekers have taken, and we will see how some of them have struggled with their choices.

Again, let us start in India.

IN INDIA

First a disclaimer. Ever since my first trip to India, I have read extensively about Hinduism, and to a lesser extent about Buddhism, but I never looked for a local center for meditation. I never even thought there would be one. I was a surgery resident, after that a practicing surgeon. My interest in Hinduism remained theoretical. I have visited Buddhist and Hindu sites all over the world, but I never moved to India or made the spiritual commitment of the Jews we are about to meet. And I admire them. Yet with all my diffidence, Buddhism has approached me:

> On a trip to Nepal in 1981, we arranged to meet the son of a physician from Detroit. One day he took us to meet a Buddhist lama whose specialty happened to be treating women who were praying for children. When I admitted that I had no children, the lama offered his services. After some hesitation, I agreed, with many smiles and nods passing between us. I nearly forgot about the incident by the time I came home, except for a nagging feeling that I was

---

[1] Goshen-Gottstein, Alon, *The Jewish Encounter with Hinduism: History, Spirituality, Identity*, (London: Palgrave Macmillan, 2016), pp. 2856ff.

about to do something wrong. Anyhow I thought, maybe he would forget.

Several weeks later, it arrived, the package from Nepal. In the package was a device consisting of a string from which were suspended two ovoid creations made of cloth, each tightly stitched into a facsimile of an ovary. Clearly I was to wear this every day with the little ovaries hanging in front of my own. Also in the package were what looked like innumerable pills made of tiny wads of paper, each inscribed with miniscule Nepalese letters. This had taken him a long time to prepare, and he had lovingly written it all out for me, sending it at his own expense.

But I could not get over the feeling that wearing it would be a forbidden violation of my religion. It seemed like worship – using foreign prayers – of a foreign god. I kept it. I looked at it. I turned it over and looked more carefully, maybe even wistfully. I put it in a drawer. A few months later I took it out, and I threw it away.

I threw it away, but not everyone would have. Some would have embraced it.

In an old joke, a Jewish lady living in an Orthodox community outside of New York city let it be known that she was collecting money for a trip to India, a trip she had to make before she died. Members of the community did not understand why she needed to go, but they compassionately provided the money. She then traveled to India, took the arduous trip to an ashram in the north, and joined it. While there, she learned that the famous guru who led the ashram was in the habit of making a formal progress among his admiring followers at a fixed time every day. One day she managed to position herself in the front of the crowd and, as he passed, she called out to him, "Moishele, Moishele my son, when are you coming home?"

The following account is true. One writer describes a trip he took to Haridwar, India to visit an ashram headed by one Swami Vijayananda. In fact, this swami was a rabbi's son who was born in Alsace, France, named Abraham Jacob Weintraub. His grandparents were Hasidim; his stepfather was a rabbi, and as a boy he had been sent to an Orthodox religious school. As a young man, he became a doctor, and he practiced medicine during the Second World War. Meanwhile he was drawn to Hinduism, and in 1951 after the liberation of France, he left for India, never to return.

His major guru was a great female 'saint,' Sri Sri Anandamayi, and under her direction he became a revered swami. When Goshen-Gottstein met him, he had a room full of Jewish holy books, including commentaries on the Torah, which he was able to read and understand in Hebrew. He told western students who came to him that they need not worship Hindu gods. He believed that different religions have different rituals, all of which are equally valid for reaching spiritual understanding, but once this understanding is reached, ritual is no longer necessary.

Two Hasidic Jews once visited him in his ashram, and they urged him to sing a well-known Hebrew melody. As they knew, this was a song his family sang on Friday nights when he was young. As they reported, he still remembered it, and tears ran down his face as they sang together.[2]

The swami was 92 when the writer Nagen met him, and he had lived in the ashram for 55 years. In his library, Nagen saw a Hebrew bible. Vijayananda told him he saw no contradictions between Judaism and Indian Vedic philosophy. One of Vijayananda's students once asked whether it was true that he used to be Jewish. Vijayananda straightened his back proudly and exclaimed, "I *am* Jewish!"

Four years later, the swami died. At his instruction, he was not cremated according to Indian custom; cremation is against the Jewish religion. His body was sent home to his family in France, where they buried him and said Kaddish, the prayer traditionally recited by Jewish mourners.[3]

It would be difficult to list all the Jews who have found their way to Hinduism, a number of whom have chosen to live in India.

---

[2] Rigler Sara Yoheved, 'The Guru and the Hasid,' Jan. 28, 2012, *Aish.com.*
[3] Nagen, Yakov, 'The Rabbi's Son who Became a Swami', Nov. 7, 2019, *The Times of Israel,*
https://blogs.timesofisrael.com/the-rabbis-son-who-became-a-swami/?utm_source=The+Blogs+Weekly+Highlights&utm_campaign=blogs-weekly-highlights-2019-11-07&utm_medium=email

One was Baba Rampuri, who was born William Gans in Chicago, and who founded the Hari Puri ashram in Haridwar, India. We could include many other examples. Radhaneth Swami, born Richard Slavin in Chicago, became a founder of the Bhaktivedanta Hospital in Mumbai, which started with medical camps in the slums of Bombay and grew to become a 200-bed multispecialty hospital with a premier research institution.

Swami Bharatananda, born Maurice Frydman in Warsaw, moved to India, converted to Hinduism and became a sanyasi, a holy man. He became a disciple of Mahatma Gandhi, lived in Gandhi's ashram and made several protypes of Gandhi's symbolic spinning wheel. Jayadvaita Swami, born Jay Israel, started out life as a Reform Jew in New Jersey. Notably, he founded the International Society for Krishna Consciousness (ISKCON), commonly called the Hare Krishna organization. He edited *Back to Godhead* magazine for years, wrote major books about Hinduism and edited many more.[4]

Sadhvi Bhagawati Saraswati was born in Hollywood California. While finishing her PhD, she went on a trip to India, and she ended up living for over 24 years on the Ganges River at Parmarth Niketan Ashram. She now is president of the Divine Shakti Foundation and is a motivational speaker on Hinduism.

Shyamdas, born Stephen Theodore Schaffer in Connecticut,[5] came to India at the age of 18 in 1971, and he lived there until his death. According to his biography, while still a boy, he was taken to a psychologist because he kept talking about a beautiful little blackish boy who always followed him. He had visions of the little boy throughout his childhood, until he finally came to an understanding that the boy was Krishna.[6] Shyamdas became fluent in Sanskrit, Hindi and Gujarati, and he became a translator, writer, teacher, lecturer and much-loved interpreter of Indian music, with a distinctly Jewish sense of humor.

---

[4] Swami also wrote *Vanity Karma: Ecclesiastes,* and *The Bhagavad-gita, and The Meaning of Life,* (Bhaktivedanta Book Trust, 2015).
[5] Shyamdas Foundation website, 2020, https://shyamdasfoundation.com/bio/
[6] Vani, Gaura, 'Shyamdas (1953–2013)' – In Memory', January 28, 2013, Shyamdas (1953–2013) – In Memory | GauraVani.com

We will have to leave out many Americans, including many who were neither born in the U.S. nor lived in India. One who should not be forgotten though, is Sivarama Swami,[7] who was born Peter Letai to Holocaust survivor parents in Hungary. The family subsequently moved to Canada, where Peter discovered ISKCON. He became increasingly active in the Hare Krishna movement, and he finally returned to Hungary to develop its Hare Krishna branch.

Another unforgettable, and uncategorizable, character was Mirra Alfassa. She was the daughter of a Turkish Jewish father and an Egyptian Jewish mother, born in Paris into a bourgeois life in 1878.[8] She began her career as an artist, and there she fell into the intellectual circle of a charismatic occultist, Max Theon, and his wife. Theon was born a Polish Jew originally named Eliezer Biemstein. Alfassa divorced, remarried, moved to Pondicherry, India and met the famous Hindu philosopher Aurobindo Ghose. Entranced, she devoted the rest of her life to him, taking the responsibility of building up and running his ashram.

Aurobindo gave her the title "The Mother," and, during the times when he went into seclusion, he only communicated with his followers through her. After the death of Aurobindo, she continued running the ashram, and she built Auroville, a utopian community, nearby. The Mother was worshipped as a great spiritual leader until her death. It must be said though that when we visited Auroville 15 years ago, the architecture was looking distinctly seedy.

S.S. Cohen was born in Iraq in the late 19th century, and at the age of 39 he moved to the city of Tiruvannamalai in Tamil Nadu,

---

[7] Sivarama Swami Official Website,
https://sivaramaswami.com/?fbclid=IwAR0ZYCIwCHi1YSzvCXtqnXNTA 9DJPARTAZxXzZb0mZ7RIMDcWpD9ZKiQX60
[8] Beldo, Patrick, 'The Mother (nee Mirra Blanche Rachel Alfassa)', *World Religions and Spirituality*, Places and dates vary according to the source. I have chosen these as representative.
https://wrldrels.org/2018/10/13/the-mother-nee-mirra-blanche-rachel-alfassa/

not far from Pondicherry.[9] He became an author, and he was active in the Theosophical Society as well as in the Association of Hebrew Theosophists in Adyar, close to Pondicherry. He once described himself as "a Jew living in an ashram." That ashram was Ramanashram, where he ultimately was buried.

Though the Theosophical Society may seem far afield of our topic, the roots of this philosophy were in Hinduism, Gnosticism and the Jewish Kabbalah.[10] Many of the active members all over the world, and some of the founders, were Jewish. The Israeli Theosophical Society alone has three branches, located in Haifa, Tel Aviv and Jerusalem, and of late the subject has become popular as a subject of academic study. Boaz Huss, Professor of Jewish Thought at Ben Gurion University, studies Jewish spirituality, and he has researched S.S Cohen as well as the Theosophical Society.

In 2012, a riveting Israeli television series came out, *Katmandu*. The key characters were a Chabad couple in Katmandu, Nepal and the Israeli backpackers and others who they helped. Based on real lives of Chabad emissaries to Nepal – Chezki and Chani Lifshitz – it told stories that Israelis hear from each other in that part of the world. One episode focused on an Israeli expat who exiled himself to Katmandu after a tragic accident in the Israeli army. Others dealt with the follies of a selfish playboy who proposed a frivolous marriage; the perils of Katmandu during a time of civil unrest, and the dangers faced by Israeli backpackers stranded in the Himalayas. Above all, the series showcased the role of the Chabad in India, and it demonstrated why it is held in such high regard. At the real Chabad House in Katmandu, the Lifshitz family gained fame for regularly putting on what was believed to be the largest Passover seder in the world, cooking for

---

[9] Huss, Boaz, "'A Jew Living in an Ashram": Philosophy, Advaita, and Jewish Nationalism in the Life and Writings of S.S.Cohen,' *23th European Conference on South Asian Studies*,
https://nomadit.co.uk/conference/ecsas2014/paper/18558
[10] Huss, Boaz, 'In Search of the Jewish Theosophists,' *Newsletter of the Friends of the Theosophical Archives*, Spring-Summer 2016,
https://www.academia.edu/26948504/In_Search_of_the_Jewish_Theosophists

over 1,500 guests.[11] This required them to import 2,000 pounds of matzo and 2,000 bottles of kosher wine from Israel for each Passover season.

If you want to see how pervasive Chabad is in that part of the world, check the internet for a map of Chabad Houses in India.[12] The Chabad website lists at least 16 centers, located in Delhi, Pune, Dharamshala, Kasa Devi, Kasol, Pushkar, Varanasi and Rishikesh in the north; also in Mumbai and the Andeman Islands, finally in Sri Lanka, Vata Canal, Goa, Palolem, Bangalore, and Cochin in the south. Katmandu is no longer listed on the 2020 website. It must be difficult to maintain constant staffing there. In all these houses, just as in the TV series, the ever-patient Lubavitchers feed, comfort and support Israelis. They find them when they are lost – in every sense – and they show them that their own Jewish culture can provide much of what they are looking for in India.

Some Israelis simply go to India, stay for a while, and come home. Most of them travel in packs, exchanging information as they go. One article estimates that somewhere between 40,000 and 80,000 Israelis go to India each year.[13] Among the comforts they find are Chabad Houses, Israeli food in many places, the near-ubiquitous presence of other Israelis, and often signs in the Hebrew language. Also helpful are Facebook groups for exchanging information about travel routes, which are called the Humus Trail. According to one article, "Going to India has become a 'goes without saying' thing. It's entrenched in Israeli

---

[11] Liphshiz, Cnaan, 'In Wake of Tragedy, a Passover Seder in Nepal Offers Respite', *Times of Israel*, Mar. 30, 2016,
https://www.timesofisrael.com/in-wake-of-tragedy-a-passover-seder-in-nepal-offers-respite/ This is one of many articles that have been written about the Lifshitz family.
[12] Leviov, Geula Nachmenson, 'Chabad house Lubavitch in New Delhi on main bazaar street,' *Chabad Lubavitch of India,*
https://www.thinglink.com/scene/999448859627225091?buttonSource
=viewLimits
[13] Tamar Lafontaine, 'Why Do Israelis Flock to India?' *Jerusalem Post*, Dec. 8, 2018, Estimates vary according to the source, but this is in the midrange of estimates,
https://www.jpost.com/jerusalem-report/mother-india-573686

culture." Israelis call India 'Mama India.' Lately the flight between Israel and India has become even shorter, using a new route over Saudi Arabia.

The same article writes "Lev Yehudi, which is an initiative funded by the National-Religious movement in Israel, is joined by like-minded initiatives in India, albeit from different areas on the religious spectrum. Another is Beit Bina, a project of the pluralistic Jewish Movement for Social Change, and, of course, Beit Chabad, a project of the Chabad Hasidic movement that has branches in most major cities around the world. Sigal and Shai Levy, a couple in their 60s from Tel Aviv, have been managing Beit Bina in the northern Indian village of Dharamkot for the past two seasons. The village has become one of the most popular stops on the Humus Trail."

In his blog, Alan Brill, gives a rather negative take[14] on a Shabbat dinner he attended at the Chabad House of Rishikesh, along the Humus Trail. He was neither impressed by the religious instruction given there nor by the Israelis who attended, many of whom were stoned. He has visited other Israeli outposts in India, including branches of other Israeli organizations, but he does not comment on them in this article. Generally, his criticisms reflect his own background. He is observant, and he views the community in Rishikesh as decadent.

Most stories are more upbeat. Amanda Miller wrote a popular play about her own experiences, and she plays the part of herself in it.[15] It tells of her journey from anxiety and depression, a journey that led her through yoga and massage to a lengthy stay in an ashram in India, then home again to the U.S. Surprisingly, at least to her, when she returned home, she felt herself drawn back toward her Jewish roots. That is the round-trip that she presents in her

---

[14] Alan Brill, 'Rishikesh: Israelis, Chabad, and Theology', November 30, 2013, https://kavvanah.blog/2013/11/30/rishikesh-israelis-chabad-and-theology/

[15] Ellin, Simone, 'Charm City Fringe Festival to Present 'The Jew in the Ashram,"
https://www.jmoreliving.com/2019/10/14/charm-city-fringe-festival-to-present-the-jew-in-the-ashram/

play, a full circle that many other American and Israeli Jews have made.

> *Once a small group of us from Michigan arranged to visit a young couple in Safed for a typical Israeli home-cooked dinner. Meeting the charming family, the Jewish grandparents among us smiled warmly to see such a lovely religious couple and their sweet baby. We asked how they had met. It was in Rajasthan. He was spending his post-military year in India, and he had postponed his departure for months as he was on the verge of becoming a Hindu. She was an American Jew who had come to India for a short trip that became a long trip. By happenstance, her room was next to his in a Rajasthan desert hotel. One day a local Chabad representative saw them walking around town, and he asked if they wanted to come over on Friday evening for Shabbat dinner. Well, yes, they did. They began to come over more often, and the Chabad slowly reeled them in. Over time they married, moved to a religious community in Safed, and started a family.*

We could tell many more stories, but now we will turn to American Jews. After that, we will discuss Israelis, and we will see the remarkable parallels with Americans.

In the U.S.

Some American Jews have turned toward Hinduism, and, as we will see when we discuss Israel, even more have looked toward Buddhism. Some have explored both Hinduism and Buddhism, so we will discuss the two spiritual quests together, instead of dwelling pedantically on the distinctions between them. Before that though, we might mention some who may not have been seeking enlightenment, but who have found the love of their lives.

It is not unusual for Americans to meet partners from other cultures in the American melting pot, but what many may not know is how many Jewish-Hindu couples have resulted. There even is a name for their offspring – Hinjews. The Urban Dictionary provides a typically Jewish-sounding definition: "A person of half-

Jew descent, that is, someone who always disappoints their mother no matter how many times they reincarnate."[16]

Articles about Hindu-Jewish marriages are all over the internet. One summarizes potential pitfalls,[17] most of which are problems that any intermarriage might encounter. Examples are decisions about names of children, child-rearing, circumcision, Bar Mitzvah, and burial customs. This article raises fears that the couple would face a troubling question of whether they intend to be monotheistic or polytheistic, yet one rarely hears of a marriage that flounders over this. That discussion normally takes place in the very beginning of the relationship. Usually mutual interests unite the couples. Members of both religions share many of the same family values, a love of learning, often even liberal politics. Both spouses are delighted to explore each other's food and culture. Commercial outfits advertise their ceremonies: "Looking for Personalized, Fun & Unforgettable Wedding Ceremony?" You can organize your Hindu-Jewish marriage through the internet.

And you might find some local help with your menu. Katz writes[18] that "Any number of enterprising Tamil restaurateurs [sic] in New York City... in Brooklyn and Queens as well, sell "kosher dosas" and proudly display hechshers [certificates] from the various kashruth organizations. In fact, Hindu "brahmin" restaurants afford a kosher dining alternative for the observant Jew."

The first American to become a Buddhist was Jewish, a man named Charles Strauss, who[19] declared his conversion to Buddhism at the 1893 World Parliament of Religions in Chicago. But Jewish interest in Buddhism has not just been an American trend. In 1985, George Dreyfus, a Swiss Jew, was the first foreigner ever to receive the highest Tibetan Buddhist scholastic title, *geshe.*

---

[16] https://www.urbandictionary.com/define.php?term=hinjew

[17] 'Hindu-Jew Marriage,' *Interfaith Shaadi,* 2019,
http://interfaithshaadi.org/hindu-jew-marriage-2/

[18] Katz, et al, p. 119.

[19] Kamenitz, Roger, *The Jew in the Lotus,* (San Franciso: HarperSan Francisco, 1995), p. 8.

As far back as the twelfth century, Abraham Maimonides, the son of the great philosopher Moses Maimonides, was the head of the Egyptian Jewish community, and he founded a Jewish-Sufi school of religion at the same time that he continued to write legalistic treatises on Jewish law. Pointing out that many Sufi ideas came originally from Judaism, he introduced many Sufi teachings back into Judaism in the tolerant atmosphere of Cairo during those years. And his mystical ideas – in the opinion of the Sufis too – contributed to the development of Kabbalah over the next two hundred years.[20] One writer asserts that, "As improbable as it sounds, the Sufi innovations in the Jewish religion begun by Abraham Maimonides were almost assuredly the single most important thing to happen to Jewish spirituality since the destruction of the Second Temple in 70 C.E."[21]

In America as in Israel, Buddhism and Hinduism have morphed. Both appeal to Jews, but Jews have streamlined and reshaped them to fit the American lifestyle and to make them appear less foreign. Idols have disappeared from many of the meditation rooms. Prayers or obeisance to foreign gods may be deleted or deemphasized, and meditation may be reconfigured into a type of medical or psychologic therapy. We soon will learn more about this.

Linzer[22] found that at one Zen center on the west coast, over half the members were Jewish, and so were most of the priests. At a Zen center on the east coast, a woman told her she was the only shiksa (non-Jewish female) there. She also writes that "During the 60s and 70s, fully one-third of the members of Zen centers I knew were Jewish."

A former Hasid from the strictly Orthodox Satmar community was a Zen priest when she interviewed him. He told her that ten of his sixteen priests were Jewish, and 29% of his

---

[20] 'Abraham Maimonides: A Jewish Sufi', *Sufi Magazine,* London, Winter 2001, http://tomblock.com/shalom_jewishsufi

[21] Ibid. 'Abraham Maimonides: A Jewish Sufi', *Sufi Magazine.*

[22] Linzer, Judith, *Torah and Dharma – Jewish Seekers in Eastern Religions* (North Bergen: Jason Aronson Inc., 1996). Much of this research was done as part of her PhD thesis, and it was based on multiple interviews with those quoted or referred to in the book.

staff were Jews. He still felt Jewish too, adding "I think there are obviously a lot of Jews here at the Zen center. Most of them don't come from any sort of religious background...They were lacking any sort of religious exposure, spirituality. I'd say there was a lack of spiritual experience. It was a lack of something with a certain amount of depth. And there was a lack of real relating."

One participant in such a Buddhist center has said that they could have a minyan every day if they included the priest. A minyan is the ten-man quorum required for formal Jewish prayer.

Actual surveys vary, but most confirm that from 6 to 30 percent of the participants in American Buddhism are Jews. This is in a country that is no more than 2 ½ % Jewish.[23]

A sociologic argument for this[24] starts from the observation that in America Jews are overrepresented in the highly educated upper middle class. They often are left-leaning intellectuals, artists or bohemians, the very people who most likely would be interested in Buddhism. Conversely, when Indians come to America, while they may not realize it, it is the Jewish lifestyle that they seek. In many cases this is exactly what they achieve, and there are 3.2 million Indians living in the U.S.,[25] the third largest Asian community in the country.

I must add, however, that a Hindu colleague who read this manuscript commented, "Although I had heard of Jews (had a Jewish teacher in medical school), I knew them only after I came to the U.S." Still, I would opine, had he known while he still was in India that the Jews in the U.S. sought the same education that he wanted to acquire, he would have seen immediately that their aspirations were the same. And, after a life devoted to medicine, academia, and research, he would make any Jewish mother inestimably proud.

Indians are one of the most successful immigrant groups in America, one of the best educated and the highest earners of all

---

[23] Kamenetz, Rodger, *The Jew in the Lotus*, (New York: HarperSan Francisco, 1994), pp. 7–9.
[24] Sigalow, Emily, *American JuBu*, (Princeton: Princeton University Press, 2019).
[25] Facilitating Bonds: India, Israel, and the Jewish People | The Jewish People Policy Institue (jppi.org.il)

minority communities, with the highest incomes of all Asian communities. As a result, when Indians meet Americans, it is as equals, colleagues, neighbors and classmates, so it is perfectly natural for them to mix, meet, and to adopt many of the same social and political ideas. This introduces them to the Jewish world, and it introduces American Jews to Hinduism.

A complete list of Jews who have become serious about eastern religion would be long, but at least we can meet some examples. They might include Sojun Mel Weitzman Roshi. Born Mel Weitsman in Los Angeles, he became an artist, formerly was the co-abbot of the San Francisco Zen Center, and most recently he has been Abbot of the Berkeley Zen Center[26]. Another is Hozan Sensei Alan Senauke. Born in Brooklyn, he is a folk musician and a poet, a former Executive Director of the Buddhist Peace Fellowship, a founder of Think Sangha, and now Vice-Abbot of the Zen Center. One more is Seishi Tetsudo, born Ross Blum, a student and lecturer at the same Center.

Any list of major Jewish figures in American Buddhism must include the following: Bernie Glassman (now Sensei Tetsugen) born at Brighton Beach New York to immigrant parents, who later became a Zen Buddhist. He founded an organization known as Zen Peacemakers, and he was one of the founders of the Zen Centers of Los Angeles. He had been greatly influenced by the Zen master Philip Kapleau. In addition, there is Brenda Shoshanna – born of an Orthodox family in the religious community of Borough Park, Brooklyn – who also practices Zen in the Mahayana Buddhist tradition.[27]

A question of definition arises. Drescher distinguishes between the genuine Buddhist who happens to have been born Jewish and the JuBu, "someone who, while engaging in Buddhist practices, affirms his Jewish descent and identity." His example of a JuBu would be Bernard Glassman. He does not include in that

---

[26] Berkley Zen Center website, led by Abbot Sojun Mel Weitsman, https://berkeleyzencenter.org/teachers/

[27] Drescher, Frank, "Jewish Converts to Buddhism and the Phenomenon of "Jewish Buddhists" ("JuBus") in the United States, Germany and Israel", *German National Library, Open Publishing*, 2012.

category one who dabbled in Buddhism and returned to Judaism or one who simply is interested in Buddhism.

A number of rabbis have combined their Judaism with an interest in certain aspects of Buddhism, usually meditation and mindfulness. The rabbi at my own synagogue does not seek any publicity, though he quietly leads meditation sessions at the synagogue once a week, and he assists with weekly yoga sessions. Rabbi Don Ani Shalom Singer is a reform rabbi who had become known for leading contemplative Jewish meditation sessions and Zen sitting practices in a number of locations.[28] Rabbi Sheila Peltz Weinberg is a reconstructionist rabbi, also the creator and co-leader of the Jewish Mindfulness Teaching Program in New York. Rabbi Rami Shapiro majored in Buddhist studies in college, after which he was ordained as a rabbi at Hebrew Union College. He studied Jewish humanism with Rabbi Sherwin Wine, and later he studied Jewish spiritual practices with Rabbi Zalman Shachter-Shalomi. He is a cofounder of the One River Foundation, which combines Jewish teachings with eastern studies.

Sigalow writes that in 2001, 16.5% of the practitioners in several North American Buddhist centers were Jewish,[29] and in 2005, nearly a third of the participants in the Cambridge Insight Meditation Center were Jewish. That conforms to the figures we looked at already. Four American Jews – Sharon Salzberg, Joseph Goldstein, Jack Kornfield and Jacqueline Mandell-Schwartz – have played a key role in popularizing the practice of mindfulness, a term chosen artfully, to avoid any religious connotations. Oxford Languages publishes an on-line Oxford English Dictionary, and this defines mindfulness as: "a mental state achieved by focusing one's awareness on the present moment, while calmly acknowledging and accepting one's

---

[28] Rubin, Linda, 'Not Your Typical Rabbi: A Sit-down with Sensei Don Singer', April 3, 2011,
https://patch.com/california/pacificpalisades/not-your-typical-rabbia-sit-down-with-sensei-don-singer

[29] Sigalow, Emily, *American JuBu*, (Princeton: Princeton University Press, 2019), pp. 1, 74–75. I am quoting these numbers as written, even though the numbers vary from source to source. They should be regarded as estimates.

feelings, thoughts, and bodily sensations, used as a therapeutic technique." Or, mindfulness has been called the awareness of something, as opposed to meditation, the awareness of nothing.

Allen Ginsberg was a poet, a prominent voice of the counterculture and a leader in the anti-war protests that dominated the sixties. He became involved with the Hare Krishna movement and with Tibetan Buddhism, although he is most famous, along with William Boroughs and Jack Kerouac, as one of the icons of the Beat Generation.

Among the many American Jewish followers of Zen Buddhism was Ram Dass, who, when he still was Richard Alpert, became famous for participating in Timothy Leary's experiments with psychedelic drugs. For that caper, both were dismissed from Harvard. The name Ram Dass was conferred on him by a guru in India, and he became a major Hindu countercultural figure.

Krishna Das, born Jeffrey Kegel, received his Hindu name from the same guru, and he achieved wide recognition for his beautifully chanted Hindu and Buddhist devotional music. Surya Das, born as Jeffrey Miller, was younger than the other two. He first explored Hinduism, then he turned to Tibetan Buddhism. He founded the Dzogchen Foundation and Centers and the Dzogchen Osel Ling Retreat Center in Texas. It should become apparent that many of these figures were not only involved in their own personal practice, they also went on to become founders of institutions. Despite the change in religion, this is very Jewish.

Daniel Goleman also studied in India with the same guru who taught Ram Dass, Krishna Das, and Larry Brilliant. Parenthetically, I remember that Larry was a freshman when I was a senior at Wayne State University School of Medicine, but he went on from there to have a career that has been, well, brilliant. And it all was inspired by his exposure to pressing public health needs during his early travels in India. Goleman too returned from India and wrote several books, one of which is *Emotional Intelligence.*

Cheryl Greene, now Bhikshuni Thubten Chodron, is a Tibetan Buddhist nun, and she is the founder and abbess of Sravasti Abbey, a center in Newport, Washington for training Buddhist nuns and monks. This has given her the unique opportunity of co-authoring a series of books with the Dalai Lama.[30]

Sensei Norman Fischer, now known as Sensei Zoketsu, was born to a Conservative Jewish family in Wilkes-Barre, Pennsylvania. He became a student of Sojun Mel Weitzman Roshi at the Berkley Zen Center, and he received dharma transmission from Weitzman. Fischer founded the Zen Hospice Center in San Francisco, and his publication list has more than 25 books. Fischer in turn worked with Jon Kabat-Zinn, who received a PhD in molecular biology and now is an emeritus professor of medicine. Kabat-Zinn had studied Buddhist meditation with several teachers, including at the Insight Meditation Society, where he later taught. Fischer helped Kabat-Zinn create the Stress Reduction and Relaxation Program at the University of Massachusetts Medical School, which later became an eight-week program – the Mindfulness-Based Stress Reduction program – with a new emphasis on a scientific framework. This has become one of the premier academic programs teaching mindfulness as medical therapy.

Rabbi Alan Lew, born in Brooklyn, became known as "the Zen rabbi."[31] He was a practicing Zen Buddhist for 10 years, and he was preparing for ordination as a lay priest when he had a sudden epiphany that led him to enter the Jewish Theological Seminary in New York. My own rabbi says that Lew made a profound and indelible impression on him when they both were students at JTS. After ordination as a Conservative rabbi, Lew became the rabbi of Beth Sholom synagogue in San Francisco. There, along with Norman Fischer, he founded Makor Or, a synagogue-based Jewish Meditation Center that played an important historical role in defining the concept of Jewish meditation. His book, *One God Clapping: The Spiritual Path of a Zen Rabbi*, is as good an explanation as one ever could find of why a Jew would become a Buddhist, and why a Jew would return from there to Judaism.

---

[30] Sravasti Abbey website, https://sravastiabbey.org/
[31] Fishkoff, Sue, 'Zen rabbi Alan Lew dies', Jan. 13, 2009, https://www.jweekly.com/2009/01/14/rabbi-alan-lew-influential-zen-rabbi-dies-suddenly-at-65/

In this book, Rabbi Lew tells of coming to study at the monastery Tassajara just as they were installing a new head monk, or *shuso*. The monk was Steve Weintraub, from the same neighborhood in Brooklyn that Rabbi Lew and Brenda Shoshanna came from. Weintraub had received dharma transmission in 1994 from Mel Weitzman, the very same Zen master who Fischer studied under. Weintraub began living in the Berkeley Zen Center in 1968, where he gave regular dharma lectures while continuing to practice as a psychotherapist. The reader will notice a pattern here. Many of the same people, from the same backgrounds, repeatedly intersect. Much of this spiritual flowering took place in the 60s and 70s, and several of these practitioners have written powerful books about that period.

One writer[32] began, as I have, by asking why so many Jews turn toward Buddhism. First, he opined that Buddhism lacks binding restrictions. Then he wrote that Buddhism does not require belief in a God, so it does not discomfit Jews who have lost faith in God. But there were other reasons. Buddhism has no history of conflict with Jews, no history of prejudice against them, and none of the historical baggage of Christianity. Buddhism does not exert pressure to convert, and it does not attempt to embarrass or shame anyone who does not convert.

Buddhism does not need to be practiced as a religion at all; it simply can be studied as a philosophy of living. As we will explain later, Buddhists have a unique view of suffering. They do not blame or berate. They simply help the sufferer let go of his pain, offering gentle guidance to one who seeks peace of mind.

Rabbi Zalman Schachter-Shalomi (Reb Zalman) was born in Poland. He attended a Zionist high school, was ordained by the ultra-Orthodox Jewish Lubavitchers and also by a sheikh of a Sufi order. He fled the Vichy government of France and the Nazis, came to America and obtained a PhD from the Reform Jewish Hebrew Union College. He experimented with LSD, founded a Chavurah (a small Jewish study group) in Massachusetts, and he

---

[32] Rifkin, Ira, 'The Jewish-Buddhist Encounter',
https://www.myjewishlearning.com/article/the-jewish-buddhist-encounter/

taught Kabbalah in California. Reb Zalman taught Jewish mysticism and the psychology of religion at Temple University, and he taught at Naropa University.[33] He is considered the father of the Jewish Renewal Movement. In 1976, he founded ALEPH, the Alliance for Jewish Renewal, an institution that combines Hasidism, Jewish mysticism, orthodoxy, Sufism and eastern religion. It also is part of a movement that encourages Chavurahs, and it facilitates their formation. Reb Zalman was part of the group who met the Dalai Lama, as described in the book *The Jew in the Lotus*, which we will come back to soon.

The Nathan Cummings Foundation was founded in 1989. The first president was Charles Halpern, who grew up in a Jewish home in Buffalo, New York.[34] He says that this is where he learned his sense of justice. Later, he was the founder of the City University of New York School of Law. The Nathan Cummings foundation characterized itself as "rooted in the Jewish tradition, committed to democratic values and social justice, including fairness, diversity and community". It has funded Jewish-Buddhist dialogues and conferences, and it sponsored the dialogue between the Dalai Lama and Jewish leaders that was described in *The Jew in the Lotus*. Halpern became a strong advocate for bringing mindfulness into the practice of law.

Sylvia Boorstein, from Brooklyn,[35] is an author and teacher of Buddhism who co-founded the Spirit Rock Meditation Center in Woodacre, California and who has organized conferences at the Barre Center for Buddhist Study. The Barre Center is located near the Insight Meditation Society, in Barre, Massachusetts; both of these organizations emphasize early Buddhist principles. Her

---

[33] Vitello, Paul, 'Zalman Shachter-Shalomi, Jewish Pioneer, Dies at 89', *The New York Times*, July 8, 2014, Zalman Schachter-Shalomi, Jewish Pioneer, Dies at 89 - The New York Times (nytimes.com)

[34] Awakin call editors, 'Charles Halpern: Cultivating Wisdom for Justice', *DailyGood*, July 13, 2017,
https://www.dailygood.org/story/1618/charles-halpern-cultivating-wisdom-for-justice-awakin-call-editors/

[35] Sylvia Boorstein website: www.Sylvia Boorstein.com.

book, *That's Funny, You Don't Look Buddhist...*[36] gives a highly personal account of her journey into Buddhism, and then even more deeply into Judaism. One of her explanations for these ventures is that Judaism encourages questioning.

Another organization, the Institute for Jewish Spirituality,[37] was formed to teach spiritual aspects of Judaism, in reaction to the number of American Jewish teachers and students who had left to join Buddhist institutions. It emphasizes traditional Jewish practices, but it combines them with mindfulness, meditation and yoga.

It is no wonder that the founders of the Institute for Jewish Spirituality were worried about losing Jews to Buddhism, or Hinduism. There were so many Jewish attendees in a kundalini yoga group at one Hindu ashram that they could conduct services on Jewish holidays, and they held a vegetarian Passover dinner. One American Jew who was studying Buddhist meditation discovered that at least half his teachers were Jewish. In some ashrams, they all were Jewish. One American Jew who had grown up in a small town found himself in contact with Jews for the first time when he began studying with Maharishi Yogi.[38] Another heard Israeli Hebrew for the first time at a transcendental meditation course, and she was deeply impressed when an Orthodox Israeli man led High Holy Day services for the Jews attending the course.

Kamenetz estimates that 30% of the faculty members in American university departments of Buddhist Studies were born Jewish. To make his point, he lists several current or former department chairs. One is Prof. Anne Klein, now Lama Rigzin Drolma, formerly Chair of the Department of Religion of Rice University and Co-founder of the Dawn Mountain Center for Tibetan Buddhism. Another is Prof. Stanley Weinstein, who taught at Komazawa University in Tokyo, in London, and again at Yale, where he had a distinguished career as the Director of

---

[36] Boorstein, Sylvia, *That's Funny, You Don't Look Buddhist: On Being a Faithful Jew and a Passionate Buddhist* (San Francisco: HarperCollins, 1997).
[37] Linzer, pp. 85–92.
[38] Linzer, p. 109.

Graduate Studies in the East Asian Studies MA Program, and he was the Chair of the Council on East Asian Studies.

Goshen-Gottstein writes that in Israel over 90% of the students taking introductory courses on Hinduism and India have visited India.[39]

Prof. Matthew Kapstein teaches Buddhist studies both at the University of Chicago Divinity School and at the Ecole Pratique des Hautes Etudes in Paris. Prof. Alex Wayman was a Tibetologist, and he was Professor of Sanskrit in the Department of Middle East and Asian Languages and Cultures at Columbia University. Prof. Charles Prebish is a professor emeritus at Pennsylvania State University, and he is an emeritus chaired professor at Utah State University, both in departments of religious studies, where his particular interest was in Buddhist studies. In a personal essay, he describes how his beloved father died of a brain tumor at age 48, when he was just 17. After that, he writes, "And I was no longer a Jew." Crushed by the loss and still hurting in college, it was a course in Buddhist studies that gave him new life.[40]

Clearly, a disproportionate number of Jews have become interested in eastern religions, practice them, read about them, write books, a lot of books, and go into academia. It figures. This has been the career path of scholarly Jews through the ages, even if they defined themselves as Buddhist, or Hindu. Here are more:

The Naropa Institute in Boulder Colorado was founded in 1974 by the Tibetan Buddhist teacher Chogyam Trungpa. Allen Ginsberg, Ram Dass, and other well-known counter-culture figures were teachers, right out of the sixties and the hippie generation! Starting as a summer school, it received accreditation as a full-time school four years later, and by 1995 it had become a four-year undergraduate college with its own campus.

So many of the students and teachers at Naropa were born Jewish that the teacher Chogyam Trungpa called it the 'Oy Vay school' of Buddhism. Rabbi Bernard Glassman taught a summer course there, but his other academic credits included being a

---

[39] Goshen-Gottstein, Alon, *The Jewish Encounter with Hinduism: History, Spirituality, Identity*, (London: Palgrave Macmillan, 2016), p. 586.
[40] Prebush, Charles S., 'A Bat out of Hell', H Net Humanities and Social Sciences On-line, Prebish, Charles S. | H-Buddhism | H-Net (h-net.org)

lecturer at Harvard and co-founder of the Center for Jewish Studies at UMass Dartmouth. Among the former students, two became Buddhist scholars. One was Prof. Robin Kornman, a professor of comparative literature at the University of Wisconsin, and an eminent translator of Tibetan to English. Another was Prof. Nathan Katz, now Professor Emeritus at Florida International University, but former Bhagawan Mahavir Professor of Jain Studies, Founder-Director of the Program in the Study of Spirituality, Founding Chair of the Department of Religious Studies, and Director of Jewish Studies! He writes, his "research focuses on Indo-Judaic studies, an area that I helped to pioneer."[41]

Not all the scholarly Jews have chosen academia. Ma Jaya Sati Bhagavati, born Joyce Green in Brooklyn, founded several institutions in Florida, where she taught a philosophy of attaining spiritual fulfillment through "selfless service" to humanity. In particular, she founded the Kashi Ashram, the River School, the River Fund, and the Kashi School of Yoga. Unfortunately, the ashram experienced several accusations of cult-like activity. Then there was Swami Rudrananda, born in Brooklyn as Albert Rudolph. He briefly became a student of Swami Muktananda in India, and then he returned to the United States, where he established an entrepreneurial chain of 14 ashrams, plus three more in Europe.

Kamenetz wrote his wonderful book, *The Jew in the Lotus,* about a trip to Dharamshala in 1990 that eight Jewish scholars and rabbis made for religious dialogue with the Dalai Lama,[42] his senior advisors, abbots of major Buddhist monasteries, youth leaders and western students of Buddhism. The Jewish participants included Joseph Goldstein, Jack Kornfield, Sharon Salzberg, Rabbi Bernard Glassman (Sensei), Stephen Levine (a colleague of Ram Dass and of the psychologist Elizabeth Kubler-Ross), and Surya Das, formerly Jeffrey Miller. For background, Joseph Goldstein grew up in the Catskills and became one of

---

[41] Katz, Nathan, 'Global Jewish Studies Program', Stephen J. Green School of International and Public Affairs, FIU, Nathan Katz | Global Jewish Studies Program (fiu.edu)

[42] Kamenetz, Rodger, *The Jew in the Lotus,* (New York: HarperSan Francisco, 1994).

America's foremost *vipassana* style meditation teachers, and Sharon Salzberg was a cofounder of the Insight Meditation Society in Massachusetts. One more participant was Alexander Berzin, a Jewish PhD in oriental studies who frequently had been the Dalai Lama's interpreter. One observer was Thubten Chodron, the Buddhist nun born as Cheryl Greene, who lived in India at the time.

In an excellent article describing the trip, Nathan Katz describes discussions that the Jewish delegation had about Jewish exile and survival[43] and about what lessons their history might have for the Dalai Lama. One example they thought of was how the Jewish home became the focus of observance and transmission of the religion, to keep it alive.

Kamenetz described misgivings that some of the rabbis had about possibly facing idols in Dharamshala and about the worry that the food there would not meet the requirements of Jewish dietary restrictions. In fact, the Tibetans took extraordinary care with the food, and it did pass muster. He also wrote of the wisdom that many of the participants shared among themselves and with their Buddhist hosts during the trip. In one conversation, Joseph Goldstein tells the group, "The Buddha didn't teach Buddhism. He just taught dharma, how he understood the truth. Really, that's about love and compassion and wisdom."

The conversation with the Dalai Lama taught them how much they all had in common. When asked why he felt it was important to establish a dialogue with Jews, the Dalai Lama answered that "I think we are both chosen people." Continuing, he said, "Another reason: when we became refugees, we knew that our struggle would not be easy. It will take a long time, generations. Very often we would refer to the Jewish people, how they kept their identity and faith despite such hardship and so much suffering." As the Dalai Lama knew very well, the Jews had lost much in the Holocaust, but 2,000 years before that, they had been expelled from their land by the Romans. Yet their religion

---

[43] Katz, Nathan, "A Meeting of Ancient Peoples: Western Jews and the Dalai Lama of Tibet", *Jerusalem Letters of Lasting Interest* VP:113, Mar 1991, A Meeting of Ancient Peoples: Western Jews and the Dalai Lama of Tibet by Nathan Katz (jcpa.org)

and culture survived, and they maintained their unity as a people. Why, and how?

The Tibetan Buddhists too had lost their land; their Dalai Lama was exiled, and 1.2 million of their fellow Tibetans were killed. Just as the Romans had destroyed the great Jewish Temple in first century Jerusalem, the Chinese had destroyed thousands of Tibetan monasteries in the mid-twentieth century. The Dalai Lama wanted to know how the Jews had survived as a people without a land for so many centuries.

The Dalai Lama started the proceedings with his question: "Tell me your secret, the secret of Jewish spiritual survival in exile." As they talked, the Jews who participated were fascinated by how the Tibetans faced their persecution with such equanimity. The Tibetans were amazed at descriptions of the Jewish Kabbalah and other spiritual practices, seeing a strong resemblance to some of their own practices. The Jewish participants, all of them well versed in Buddhism, explained Jewish practices in terms that the Buddhists would understand, "Shabbat harkens back to creation at the same time as it anticipates the messianic completion of the world. Jews live Shabbat as though the world were redeemed. The Dalai Lama draws upon his own meditational tradition of deity yoga visualization to comment, "You mean that Shabbat is your people's visualization exercise?" That is precisely what we do: through living "as though," we participate in the cosmic drama of redemption."

Both sides parted inspired.

Among the stories that Kamenetz told the group in Dharamshala, one was about the son of his friend Dr. Lieberman, who asked his father whether he was Jewish or Buddhist.[44] Dr. Lieberman answered, "I've got Jewish roots and Buddhist wings."

David Rome, the heir to the Jewish publishing house Schocken Books, was well aware that his family was descended from the great rationalist sage, the Gaon of Vilna. Yet he spent years studying Buddhist meditation with Chögyam Trungpa, and he reported that in meditation he felt "a sense that something was

---

[44] Kamenetz, p. 255.

right – just very much intuition." He said, "Though meditative practice survives in the Jewish tradition, the Buddhists are the world experts." Rome also was a co-founder of Naropa University.

Finally, after years of Buddhist studies, true to his scholarly roots, he returned to become an editor at Schocken Books, and shortly afterwards, he would be the one who received the manuscript of Rabbi Aryeh Kaplan's important book, *Jewish Meditation*, a seminal book of Jewish meditation.

Just after writing the above paragraph, my weekly Detroit Jewish News came in the mail, featuring an article about a start-up called the Nu Deli Truck. It seems that a Jewish man and his Indian girlfriend operate a restaurant in Goa during the winter, and in the summer, they come back to Michigan, where they serve Jewish deli food with an Indian flair from a truck that makes its way around neighborhoods in the Detroit area.[45] Later that week, a newsletter came from my synagogue with reminders of a yoga session on the coming Shabbat and of a meditation and mindfulness session that the rabbi would lead on Sunday. The same week, I watched a podcast of a dialogue between an American artist and an Israeli scientist, both of whom referred to their personal meditation practice. This blended tradition, Jewish-Indian, has become mainstream.

---

[45] Michael Pearce, 'Schmoozing with Matt Daniels of Nu Deli', *The Jewish News*, June 12, 2019.

CHAPTER FOUR.
IN ISRAEL

David Ben Gurion, the first Prime Minister of Israel, visited Burma in 1961. An avid student of Buddhism, he talked with Buddhist monks there, and he discussed Buddhism with Prime Minister U Nu. He asked so many questions that the Prime Minister suggested he travel to Ceylon to talk with a special Buddhist teacher. Ben Gurion asked what language they would have in common. U Nu answered, "What else? Yiddish."[1]

Ceylon now is Sri Lanka. Nathan Katz wrote an autobiography[2] detailing his Buddhist studies in many countries, including Sri Lanka. While living and studying there, he learned of a great master of Theravada Buddhism, the Venerable Nyanaponika Mahathera, called a "monk's monk." One day Katz was struggling with a verse (a *shloka*) that he found difficult to translate, and he sought out the master in his hut in a wildlife preserve. The monk solved his problem easily. In conversation, it turned out that his original name was Sigmund Feninger, or Siegmund Feniger.

Siegmund Feniger was a German Jew born near Frankfurt in 1901.[3] When he became serious about the study of Buddhism, he moved to Ceylon (Sri Lanka), where he was ordained as a

---

[1] Kamenetz, p. 165.

[2] Katz, Nathan, *Spiritual Journey Home: Eastern Mysticism to the Western Wall*, (Jersey City: KTAV Publishing House, 2009).

[3] Gomes, Jacquetta, 'Buddhism and Judaism, Exploring the Phenomenon of the JuBu', Mar. 19, 2010,
https://thubtenchodron.org/2010/03/jewish-buddhists/

Buddhist monk. While living in Sri Lanka, he began translating selected sermons of the Buddha into English, and that endeavor morphed into the highly respected Buddhist Publication Society, of which he was president until he died in 1994. When he died, he was succeeded by an American Jew who had become a Buddhist monk, taking the name Bhikku Bodhi. Both were Buddhists, but typically Jewish in their deep commitment to scholarship.

It also turned out that other Jews had followed the same route from Germany. If they came to India though, they were interned as Germans by the suspicious British, though they lived in an ashram in a lovely hill station to study Buddhism and Hinduism. Another German in India was a meditation teacher and activist for the rights of Buddhist women, Ayyah Khema, who had been born Ilse Kussel to a highly assimilated Jewish family in Berlin. Of course, that generation represented a very specific time in history, but Jews have been coming to India ever since.

Not long ago, I had dinner in Tel Aviv with one of my former Hebrew teachers. When I told her what I was writing about, she said that was a real coincidence; the next morning she was going off to attend a Buddhist retreat. It turned out that her father had been a practicing Buddhist, and he had even become a Buddhist monk in Thailand, as well as in England, at one time. Now she participates in a Buddhist sangha weekly, and from time to time she attends Buddhist retreats. She explained that the sangha was a group who meditated together, often led by an Israeli who had spent some time abroad as a Buddhist monk, perhaps in a monastery, then returned to Israel to teach. Yet, for all the years that I have known her, she had never even thought that fact was remarkable enough to mention. And mind you, she is absolutely Jewish. No question.

Newspaper articles try to estimate the number of Israelis who travel to India each year, and, not surprisingly, the numbers differ. Recognizing the wide variance in these numbers, we can simply quote some of them, without opining about which one is most accurate. In 2014, *Haaretz* published an article about Israelis who travel to the east. In it, they said the top destination was

Thailand, the second China, and the third was India, drawing 55,071 Israelis that year.[4]

Another article provides some details. "The Parvati Valley is the hotbed of this recreational immigration. The readily available drugs, peaceful environment and prospect of rave parties draws many foreigners to this hill station. There is complete freedom to do anything or nothing if you so choose." An Israeli friend reminds me that it is cold in the Himalayas during the winter, so this destination is only for warm weather months. The writer continues, "The daily expense comes to about 25 dollars (1,250 rupees), including lodging. Therefore, Israelis can easily spend six months to one year without any financial constraints, many enjoy the life so much they never return."[5] Accompanying the article are pictures of young Israelis in various versions of Indian dress and undress, partying.

Typical Israeli travelers to India are backpackers between 20 and 24 years old, who have just finished their stint in the Israeli army. Many go to remote Himalayan towns, where the locals are very indulgent of them; others go to coastal villages near Goa or to towns in South India. Many make a circuit of all these destinations, staying in India until either their money or their enthusiasm runs out. They may seek drugs, rave parties, or perhaps a peaceful environment free from conflict. "India is one of the most safe destinations with no known prejudice against Jews. Yoga and spirituality only add to India's allure"

Israelis also flock to the camel market in Pushkar, Rajasthan, as well as to other tourist locations in the Rajasthan Desert. Young travelers from other countries go there too, which adds to the appeal. Not only young Israelis travel to India either. Even their parents may come.

---

[4] Rosenblum, Irit, 'Where did the Israelis travel In the East in 2014?' *Megafon,* Jan. 13, 2015,
https://translate.google.com/translate?hl=en&sl=iw&u=https://megafon-news.co.il/asys/archives/233231&prev=search&pto=aue
[5] Arora, Anmol, 'Why young Israelis travel to India and never return home,' *Tripoto,* 2018,
https://www.tripoto.com/india/trips/why-israelis-in-india-love-india-897940

On the Quora question and answer site,[6] someone asked why so many Israelis travel to India. A long string of answers ensued: India is relatively cheap for the frugal traveler. Bargaining is normal. Israelis feel comfortable, welcome, and safe. Places frequented by Israelis often have Hebrew signs and menus. Young Israelis in India typically travel in groups, share travel information and party together. Cannabis is readily available. India is spacious compared to little Israel, and Israelis have the freedom to do whatever they want, untroubled by parental judgements about their lifestyles. India has no history of antisemitism. The food is delicious, and it is vegetarian-friendly. In much of the country, the climate resembles that of Israel. The exotic culture is amazing.

Israelis emphasize that they gave several years of their life to their country serving in the Israel Defense Forces (IDF), and, in return, Israeli society gives them something special, something not given by any other country in the world – a vacation, time, the opportunity to travel, to relax, to meet new people, to see new places. This is part of Israeli culture. Nobody thinks of going directly to university after the IDF. When they finish their service, the question they ask each other is, "And where are you going to travel?"

This is an important time in the life of an Israeli, a time with no responsibilities, no kids, no family. This trip to India is their first exposure to Asia, to exotica, to ornately carved art, and to nonwestern philosophies. It is their first and perhaps only chance to educate themselves before they go home to look for a job. And, since many do not attend college, this may be their most important post-military education.

This is a time when it is OK to stay for months, perhaps more than a year, with no pressure to return at a certain time. My teacher says, "Think how unusual this is. This is a very Israeli phenomenon. We feel free to learn a new culture, one that is approachable, but also stimulating. It also helps the young former soldier who had a traumatic experience in the IDF, who now needs to process what happened in military service, in a war, in

---

[6] https://www.quora.com/Why-do-Israelis-love-to-travel-to-India

a difficult battle. This is when they have time to understand it, to find meaning in it."

From a practical point of view, it has been easy to get a six-month visa. At one time only Israelis were able to obtain a one-year visa, an advantage that people from no other country enjoyed. In 2020 they still could obtain one-year visas and even do so on-line, but it is hard to predict what the situation will be after the Coronavirus epidemic.

Another intriguing advantage that Israelis have, especially if they are dark or sun-tanned and they enjoy wearing Indian garments, is that they blend in right in with the Indians, especially north Indians. I can attest to that, as I regularly wore kurtas – Indian shirts – and I used to be taken for Punjabi.

Family relationships connect the two countries too. So many Indian Jews have moved from Kerala or Bombay to Israel that relatives often travel between the two countries. A friend of mine who had traveled extensively in India remembers her delight when she spotted an entire family – the women dressed in beautiful Indian saris – sitting village-style, in a large group on the floor of Ben Gurion airport in Israel. When she approached them, they explained that they were about to visit the Indian side of their family.

As a result of the sizable Indian diaspora in Israel, Israelis may be exposed to Indian cultural events all across Israel.[7] The Indian community has built synagogues in 16 cities, in some cases several synagogues per city[8]. Dimona has an Indian Jewish Heritage Museum. A Marathi quarterly magazine is published in Israel for former citizens of that Indian state. There is an annual Indian cultural event in Lod. In Nevatim, the Cochin Heritage Center and synagogue[9] holds evenings of Indian Cochini folklore.

Speaking of this diaspora, "Many of them maintain emotional attachments to both Israel and India: "Israel is my fatherland, but India is my motherland," was and still is a

---

[7] Leyaqat Khan, p. 75.
[8] http://www.indjews.com/ijci_synagogues.html
[9] Cochin Cultural Heritage Center webpage,
http://cochinsyn.com/page-cochin-heritage-ctr.html

traditional saying among Indian Jews," according to a publication called *The Jewish People Policy Institute*.[10] They say that hundreds of Indian Jews come to parties at the Indian Embassy each year to celebrate Indian Independence Day and Republic Day.

Tourism to India is so common that it is essentially a societal norm. in December 2018, "Eli Sneh, the head of Consular Affairs for the Israeli Embassy in Delhi, estimated that some 80,000 Israelis visit India each year – a number, he says, that is growing".[11] That is the highest estimate I have seen. He also mentioned "Israelis [in India] on what is called the Humus Trail." The same article refers to 40,000 Israeli backpackers each year in India, a number resembling those in most other articles. The real numbers are not known. But it is a whole industry. Israeli social media groups provide tips for travelers to India. "One of the most popular of these is the Facebook group "Traveling to India with Meron," which formed two years ago with some 2,000 members and has since grown to nearly 30,000."

I asked a knowledgeable friend of mine in Israel if she could estimate the number of Israelis who visit India each year. She wrote: "In 2004, according to Ha'Aretz, 50,000 Israelis visited India...and it has probably been this way for the last 30 years... *1.5 million Israelis who have visited India. If you want to be super careful – you could say 1 million,* as many return repeatedly, although since 2004 there might be more than *50,000 Israeli visitors a year to India. That makes... 10% of Israeli population [that have] visited India! Most of them [are] young people, after their military service.*"[12] An article released from the Embassy of India shows that she is spot-on. They report that over 50,000 Israelis visited India in 2018, and over 70,000 Indians visited Israel in 2018.[13]

---

[10] Facilitating Bonds: India, Israel, and the Jewish People | The Jewish People Policy Institute (jppi.org.il)

[11] LaFontaine, Tamar, 'Why do Israelis Flock to India?' *The Jerusalem Post*, Dec. 8, 2018,
https://www.jpost.com/jerusalem-report/mother-india-573686

[12] Personal communication from Michal Ron.

[13] India-Israel Bilateral Relations, *Embassy of India* website, 2020,
https://www.indembassyisrael.gov.in/pages?id = mbk5e&subid = lejRe

An article written by a nun in a Tibetan Buddhist order begins with an expression of surprise at finding herself visiting Israel. She says, "Israel is one of the last places I'd ever expected to find myself teaching the Dharma, for a couple of reasons. One is personal: although I was raised Jewish, I have had very little contact with Jews (except for the JuBu's, the Jewish Buddhists in Dharamshala) since the mid-seventies."[14] She in fact was born Cheryl Greene, and note that she was "raised Jewish."

She then poses the question: "What draws Israelis of all ages to investigate the Dharma when they live in a land of many religious traditions? Because Orthodox Jews in Israel have become stronger politically and socially in recent years, many secular Jews feel alienated from their own religion. The Orthodox assert that either one practices their way, or one is not a proper Jew. Most people are not attracted to the Orthodox traditions, and other forms of Judaism, including the esoteric Kabala, although present in Israel, are not prominent. Thus, many people find themselves in somewhat of a spiritual vacuum."

Some might simply put it that most people in Israel are secular, non-practicing Jews who are not attracted to Orthodoxy at all.

Referring to one of the first groups to be established in Israel, the Vipassana meditation taught by Goenka, Thubten Chodron explains that this is "where they are brought back to their own raw physical and mental experiences. Here, they find little ritual and basic teachings free from cultural trappings and religious expressions such as bowing, refuge, and so forth... Others find the teachings on patience, love, and compassion in the Tibetan tradition inspiring."

Another woman we should mention is Rita Riniker, not Jewish, now usually called Losang Palmo, or simply Anila (nun) by her students. Born in Switzerland, she became a Buddhist nun in India. She lived in the Tushita Meditation Centre near Dharamshala for twenty years, where she was discovered by

---

[14] Thubten Chodron, Bhikshuni, 'Dharma- Israeli style', *Shambala Publications*, Winter 2000,
https://www.shambhala.com/snowlion_articles/dharma-israeli-style/

traveling Israelis, and since then, half of her students have been
Israelis. She spends most of her time now at her center in Bern,
but her students in India urged her to come to Israel and teach
them at a location near Mt. Tabor. Since then, for the past twenty
years or so, she has been coming to Israel yearly for three-month
sessions, teaching hundreds, if not thousands, of students every
year.

In an excellent article[15] Rabbi Goshen-Gottstein describes his
own progression from youthful explorations of transcendental
meditation to his founding the Elijah School for the Study of
Wisdom in World Religions, now called the Elijah Interfaith
Institute in Jerusalem. He also has served as head of the Institute
for the Study of Rabbinic Thought at Bet Morasha College,
Jerusalem. At the Elijah Institute, he began bringing Hindu
teachers, as well as teachers from other faiths, to Jerusalem, and
this led to forming the Elijah Board of World Religious Leaders.
Invitations to visit India ensued, and these led to his book *The
Jewish Encounter with Hinduism: History, spirituality, identity*, which
he dedicated to his extraordinary teacher, Swami Chidananda
Saraswati.

Rabbi Goshen-Gottstein describes his first impression of the
Swami: "I wish I could communicate in words the feeling of being
in this man's presence. The intensity of energy and feeling, the
uplifting of one's internal orientation and internal quest, that
occurred simply by being in his presence, are the stuff of which
stories of tzaddikim and masters of faith in all traditions are
made. One knows the presence when one is in it and someone
who has not experienced being in the presence of a great soul or
spiritual teacher will simply not understand the overwhelming
energizing and transformation one undergoes simply by being in
the presence of some individuals. Is this not in itself already a
powerful and transformative encounter with the spiritual reality
that comes from another tradition?"

---

[15] Goshen-Gottstein, Alon, 'My Jewish Encounter with Hinduism', *Tablet
Magazine*, April 13, 2018,
https://www.tabletmag.com/sections/arts-letters/articles/my-jewish-
encounter-with-hinduism

Everyone in the room was sitting on the floor when he first met Swami Chidananda, except the Swami, who was sitting on a chair. But when the rabbi sat down on the floor, so did he. The rabbi writes: "The hallmark of this contemporary teacher was humility, the kind of humility that grows from the fullness of knowledge of divine presence and that translates itself into a meticulous care taken in human relations. I do not think I ever saw or felt the depth of humility in practice as during that brief moment when Swami Chidananda descended to sit facing me."

These are the best descriptions I have ever read of a powerful Jewish encounter with Hinduism, experienced at the highest level. The rabbi wrote that this "combination of wisdom and deep humility was possibly unique" among all the religious leaders he had ever known.

It is amazing how many people in Israel have their own stories. Long gone are the embarrassed days when I was shy about admitting my own interest in India, lest I be considered a lapsed Jew. One evening in Tel Aviv, I told a successful attorney and his wife that I was thinking of writing this book. "Of course," they said. A relative of theirs had gone to India, married an Indian man and returned to Israel, where she was a university lecturer on East Asian Studies.

Our friend Michal is the brilliant daughter of good friends of ours. Her mother is a world-renowned professor of microbiology and a former Dean of Life Sciences at Tel Aviv University, and her father is a well-known Israeli engineer. Michal has strong academic credentials in Judaic studies, and she also meditates on a regular basis. On a recent trip to Tel Aviv, when I asked her, she checked WhatsApp groups to find meditation sessions for me.

One day we went to hear a visiting lecturer, Khenpo Samdrub, the head of the Garchen Rinpoche Institute in Ohio, who described several different types of meditation. Among them were *Om-ah-hung* meditation, *Shamata* and *Vipassana*. He also mentioned another Pali tradition. Some 45–50 people were in attendance, smiling in recognition as he discussed the different techniques. The next day, we joined another meditation group. I counted 15–20 attendees, mostly women. And this was only one of the many we could have attended that week in Tel Aviv alone.

In Israel, one simply checks social media to find out where and when there will be a nearby Buddhist sitting. In Tel Aviv, there are many choices. You can be included on any of several mailing lists, and you can find meditation groups, yoga classes or spiritual retreats online, since this is the way Israelis communicate. With all these overlapping lists, it is difficult to count the number of meditators, or potential meditators in Israel, but we will come back to that question.

When you arrive, a few people may be gathered for refreshments, or not. Then you remove your shoes, pick up a large meditation pillow, place it on the floor beside your fellow meditators, sit on the pillow in whatever position is comfortable, practice breathing or any other meditative exercise that you prefer, remain in the room for any teaching session that might take place at the end of the session if you wish, get up, replace your pillow on the shelf, perhaps leave a donation, and go quietly out. That is it. Or, if you want to, you may become more involved.

The Israel Insight Meditation Society (Tovana) is one of the most established Buddhist Dharma teaching organizations in Israel. The founder, Stephen Fulder, Ph.D, is a London born molecular biologist, educated at Oxford University, who became interested in alternative medicine and in meditation. After many years studying in India, he returned, and he has taught Buddhist meditation practice both in Israel and other countries for 20 years. He also has written 14 books on the subject. According to his website[16] "He is interested in the meeting point between dharma and Jewish wisdom." The Society[17] holds most of its retreats at Kibbutz Ein-Dor in the Galilee, close to Mt. Tabor, the site of the transfiguration of Jesus. In addition, retreats are held in other locations, lasting from one to several days. On their website I counted some 14 retreats listed over about 6 months. There also were two meditation classes on-line and other classes held weekly in May, 2021. In addition, in April through August there were 9 day-long courses. Attendance at retreats averages

---

[16] Stephen Fulder website, https://www.stephenfulder.com/
[17] www.tovana.org.il is the website of the Israel Insight Society, also known as Tovana or Amutat Tovana.

around 100, and Tovana says that their courses draw an average of about 40 attendees.

Dozens of weekly meditation sessions are held in towns, cities and kibbutzim all over the country, and a number also are held on-line. One that I attended was in Tel Aviv on Ovadya MiBartnoura St. This was Vipassana style, "with an emphasis on mindfulness, calm and insight," and it was only one of several locations at which Tovana holds weekly meditation sessions in Tel Aviv alone.

The mailing lists of participants in the many separate Tovana courses and retreats, taken all together, would run into the thousands. When I asked them how many they have on their mailing list, they estimated 15,000, but they pointed out that the number would be higher if they include those who just are engaged in mindfulness practice. Total numbers of individual participants would be very difficult to estimate though, because many people attend multiple activities.

Michal estimates that 50–100,000 Israelis have participated at least once in some form of activity related to eastern religions, primarily Buddhism. Many of them use Whats App groups to find lectures or meditation sessions that suit their needs and schedule. There are permanent centers too, such as the Israel Vipassana Meditation Center, also called Dhamma Pamoda. This was established in 2014 by students of S.N. Goenka, and it is located next to Kibbutz Deganya Bet, one of the oldest kibbutzim in Israel, just a short distance from the Sea of Galilee. Goenka was born in Myanmar (Burma), where he studied the technique of Vipassana for 14 years, and he also was the head of the Hindu merchant association. After that he moved to India, and he began teaching Vipassana in 1969. The Dhamma Pamoda center now holds ten-day residential courses in Vipassana meditation in a huge purpose-built hall, in English, Hebrew, and Russian.

In response to my question about how many people are on their mailing lists, the Dhamma Pammoda (or Pamoda) Center answered that, "On normal days the center can host approximately 80 students. Normally every two weeks a 10-day course is taking place in the center." On their website, I saw three ten-day courses and one three-day course to be held in about a month in 2021, all held at Kibbutz Degania. These classes are held throughout the year, which would come to over 2,000 students a year for the past six years, a potential total of 12,000. Then again, if 20–30% are returnees, as some estimate, the number would be smaller.

Michal writes: "They are one of the oldest groups in Israel...the Israeli center of the Goenka tradition. They have had their own center since 2014, but they have been running yearly courses with hundreds of people for the last 30 years plus...They are fully booked, usually, for 2–3 months in advance." Obviously during the time of the Coronavirus, these numbers and bookings have differed from those of previous years. During this period some people moved closer to home. In other cases, they went to India, the Sinai, or to a monastery in the east in order to continue their practice.

Adding to the multiplicity of retreats, In 2010, the artist and musician Itamar Newman and his wife Liora founded another Buddhist Vipassana Meditation Center, located in Yavne'el Israel.[18] The chief teacher is Ajahn Ofer Adi (Phra Ofer), an Israeli who became a Buddhist monk in northern Thailand, and for the past 16 years has been teaching world-wide, mainly in Europe and Israel. The center teaches art, meditation and the connection between art and Buddhism. This is not the same as the Buddhist Vipassana Meditation Center near Deganya Bet, which is not related. Phra Ofer teaches in several settings in Israel, and he has held numerous retreats, some scheduled on the Jewish holidays of Succoth and Pesach.

Other Buddhist centers in Israel are affiliates of world-wide chains.[19] Among these are the Diamond Way Buddhism centers, whose teachers come from the Karma Kagyu lineage of Tibetan Buddhism. The founder is Lama Ole Nydahl, a controversial and flamboyant figure[20] who was born in Copenhagen, Denmark, and

---

[18] Newman Association – Buddhist vipassana meditation center website, 2019, https://www.israelgives.org//amuta/580451466
[19] Diamond Way Buddhism Israel website,
http://www.buddhism.org.il/en/
[20] Scherer, Bee, 'Neo-Orthodox Tradition and Transition: Lama Old Nydahl and the Diamond Way', 2018, published on a site labelled Tibetan

who teaches in centers all over the world. The website calls him a follower of the 17th Karmappa, Trinley Thaye Dorje. This is the so-called Chinese Karmappa, not the Karmappa who lives in Dharamshala, but the political ramifications of that are not relevant to our discussion. Starting with seven franchises in Israel – Tel Aviv, Jerusalem, Haifa, Ashdod, Beersheba, Bat Yam and Eilat, the Diamond Way centers are part of a network of more than 650 centers across the world. On their site they estimate that they have over 200 followers in Israel, but this number seems low in view of the number of centers they report. The centers offer weekly Vajrayana meditation sessions, yoga, and coaching programs for businesses.

Many of the names are confusing. On one website is an organization called Dharma Friends of Israel, which describes multiyear Buddhist training programs and has an extensive library of literature on the Mahayana Buddhism of the Dalai Lama. I wrote to ask how many students they have taught, but I received no answer.[21]

Friends tell me that the numbers may be, for the Vipasana/Mindfulness/Hinayama/Teravada Buddhism tradition, perhaps 12,000 participants a year studying with Goenka, a thousand a year with Phra Ofer, and, as we have estimated, another several thousand with Tovana. For the Mahayana/Tibetan Buddhism tradition, Dharma Friends of Israel lists 4,000, but many come to more than one course a year.

Michal points out that many of the people who attend courses come yearly, so not all those on the course lists will be new students. For example, a mailing list may have more than 1,000 people, but every month more than 10 new people will register. Then she asks, "What about the people who are registered to more than one group?" She continues, "Someone who is registered, but never read the mails – is he involved? And

---

Buddhism in the West. As described, Nydahl follows Karmappa Trinley Thaye Dorje, the Chinese Karmappa, so called because the Chinese picked him to supplant the Karmappa who was chosen in the Tibetan tradition. https://info-buddhism.com/Ole_Nydahl_and_Diamond_Way_B_Scherer.html
[21] Dharma Friends of Israel website, www.dharma-friends.org.il

if he shows up once every few years? Someone who practices at home with a teacher... might not belong to any of the groups."

How do we count those who are on one mailing list, as opposed to those who are on duplicate lists, those who participate occasionally, those who practice daily, those who identify completely as Buddhists, those who practice mindfulness or breathing meditation without any religious reference, or those who have only participated occasionally, maybe only in the past?

Speaking particularly of Buddhist groups, Michal writes: "most groups in Israel work in co-operation... Shantideva in Herzliya Israel – which belongs to the Foundation for the Preservation of the Mahayana Tradition (FPMT)[22] is getting very big, but many of its volunteers are also active in other groups. They began to invite Chamtrul Rinpoche to come to Israel every year from his home in Dharamshala India, and he now has come at least 15 times. Later Bodhicitta Israel formed to arrange his visits. Their name means mind of enlightenment, and they teach Tibetan Buddhism." Both of these belong to large multinational organizations.

Searching on-line[23] for Buddhist organizations in Israel, the World Buddhist Directory listed 27 entries. Four are affiliated with Diamond Way, and thirteen are affiliated with the Community of Mindfulness in Israel (CMI)[24]. We already have discussed three of the centers. Among the nine remaining, three describe themselves as non-sectarian, and four as Zen.

One of the non-sectarian centers is the Simply Meditate Nondual Meditation Group in Hod Hasharon[25], taught by Jonathan Harrison. British-born, he started as a high-tech

---

[22] Foundation for the Preservation of the Mahayana Buddhist Tradition website,
https://fpmt.org/fpmt-community-news/news-around-the-world/shantideva-study-group-working-for-peace-in-israel-and-palestine/
[23] Buddha Net's World Buddhist Directory,
https://www.buddhanet.info/wbd/region.php?region_id=6&offset=25
[24] The Community of Mindfulness in Israel,
http://mindfulness-israel.org/about-2/
[25] Simply Meditate Nondual Meditation Group website,
http://www.simplymeditate.org/

manager who studied awareness techniques to relieve the stress of his job.

Another of the non-sectarian centers is the Bhavana House in Tel Aviv, which belongs to the World Fellowship of Buddhists. This was established by two Israelis, Itamar Bashan, a clinical psychologist, and Thor Gonen, both children of Holocaust survivors. The other center, Mandala Land, located in both Haifa and Yavne, was described as Vajrayana in practice, but now the website has disappeared.

The thirteen centers listed on the Community of Mindfulness in Israel (CMI) website include ones in Ein Hod, Jerusalem, Kiryat Tiv'on, Mevasseret, Modi'in, the Negev, and two in Tel Aviv. They teach in the tradition of Zen master Thich Nhat Hanh, and they are part of the Plum Village Community[26], that has affiliates in six other countries.

A website called Study of Buddhism in Israel[27] lists a number of courses and travel-study programs, one of which is a café in Tel Aviv that doubles as a Zen monastery. Another site was to be "a sacred space to be inaugurated in a high-rise building." According to the media, this was a Sri Lankan Buddhist temple that opened in Tel Aviv several years ago, very quietly, to avoid offending local sensibilities. Apparently it was quiet indeed. My Israeli friends seem to have never heard of it, and that website too has disappeared.

Do you want to meditate on Mt. Carmel just south of Haifa? The Bet Hadharma (Dharma House) is there, dedicated to Tibetan Buddhism, meditation and mindfulness.[28] And, if you look, you can also find dozens of other small groups in the area.

Since November 2014, Lama Dvora-la, born Dvora Tzvieli,[29] the daughter of Eliahu and Hana Zucker, has been teaching

---

[26] Plum Village website, https://plumvillage.org
[27] Study of Buddhism in Israel, *Study Israel*,
http://carleton.ca/studyisrael/israel-fun-facts/study-buddhism-israel/
[28] Dharma House website,
http://www.dharma-house.org.il/dh/index.php/en/home/2-uncategorised/72-about-dharma-house
[29] 'Dvora Tzvieli', Prabook, trademark of World Biographical Encyclopedia, https://prabook.com/web/dvora.tzvieli/3352101

Tibetan Buddhism at three retreats a year in the Arava Spiritual Center, south of the Dead Sea. Lama Dvora was born in Poland, moved to the U.S., studied in the U.S. and Israel, and she worked as a communications executive with AT & T in the U.S. for many years. Since then, she reportedly[30] has led 45 meditation groups in Israel, and she has offered a three-year retreat in Arizona, though none of the articles about her present any evidence of a Buddhist lineage. According to one article that announced her program,[31] "Lama Dvora Tzvieli seeks to build a spiritual university in the central Arava, under the rubric of 'Wisdom and Intelligence.'"

We should mention that she has met opposition. In January 2011, while the center was still in the planning stages, the anti-missionary society Yad l'Achim objected to hundreds of acres being given over to a "Spiritual University" in the Arava. In particular, the society condemned the potential presence of graven images of the Buddha, since according to Jewish law this is idol worship, which is strictly forbidden. Yet, Lama Dvora built her center.

The matter of Lama Dvora brings up an interesting point. Setting aside any discussion of her credentials, she raises the issue of feminism. Most female practitioners of Buddhism and Hinduism in both America and Israel say that this is important to them. It is not unusual for groups to have female leaders, and a woman in a meditation group has every reason to expect that she will participate with no restrictions. In India, almost all the Hindu priests are men, but of late a few are female. One exception to the general rule has been that yoga teachers all over the world commonly are women.

Yoga is a completely different case though. Michal says there must be more yoga practitioners than meditators in Israel – since many do yoga as a sport, like a gym class. In India though, yoga is a distinct practice, and it is more of a spiritual regime. As

---

[30] The Knowledge Base,
https://www.theknowledgebase.com/archive/en/voices-from-three-year-retreat-meditation-three-years-later/
[31] Benari, Elad, 'Warning Against Buddhist Center,' Arutz Sheva 7, Jan 13, 2011, http://www.israelnationalnews.com/News/News.aspx/141713

exhaustively described in the Yoga Sutra of Patanjali, a collection of 196 sutras compiled from 500 BCE to 400 CE, it becomes apparent that yoga constitutes an entire interwoven mode or system of practice and life, in which the mental exercises and physical exercises (Hatha Yoga) are part of a whole, with the mental portion considered to be the more advanced form. Understood in that way, the reader will realize that yoga is an entire philosophy, drawing upon both Hinduism and Buddhism. Yet, in the west, the entire mental practice often is ignored.

To properly discuss various forms of Hindu practice in Israel we would need to go into distinctions between meditation, Buddhist meditation, Hatha Yoga (the physical practice) and Hinduism itself, but that would mean trying to describe relatively small practice groups with, in the aggregate, probably not more than a few thousand participants. Again, the number would be difficult to pin down, since people may attend one, several or many programs, and each person might be counted multiple times. Still, Michal points out, when famous teachers visit, a large number of people attend.

Israel does have many yoga organizations, ranging from Iyengar yoga to Ashtanga, Vinyasa, none of which qualify as religious institutions. They are more like exercise programs, even though many of them add a few minutes of meditation at the end of the session.

There are several Sivananda Yoga Vedanta Organization Centers, founded in 1971 by Swami Vishnudevananda, a disciple of Sri Swami Sivananda of Rishikesh, India. The largest group of yoga centers in Israel, their website indicates that they have trained thousands in their centers in Jerusalem, Pardes Hana, Eilat and Tivon. Lately the Sivananda Yoga Center in Tel Aviv has diversified. No longer just a yoga studio, it also offers meditation, stress management and cooking classes.[32]

While Hinduism may be less popular than Buddhism in Israel, Hare Krishna certainly has an active presence. After first starting out in Tel Aviv on Ben Yehhuda St., it moved to the West Bank city of Ariel, where "It is spearheaded by Jagadish and his

---

[32] Sivananda Yogi Tel Aviv, https://www.sivananda.co.il/

wife, Jugala-Priti, and serves a growing community of devotees from Russia...”[33] Jugala-Priti later joined ISKCON (the International Society for Krishna Consciousness) in Tel Aviv,[34] where Hare Krishnas come to spend Saturdays on the beach, singing, dancing and selling books.

The ISKON centers are a huge enterprise, with locations all over the world. Founded in the 1960s, ISKCON is known as Hare Krishna. From the beginning the movement was particularly attractive to Jews, especially Russian Jews, and at one time much of the leadership was Jewish. Before they dialed it down a bit, the Hare Krishnas were well known around the world as street-side chanting, orange-draped groups much like the “Na, Na Nachman” Hasidim who hop out of their cars to dance in the middle of the road in Jerusalem.

The colorful Krishna Janmashtami festival,[35] patterned after yearly Hindu festivals in India, is very popular in northern Israel. The festival features theatrical presentations of scenes from Krishna’s childhood, accompanied by singing, dancing, and a feast of 108 dishes. A highlight of the festival is a nine-tier human pyramid with a little boy who has climbed to the top. The festival is held in Kibbutz Barkai, close to the town of Harish, south of Haifa.

The Sathya Sai Organization was established in 2001 in Ein Hod, near Haifa. A Youtube presentation[36] of theirs emphasizes their devotion to the education of children, community service, disaster relief and free medical care, characterizing the organization as completely non-denominational. The film says

---

[33] Dhanurdhara Swami, ‘Ariel, Israel, There is Another, *Waves of Devotion*, May 18, 2002, https://wavesofdevotion.com/2002/05/18/ariel-israel-there-is-another/

[34] The International Society for Krishna Consciousness website, www.iskcon.org

[35] ‘Krishna Janmashtani 2020: History, significance, date and time of celebration’, Hindustan Times, Aug. 11, 2020, https://www.hindustantimes.com/more-lifestyle/krishna-janmashtami-2020-history-significance-date-time-interesting-facts/story-YunHjzynOhs6KRPx6wuEbI.html

[36] ‘Sathya Sai International Organization’, https://www.youtube.com/watch?v=EasB6uCgVmE

clearly that none of the portrayed activities have religious content. Yet clips on their Facebook site[37] feature a guru delivering devoutly Hindu religious messages, leaving the viewer wondering whether the Youtube presentation is disingenuous.

Hinduism is especially prominent in Israel because of the many Israelis who have spent time in India. My husband once had dinner with a prominent Sikh politician at the Indian Embassy in Washington, and he said that he had been the Chief of Mission of the Indian Embassy in Israel, where he felt very much at home, enjoying the many greetings from Israelis who approached him on the street, put their hands together in the typical Indian namaste and greeted him in Punjabi.

If all the Hindu and Buddhist practitioners are taken together, the aggregate number is large, which raises an interesting question. Why does Israel tolerate them with so little resistance? My husband and I have visited the Mormon center in Jerusalem twice, where they told us that, as a condition of being allowed to build their center, Israel required them to foreswear proselytizing. This is hard for Mormons to promise, but they knew they had to. In June 2020, Israel pulled the license from GOD TV, an evangelical radio station that actively promoted conversion to Christianity. Of course, neither Hindus nor Buddhists proselytize.

Israel may worry less about incursions by eastern religions than it does about religions that actively proselytize, such as Mormonism. Remember, *neither Buddhism or Hinduism presents itself as a substitute religion.* Most Jews regard them primarily as enhancements or enrichments to existing Jewish spirituality.

But there has been push-back. Srila Dhanurdhhara Swami discussed this in a 2002 journal article,[38] saying "Because Krishna consciousness is a cultural revolution, it threatens that identity and thus subtly threatens the country's survival at least in the mind of the common citizen. Thus, to become a devotee in Israel, one must not only overcome one's philosophical doubts, but also

---

[37] 'Sri Sathya Sai Baba Official Facebook Page.
[38] Srila Dhanurdhhara Swami, Harish, Israel, 'Waves of Devotion Archives', May 17, 2002,
https://www.wavesofdevotion.com/journal/2002/05/

a sense of betrayal to one's country." In the end, he says, he was able to teach his students without undue interference.

Buddhism and Hinduism have been fertile fields for scholarly work in Israel. Many prominent Israeli academics study and teach both subjects, and some of them are known world-wide. We might want to learn about a few of them.

Jacov Raz is a professor emeritus of Buddhism, Zen Buddhism and Japanese culture at Tel Aviv University.[39] Professor Raz was born in Tel Aviv to parents from Thessaloniki who were professed communists, but he rose to become Head of East Asian Studies at Tel Aviv University, perhaps the largest department of its kind in the world, with 650 students. He leads Buddhist meditation groups and is a cofounder of a center for Buddhist therapists. In an interview for Haaretz in the Tel Aviv coffee shop that doubles as a Zen monastery, he explains that he is interested in demonstrating the practical relevance of Buddhism to everyday problems we face in the modern Western world.[40]

Professor David Dean Shulman is the Renee Lang Professor of Humanistic Studies at Hebrew University in Jerusalem, and one of the most renowned figures in the world in the field of Sanskrit and Hindu cultures. His interests range from Indian poetics, to Sanskrit theater, to the 16–17th century culture of South India, to the classical music of Karnataka, to Islam in South India. He was elected to the Israel Academy of Sciences and Humanities, received the Israeli EMET Prize for Art, Science and Culture and received the Israel Prize. In addition to Hebrew and English, he is fluent in Sanskrit, Hindi, and the south Indian languages of Tamil and Telugu. Prof. Shulman also reads Arabic and Malayalam. He has published Hebrew poetry, and he has written or co-authored more than 20 books, many of them on South India.

---

[39] Sela, Maya, 'Finding Zen at the Heart of Tel Aviv', *Haaretz*, Sept. 28, 2013, https://www.haaretz.com/.premium-zen-and-the-art-of-buddhism-in-tel-aviv-1.5340871
[40] Study of Buddhism in Israel, https://carleton.ca/studyisrael/israel-fun-facts/study-buddhism-israel/

Prof. Shulman's son Eviatar Shulman has a PhD in Buddhism, and he also writes about Buddhism. Of all the prizes that the father was awarded, it should be obvious that these honors were awarded by the Israeli establishment in honor of his works about Hinduism and eastern spirituality, despite the issue of idol worship.

That does not mean that idol worship is no problem for a Jew who is interested in Hinduism. I have felt that exact discomfort:

> *My husband and I were in Bangalore with Ram, a friend of his, and our two close physician friends from Detroit, who had come to India for a conference. Ram's friend, a pious south Indian, learned that we could join morning prayers at a beautiful temple near our hotel, and she urged us all to go together. At this private ceremony, or puja, we all stood behind the priest while he ladled offerings into a gaping aperture in the side of the temple, flames visible inside. By that time, I had dragged my husband to practically every famous temple in India, where he would stand by patiently while I admired elaborate sculptures of gods. We even had visited this same temple before, but only to see the carvings. Still, this was different.*

> *"Come in closer," Ram's friend said. "Here, let the priest bring you into the puja. You can hold the handle."*

> *I was shocked at how I felt. Participate? That would be unabashed idol worship. No caveats. I was standing in a tight knot of very dear friends, who felt like family. There was no question that I was there willingly, that my participation could be construed as signifying homage to Hindu gods. But what about the Ten Commandments and the prohibition against worshipping graven images? No. I could not. I shrank back as far as possible. They warmly invited me to come closer, and I moved even farther away. I could admire the artistic merit of a graven image, but never could I worship it.*

It is possible though to walk this line. Rabbi Alon Goshen-Gottstein found comfortable footing on both sides of it. He not only created the Elijah Interfaith Institute, but he also taught at

Tel Aviv University. He also served as director for interreligious affairs at the respected Shalom Hartman Institute for Advanced Studies in Jerusalem. Here is an Israeli who has found no conflict between interfaith studies and his Judaism.[41]

So far, we have learned about person-to-person contacts, but a remarkable number of country-to-country relationships have formed, in a relatively short time. This just demonstrates the exceptional affinity Israel and India have for each other. Remember, official connections did not start in 1950 when India first recognized Israel. They did not start in 1970 when – as we are about to read – Ram Jethmalani worked with the Indian Consul to Bombay, Ya'akov Morris, to establish ties between the two countries and to make use of a building that was essentially an informal Indian embassy in Delhi. Recognized and acknowledged connections had to wait until the establishment of formal diplomatic relations, which only began in 1992, when India finally opened an official embassy in Israel. But after that, they took off apace.

And this is despite the reality that the two countries had a common colonial history, were born at the same time, had many of the same enemies, were given the same legal system, used the same English language for administrative purposes, and in many ways were influenced by the same societal norms. So what could be the problem?

---

[41] The Elijah Interfaith Institute website,
http://elijah-interfaith.org/about-elijah/our-staff

CHAPTER FIVE.
POLITICAL AND ECONOMIC TIES

Both India and Israel were born, actually reborn, at the same time, from the same mother.

THE BRITISH

Both India and Israel are ancient lands, with ancient peoples, and both were former colonies of the British Empire, the largest empire in the history of the world, an empire so large that the sun never set on all its lands. The empire began in about 1500, and it did not wind down until after the Second World War. Just before the First World War, the British Empire held almost a quarter of the population of the world. Just after that war, it covered almost a quarter of the area of the earth.

The empire disseminated the English language, the English legal system, the Parliamentary system of government and the conventions of the British military all over the world. In as many areas as possible, wherever the British ruled, they built roads, railroads, courts and civic institutions. As a result, their former colonies have much in common, the British elements strong and recognizable. Visitors from one country to the other will find much that is familiar about the laws, the courts, and the commonly understood sense of values.

The British East India Company formed as early as 1600, and by 1757 this private company effectively ruled portions of India. By the 1800s, its army was twice the size of the regular British army. The Indians finally rebelled. The turning point was the Sepoy Rebellion of 1857. After that, the British East India Company was disbanded, and in 1858 the British began to rule India directly. This period was called the British Raj, in which Queen Victoria became the Empress of India. By the end of the Second World War, the Indians were pushing out the British as fast as they could; the British were reduced to borrowing money from the U.S., and they were ready to leave India. Ultimately, they boarded ship in Bombay on August 15, 1947, and they went home.

The land of Palestine was part of the Ottoman Empire for 400 years, but in the Battle of Beersheba on October 31, 1917, General Allenby wrestled the Holy Land away from the Turks. From there, he marched into Jerusalem. At that same time, the Jews were pressuring the British to grant them Palestine as a homeland. The Balfour Declaration was issued on exactly October 31, 1917, in the form of a letter from Lord Balfour to Lord Rothschild, and it affirmed the intent of the British to establish a national home for the Jewish people in Palestine.

In 1919, the Treaty of Versailles officially created a Mandate for control of Palestine, and it handed Palestine to England. After that, it becomes complicated. Leaving the rest of that story aside, the end of the Mandate came when the bankrupt British left the land of Israel. This was on May 15, 1948, nine months after they left India.

Thus, India and Israel shook off their British overlords at nearly the same time. Theodor Herzl predicted the rebirth of Israel in his book, *Altneuland*. The title means old-new land, and that description also fits India. Both countries had rich cultures that predated that of Britain, their colonizers and erstwhile superiors. Now both had to start anew, and that meant war.

As soon as they emerged as independent nations, both India and Israel suffered catastrophic sectarian violence at the hands of Muslims. India was partitioned into two parts, and when it achieved independence from the British on August 15, 1947, its Muslim population violently split away to form a new country called Pakistan. Ever since, Hindu India and Muslim Pakistan have been intermittently at war.

Less than one year later, on May 14, 1948, Israel declared independence from the British, and the country of Israel was attacked by the surrounding Muslim countries. Ever since, Israel has been attacked intermittently by Muslim nations or by Arabs living in the Palestinian territories. Thus, the two countries have much in common, but up to 1992, the Indian government was more concerned about the Muslim vote than it was about Israel.

Before India established full diplomatic relations with Israel, relationships between the two countries did exist, but they were under the radar, subject to the political whims of the Indian government.[1] Israelis did travel to India, but there is no comparison with the time after 1992, when travel blossomed. All this might seem surprising, since there always had been quiet cooperation when times were tough.

India enjoyed agricultural assistance from Israel during the period of diplomatic drought. Israel was one of the few countries to offer military help to India in 1962 during its conflict with China in the Himalayas, and Israel quietly helped India again in 1965 and in 1971 in its wars with Pakistan.[2]

But India still hesitated to engage with Israel, even though both countries obtained independence from the same colonizer, underwent partition, were birthed in war, received a flood of refugees, and they continued to face hostilities from similar neighbors. The problem was that, before partition, India had the largest number of Muslims of any country in the world, and even after partition, it had the third largest, representing over 12% of the Indian population.

In Israel, the Muslim population opposed the Zionist dream of a Jewish nation. In India, recognition of Israel was a wedge issue between the two major political parties, both of which needed Muslim votes. This issue also affected Indian relationships with Pakistan, Kashmir, the Muslim-majority nations of Asia and the Middle East. For instance, India wanted the support of Arab states in the UN in the ongoing dispute with Pakistan over Kashmir. Making things worse, India turned toward Russia, and Israel was aligned with the U.S.

---

[1] Kumaraswamy, P.R., *India's Israel Policy*, (New York: Columbia University Press, 2010). An excellent summary of important milestones in the India-Israel relationship.

[2] Kumaraswamy, P.R., *India's Israel Policy*, p. 215.

Despite the worry over the Muslim vote, quiet warmth existed between the two countries all along. Kumaraswamy writes[3] that "Even before the formation of the Jewish state, India was functioning as a transit point for the emigration of Jewish refugees from Iraq, Afghanistan, and Europe. Shortly after Indian recognition, an *aliyah* office opened in India to facilitate refugee emigration." And in 1951, the Jewish Agency appointed a representative in Bombay for that purpose. After that India established a consular agency in Bombay.

From 1969 to 1971 Ya'akov Morris was the head of the Israeli consulate in Bombay. The father of the Israeli historian Benny Morris, he was an extraordinarily active consul, often working impishly with our lawyer-politician friend, Ram Jethmalani.[4] Together with other prominent figures such as the author Khushwant Singh, they formed an Indo-Israel Friendship Association with over 90 branches all over India. Morris socialized and held major events, sometimes using a house that the Jethmalani family had purchased for that purpose in Delhi. Ram called it the de facto Israeli embassy. Encouraged by Ram and his other enthusiastic supporters among the Indian intelligentsia, Morris attracted so much publicity with his activities that finally he pushed his luck, and he was invited abruptly to return to Israel. His successors were kept under tighter rein.

On a personal note, my husband and I met Ambassador C.S. Jha at the engagement party for Ram's daughter Rani. Jha was the father of the groom, but more to the point, he had been a former ambassador to six countries and to the UN; his stories captivated my husband for the entire evening. In his book, Kumaraswamy specifically mentions Israeli contacts with Ambassador Jha, saying that he and other Indian politicians had

---

[3] Kumaraswamy, P.R.,' India and Israel: The Diplomatic History,' Chap. 12, in Katz et al. India recognized the Jewish state in 1950, but it did not establish full diplomatic relations with Israel until 1992.

[4] *After Saturday Comes Sunday*. In this book I devote a chapter to the story of Morris in India, courtesy of materials furnished by his son, Benny Morris, but I only give the highlights here.

facilitated Israeli meetings and diplomatic contacts with key Indian politicians long before normalization.

Finally, in 1992 all the diplomatic tiptoeing around ended, and today there are many important relationships in multiple fields between Israel and India.

RECENTLY

Twelve or thirteen years ago, when we were eating dinner in our hotel in Delhi, our waiter told us that the hotel was exceptionally busy. It was full because that week the Indian government was taking bids from international arms dealers. My husband and I looked at each other, certain there would be Israelis among them. After dinner, we pressed the elevator button to go to our room, and when the elevator door opened, it was full of Israelis talking Hebrew. I greeted them in Hebrew, and we talked briefly. At breakfast the next morning, one of the Israeli women asked if I was busy that day or if I would be able to go around with them.

A woman from another hotel was in the car that picked us up that morning. She explained that, because of the nature of their business, all the Israelis were not allowed to stay at the same hotel. The driver was Indian, but he spoke Hebrew. We drove to his office, got out and walked down a wide lane through one of the main markets of Delhi, passing several signs in Hebrew. Then we walked upstairs to a leather shop where young Israeli backpackers were lounging indolently, smoking weed. The Indian proprietor took orders for merchandise in Hebrew. My companions finished negotiating their purchases, and we returned to the office, where they asked if I would join them for lunch, pointing to a restaurant across the way. On the door was a Star of David. I demurred, since I had plans for the afternoon.

The woman from my hotel offered to have the driver take me back, but the other woman said, "Lo, lo, lo; I promised my husband that I would never be out of his sight. I have to stay with the driver." Ah yes, he would be the security guard. These were arms dealers after all.

In relations between India and Israel, the most conspicuous cooperation has been on matters of defense, internal security and counterterrorism. Between 2002 and 2012, Israeli sales to India in the field of defense exceeded $10 billion.[5] According to political scientists at Aligargh Muslim University, "India constitutes Israel's third largest export market for arms and defence [sic] equipment."[6] By 2010, Israel was India's second largest defense supplier after Russia, and India was Israel's largest export destination for Israeli arms. In 2019, India purchased 46% of all Israeli arms exports.[7]

Meanwhile, in part because of these military ties and the relationships that formed between the parties, other business, commercial and cultural ties developed. Some of the original relationships had been personal, starting with contacts made by young Israelis travelling in India. However it started, from 1992 on, bilateral trade rose by 50% a year, topping one billion dollars by 1999, as reported by Aligarh Muslim University. By then, Israel was India's fourth largest trading partner in the Middle East. Kumaraswamy writes that bilateral trade was close to $4 billion by 2010.

In 2014, bilateral trade was about 4.4 billion, even though Indian products still only represented 3.2% of all Israeli exports and 3.1% of Israeli imports. In return, India's trade with Israel still was only 3% of all its Middle East trade.[8] Though these

---

[5] Ullekh, '$10 bn business: How Israel became India's most important partner in arms bazaar', *The Economic Times*, Sept. 24, 2012, https://economictimes.indiatimes.com/news/economy/foreign-trade/10-bn-business-how-israel-became-indias-most-important-partner-in-arms-bazaar/articleshow/16507523.cms?from=mdr

[6] Khan, Leyaqat, 'India-Israel Relations', *Aligarh Muslim University Department of Political Science*, https://shodhganga.inflibnet.ac.in/bitstream/10603/110707/9/13_chapter4.pdf

[7] Wermenbol, Grace, 'A passage to India: Israel's Pivot East', Jul 24, 2019, https://www.atlanticcouncil.org/blogs/menasource/a-passage-to-india-israel-s-pivot-east/

[8] 'India, Israel and the Jewish People', Chap. 2, *The Jewish People Policy Institute*, Economic Exchanges | The Jewish People Policy Institute (jppi.org.il)

percentages are low, increasing numbers of Indian trade delegations have come to Israel since 2012, and interest remains high, especially in IT and telecommunications, agriculture, water, renewable energy, pharmaceuticals, homeland security and infrastructure projects. Much of this has been since 2014, when Narendra Modi was sworn in as Prime Minister.

By the end of 2020, according to the Jewish News Service on October 18, 2021, bilateral trade had reached $4.67 billion.

With all the demand for high-tech alliances, three quarters of the Indian exports to Israel still have consisted of cotton and diamonds. By 2010, two thirds of the bilateral trade between the two countries was in diamonds. Herein lies a story.

In the not so distant past, Orthodox Jews in Antwerp, Belgium and Amsterdam dominated the world diamond trade. Gradually a group of Indian merchants and diamond cutters became increasingly skilled in the business, and in a relatively short time they took over a huge percentage of it. These were the Jains, most of them living in the state of Gujarat, in northwest India. They do most of their diamond cutting in India, and they export more than 90% of all the world's cut diamonds, primarily to Antwerp, Tel Aviv, the U.S. and Hong Kong. This is no small matter. Though it lost ground during the Coronavirus epidemic, the diamond trade still represented over a quarter of Israel's total exports.

The Israeli Diamond Exchange is a large complex of four interconnected buildings in Ramat Gan – next to Tel Aviv – and this where the diamonds are cut, traded, marketed and sold. Tours are available, and at the end of the tour, the tourist is led to the huge diamond store.

Nearby lives a community of 30 Jain families who have been in Israel for decades. This is where they ply their trade, and here they continue their Indian culture, religion and yearly Diwali party. The patriarch of one of these families, when asked why he came to Israel, told a reporter that he[9] felt an affinity with Israel.

---

[9] Behrmann, Anna, 'Israel's Indian Diamond Dealers', *Tablet*, July 30, 2018, The Indians have successfully taken over the bulk of this trade from the Jews, but relations between the two communities remain cordial.

"I liked the people," he told me, "maybe because the Indian and Israeli mentality suit each other. Nowhere else in the world, apart from Israel and India, can you knock on someone's door and walk in without making a prior arrangement. You feel like family here."

Incidentally, like all diamond merchants all over the world, when the Jains sell a diamond, they seal the deal with a handshake and a time-honored phrase "mazal u'bracha." This is Hebrew, meaning "luck and blessing." I first heard this expression from my uncle and cousin, who sold diamonds in the U.S.

Israeli-Indian trade has gone far beyond diamonds today. Joint business ventures have proliferated in solar power, water technology and irrigation. Just as Israelis have learned how to make the desert bloom in the Negev, the farmers in Rajasthan, India want to learn how to make their desert bloom.

India and Israel have set up a Joint Business Council and an India-Israel Business Alliance. The World Jewish Congress opened an office in Delhi in 2003. An "International Seminar on the Jewish Heritage of Kerala" was convened in Kochi in February of 2006.

In early 2021, an article appeared about an Indian entrepreneur who is marketing Israeli innovations to India.[10] He says, "Indian companies were scaling fast and all of them were looking for solutions across five buckets – cloud, data science, AI, cybersecurity and marketing. So we created a stack of 15 Israeli companies in each of these categories and bundled them for our customers." He approaches Indian companies and introduces them to the Israeli solutions to their most pressing needs, "using the best of [the] Israeli tech ecosystem." This is cross-fertilization between the two countries.

Exchange students from both countries have been granted scholarships to visit and study each other's cultures, language and religions. In 2018, 550 Indian students were studying in Israel,

https://www.tabletmag.com/sections/community/articles/israels-indian-diamond-dealers

[10] Leichman, Abigail Klein, 'The Man Who Meet's India's Business Needs with Israeli Products,' *United with Israel*, Feb. 12, 2021.

according to the Indian Embassy[11]. By 2020, over a thousand Indian students were studying in Israel at the Weitzman Institute, Tel Aviv University, Hebrew University and the Technion.[12] Under a program initiated by the Israel Council of Higher Education in 2012, post-doctoral scholarships were awarded to 235 Indian scholars in the first three years. Among a few such programs in India is the Jindal Center for Israel Studies at the Jindal University New Delhi campus.

At the same time, some 40,000 Indian tourists have come to Israel each year.

Almost as soon as the two countries began formal diplomatic relations, they began working together on scientific and technical projects.[13] Leyaqat Khan writes that "Way back in 1993, an agreement on Science and Technology was signed between the two states during the visit of the then Israeli foreign minister, Shimon Peres." The earliest cooperative arrangements were in technical areas – biotech, lasers, and electro-optics. A Joint Working Group was formed, and it met yearly in the 1990s, moving into subjects such as genetics and the human genome. From there, the cooperation extended to include engineering, ground water management, desalination and agro-industries.

An agreement was made between the Indian Science Academy and the Israeli National Academy of Science and Humanities, and cooperation between the two countries extended to solar energy, electronics, IT and space research.

The Indian Embassy lists several joint scientific projects, describing them in language that only a government will use. It also announced that "India and Israel launched a new funding

---

[11] Embassy of India, Tel Aviv,
https://www.indembassyisrael.gov.in/pages?id = mep2b&subid = PdRqb
#:~:text = Currently%2C%20there%20are%20around%20550,post%2Dd
octoral%20and%20doctoral%20studies.&text = Currently%2C%20there%
20are%20six%20joint,receiving%20funding%20under%20the%20progra
mme.
[12] Dasgupta, Sandipan, 'Chapter Two of India-Israel Relations: Beyond Defense and Diamonds', *Times of Israel Blogs*, Aug. 17, 2020,
https://blogs.timesofisrael.com/chapter-two-of-india-israel-relations-beyond-defense-and-diamonds/
[13] Khan, Leyaqat, 'India-Israel Relations', chapter 4.

programme for joint academic research and development in May 2013, with University Grants Commission (UGC) and the Israel Science Foundation (ISF)...administering the fund. Each government is contributing USD 12.5 million over a period of 5 academic years starting from 2014–15. The programme provides support of up to USD 300,000 for an experimental project and USD 180,000 for a theoretical project for up to three years."

Commercial relationships have also burgeoned, now including not only agriculture, but also telecom, software, pharmaceuticals, and medical equipment. High-level trade delegations visit back and forth regularly, and multiple research and development centers are working on ventures in nanotechnology, biotech, renewable energy and aeronautics.[14] The State Bank of India opened a branch in Tel Aviv.

In the middle of the coronavirus epidemic, a group of Israeli scientists worked closely with a group of Indian scientists to develop a rapid test for the virus.[15] To validate their work, the Israelis went to India in October of 2020, where they were able to recruit 25,000 test subjects in one week. This is only one of many joint scientific projects.

Last, as we consider links between India and Israel, let us not forget the many cultural exchanges between the two countries. There is an Israeli Cultural Center in Delhi. Dance groups, symphonies and other musical groups play in each other's countries. Indians participated in the International Women's Film Festival. An Israeli dance group performed in Gujarat, and an Indian poet was invited to a poetry festival in Jaffa, all in 2006. And a delegation of Indian archeologists met their counterparts in Israel, in the same year.

Two Indian festivals were held in Tel Aviv in 2007, one of them a film festival. In 2008, an Indian dance group performed in Karmiel, and in 2009 an Indian vocal group and a dance group performed in Israel. Goshen-Gottstein[16] writes that the Israelis

---

[14]Ibid. Khan, an economist, provides a lengthy treatment of this material. This is a brief summary.

[15] https://unitedwithisrael.org/watch-israeli-indian-scientists-developing-game-changing-corona-test/

[16] Goshen-Gottstein, p. 1538.

even have what they call a boombamehla, shades of the Indian Kumbh Mela, but really a festival for young people who want to have fun, with an Indian theme.

Yudit Kornberg writes of conferences she attended recently.[17] One was a meeting in Jerusalem in September 2016 called Asian Traditions, Contemporary Realities: A Meeting of Israel-Asia Faith Leaders, sponsored by the Israeli government, and another was in Delhi, the India-Israel Academic Dialogue conference: Political and Cultural Crossings. Holdrege points out that the Hinduisms and Judaisms Group within the American Academy of Religion was established after a 1995 conference. The Journal of Indo-Judaic Studies was established in 1998, and the volume called *Indo-Judaic Studies in the Twenty-first Century* was edited by Nathan Katz and others. This book is excellent, and I recommend it to the interested reader.

In August 2020, Israel and India signed a three-year cultural agreement,[18] which anticipated a film project between Israel and Bollywood. The agreement also proposed cooperation between the Israel Antiquities Authority and the Archaeological Survey of India. Further envisioned were literary fests, book fairs, youth festivals, museum exhibitions, dance performances, theatre, exhibitions of the visual arts, cooperation between book publishers, and film festivals.

Speaking of film, in the early days of Bollywood there were cultural prohibitions against Hindu or Muslim actresses appearing on screen. That was where Jewish actresses came in.[19] The Times of Israel writes of a 2018 movie, *Shalom Bollywood*, that gives the history. It turns out that there not only were Jewish actresses, but some of them were superstars. One of the first was Sulochana, born Ruby Myers. When the talkies came in, she was succeeded by Miss Rose, born as Rose Ezra; by Pramila, born as Esther

---

[17] Theodor, Ithamar and Kornberg, Yudit, *Dharma and Halacha: Comparative Studies in Hindu-Jewish Philosophy and Religion*, (Lanham: Lexington Books, 2018).

[18] 'India, Israel sign cultural agreement to further strengthen people-to-people ties', *Times of India*, (indiatimes.com)

[19] Tenorio, Rich, 'When Jews Ran...Bollywood?', *The Times of Israel*, April 4, 2018.

Victoria Abraham; by the famous Nadira, born as Florence Ezekiel Nadira, and more. There even were Jewish male stars, just as there were in Hollywood.

Before we leave this subject, we must not forget the musical love between Zubin Mehta and Israel. Mehta is a Parsi from Bombay, where his father was the founder of the Bombay Symphony Orchestra. Zubin Mehta began making guest appearances with the Israel Philharmonic Orchestra in 1961, and he was a big hit from the beginning. Israelis loved him more than ever when, during the Arab-Israeli war of 1967, he rushed back to Israel to conduct solidarity concerts. He was appointed music director of the Israel Philharmonic in 1977, and he became music director for life in 1981. Famously, he conducted in 1991 during the Gulf War in front of an audience that sat with gas masks on their laps. From the start, he always felt a deep kinship with the country of Israel, and they with him. Soon we will learn why his Parsi background is relevant.

That leads us to the next chapter. Most of us do not realize that, throughout history, the Jews in the Land of Israel, the Persians in Iran, and the Parsees in India had anything in common, but for thousands of years vast empires stretched from the Mediterranean to India, and within their purview they interchanged philosophical ideas, myths, and languages. Their vassals even labored under the same bureaucracies.

As you read about these empires in the coming chapter, the key is to visualize how enormous those empires were and how they connected the known world. Surely if peacock feathers from India were brought to Israel in the time of King Solomon, religious ideas may have been too.

CHAPTER SIX.
ANCIENT CONNECTIONS, ANCIENT EMPIRES

Israel and India were not just part of the British Empire, both once were part of ancient Persian empires, the empire of Alexander the Macedonian, the Timurid Empire, and the Muslim empires that followed.

One writer says "India was invaded nine times in one millennium by Achemenides [sic], Macedonians, Bactrians, Greeks, Sakas, Kusans, Sassanids, Yuezi, and Hephtalite Huns, just in antiquity. And then, of course came the Turks, Mongols, Afghans, Portuguese, French and British."[1] Many of these invaders came from the west, and many of them conquered Israel first.

Modern-day ties between Israel and India are part of a continuum that goes back almost three thousand years. Their lands were conquered by the same conquerors and ruled by the same empires. They blended with each other's cultures, and they borrowed from each other's religions to an extent that we still do not fully understand. And in that foggy past, Israel and India more than once served as the eastern and western poles of one single empire.

I invite you now to travel back with me at least to the year 2747 BCE. I hope that you enjoy the trip, even if you, like me, hated high school history class. At the time, it seemed like our teachers force-fed us a steady diet of battles, dates and names of

---

[1] Bryant, Edwin, *The Quest for the Origins of Vedic Culture – The Indo-Aryan Migration Debate*, (Oxford: Oxford University Press, 2001), p. 237.

kings that we had to memorize and regurgitate back on tests. We never stopped to imagine how these kings, conquerors and emperors could have marched through history creating empires that extended from one end of the known world to the other. We never thought about how they could have swallowed multiple countries that today seem incredibly far from one another, especially if they travelled on horseback.

At first, they probably spread out in search of better grazing areas, richer farmland or safety from attackers. Later they turned to conquest. In my own mind, I see warriors riding their horses, pulling chariots behind them, armed only with swords and shields, but still able to sweep in all directions from the Mediterranean to unite their world with both Europe and Asia. I even have felt that I saw the notable man who gave Ram's family its name.

> *I used to have a persistent vision of Ram Jethmalani's most revered ancestor, Jethmal. I was reluctant to ask Ram about it, but I just had to know if the image could have been true. One day I diffidently described it to him. I saw Jethmal, the progenitor of his family, on a horse, riding through a desert. I asked if there was a desert in Sindh, his ancestral state. He said yes. I saw Jethmal wearing flowing white robes that fluttered in the wind, wearing a white turban. I asked Ram if he would have worn a turban. He said yes. Would he have ridden a horse, not a camel? Yes. In sum, Ram said that the whole vision was absolutely authentic. Many years later I learned that on the eastern border of Sindh lies the great Thar Desert, and it ripples with sand dunes.*

From the very first beginning of human time, waves of tribes, kingdoms and empires washed across the Middle East and Asia, carrying their myths and their gods. In time, able and ambitious rulers arose to create extraordinary empires. In these empires, between the world of the Mediterranean and that of the Indian subcontinent were a spectrum of cultures, religions, languages and traditions. Do Israelis today find something familiar about India? Do Indians who travel to Israel feel strangely at home? Is there a reason? Remember, between Israel is the Iranian Plateau. It must have played a role.

Between 2000 and 1000 BCE, most experts tell us, groups of nomadic tribes migrated out of the southern Russian steppes,[2] bringing tales of a wintry land that had 10 cold months a year. This land may have been the Ural Mountains or the Pontic-Caspian region, and the migration may have started even earlier, perhaps between 5000–3400 BCE, some say as early as 7000 BCE.[3] Or, they may have come in successive migrations over the centuries. Scholars call these tribes Indo-Aryans. Some of these tribes ventured over the forbidding Hindu Kush mountains into India. Others, the ones now called proto-Iranians, continued to the Iranian Plateau. They called themselves *arya*. This is the root of the word Aryan, which means 'a member of our group.' It also is the root of the name Iran.

Aryan does not mean Germanic, nor does it have anything to do with a caricature of tall masterly blondes. That was purely nationalistic propaganda. The Aryans who migrated to the Middle East and to South Asia probably resembled the current inhabitants of these lands, their descendants. In fact, a body of Indian scholarship argues that the Aryans originated from between Afghanistan and the Punjab.[4] According to this theory, they would have spread from there to the rest of northern India.

Between 3500 and 2500 BCE, the Aryans made one of their greatest discoveries. They domesticated the horse. But that was not enough. They learned to build and drive chariots. Now they could conquer any foes, and they could create empires. In homage to their equine assets, tombs in the Indian subcontinent show that they made horse sacrifices as far back as the fourteenth century BCE.[5] The ancient Persians also sacrificed horses, but usually they offered their gods the blood of a bull. And in the Jewish Temple

---

[2] Parpola, Asko, *The Roots of Hinduism–The Early Aryans and the Indus Civilization* (Oxford: Oxford University Press, 2015). Parpola discusses these and other relevant dates in his introduction and in several chapters of the book
[3] Bryant, Edwin, *The Quest for the Origins of Vedic Culture – The Indo-Aryan Migration Debate* (Oxford: Oxford University Press, 2001), p. 41.
[4] Bryant, p. 63.
[5] Parpola, p. 36. Starting on this page and continuing on, he discusses the importance of the horse in the archeology and history of the steppes.

in Jerusalem, the Jews would sacrifice an unblemished bull. Was there a connection?

The earliest Indo-Iranians had oral traditions as well as written records that have been traced to the fourth through the third millennium BCE, and researchers show that their languages may be derived from one presumed primordial language. For instance, the oldest Persian texts linguistically resemble the oldest Sanskrit texts of the Hindus. The names of several rivers are similar in the two countries. The Persian Harahvaiti and Haroyu rivers are the same linguistically as the Sanskrit Sarasvati and Sarayu rivers. The very word river is *ranha* in the Persian Avestan language and *rasa* in Sanskrit.

The Indus Valley (Harappan) Civilization northwest of India flourished from 2300 to 1750 BCE, and archeologists believe that it "formed a trading and cultural zone with central Asia, Afghanistan and Baluchistan in the third millennium BCE." Amulets and ceramic objects that resemble each other have been found in graves of eastern Iran, northwest Afghanistan, southern Uzbekistan and Baluchistan, which now is split between Afghanistan and Pakistan.

Traders from the Indus Valley had crossed the Iranian Plateau and arrived at the Persian Gulf by the second half of the third millennium BCE.[6] Ancient troves of seals and jewelry demonstrate this. Meanwhile in Europe, Aryans migrated from the Russian steppes north and west as far as Lithuania, and that land has a remarkable backstory. Some Lithuanian words are the same as Sanskrit, and some Lithuanian pre-Christian traditions are the same as those of pre-Islamic Iran. We will come back to visit Lithuania.

Back to Persia. The ancestors of Persians and Medes settled first in northwestern Iran, but they had a gluttonous eye fixed on the riches of Mesopotamia, the kingdom of Assyria, and the pearl of all, Babylon. In 612 BCE, the Medes and Babylonians overthrew the Assyrian capital of Nineveh. Perhaps you do not know where it was, but one day I learned. It once was the dominant city of the

---

[6] Parpola, pp. 213–14.

entire Middle East. Even today the portion of Iraq north of Mosul is called Nineveh Province.

> *Many years ago, while sitting in the kitchen of Chaldean friends, I asked a member of their community where their home had been in Iraq. Their village, he told me, is Telkef. That meant it had a tel, meaning a large mound of rocks that signifies to an archeologist that there once was a city or a monumental building there. I asked him if he knew what city was under the tel. Nineveh, he said, with great pride. It sounded like the refrain of a song from the musical play Kismet: "Not since Nineveh..." I ran home to look it up. It turns out that Telkef was built on one of the massive outer walls of the famed Assyrian capital, Nineveh.*

Before we take our trip through the empires of old, let us stay with the Chaldeans for a moment. It was the Chaldeans, led by Nebuchadrezzar, who formed the bulk of the Babylonian army that conquered Jerusalem in 586 BCE, but that is not the only reason for remembering them. There is a splendid and unique museum in the Chaldean Cultural Center of West Bloomfield, Michigan that displays an exact replica of the famous Hammurabi Code.

This is a black stele as tall as a man, and it is inscribed with the most famous ancient code of law, one that was promulgated by a Babylonian king – my friends would say a Chaldean king – who reigned between 1792 and 1750 BCE. The original is in the Louvre, but the accessibility of the one in Michigan allows the visitor to look closely at the beautifully inscribed cuneiform, with its 282 edicts – in Akkadian – that made it so famous. Other codes existed before this one, two of them written by the Sumerians, but scholars have concentrated their research on comparisons between Hammurabi's code and the laws of the Torah.

Thus, the Chaldeans left one of the earliest historical records of the Middle East, but they were not alone. Their partners in conquest were the Medes, who founded one of the earliest of the great empires.

THE MEDES

The Medes were an Iranian people from an area that now is split
between northwest Iran, parts of Azerbaijan and Kurdistan. Their
capital was built in the same location as Hamadan, one of the
oldest cities in Iran. Hamadan may date back to 1100 BCE, and it
is mentioned in the biblical Book of Ezra.

By the end of the seventh century BCE, the Medes were ready
to rebel against the Assyrian Empire, and they joined forces with
the equally ambitious Chaldeans, called by historians the neo-
Babylonian Empire. Together these two armies conquered
Assyria's capital, Nineveh, the greatest city in the known world,
in 612 BCE.

By the mid-second century BCE, the Medes had created the
Median Empire, which stretched across southern Anatolia,
northern Iraq, northeastern Iran and into the Caucasus. It is hard
to imagine, but they accomplished this from a starting point just
east of the impressive Zagros Mountains, whose peaks reach to
over 14,000 feet. These feats of conquest were amazing achievements for mountain people only armed with primitive weapons,
communications and transportation systems. But as historians tell
us, they were more sophisticated than their enemies, because they
were horse breeders. The ability to ride horses was their big
advantage.

The Medes were more than horsemen. In the area of today's
Tehran was a Median priestly caste, the Magi, who passed their
duties from father to son. When the Zoroastrian religion appeared
in ancient Persia, it was through the power of the Magi, the sacred
Median priests. When word went out that Jesus was born, he was
visited by the Magi, famed throughout the Middle East as wise
men, kings, astrologers, astronomers, and magicians.

Zoroastrian prayers and ceremonies were conducted in the
Median language, an old Iranian language, used for ceremonial
purposes even when it no longer was spoken in Persia. This would
be like conducting services in Latin, or in Hebrew in countries
where the congregants did not speak the language. Shadows of
this language remain with us today. The Greek name for the magi
is 'magoi,' the origin of our word magic. The Median word
Paridaiza meant paradise.

The Median Empire fell to the next army of conquerors, led by Cyrus the Great, but the Medes retained great respect, the priesthood, and many positions of honor in future Persian empires. The Magi also retained the power to quash new religions that competed with theirs, for centuries. The effect of this power on the subsequent development of religion in Iran is not to be disregarded.

Cyrus and the Achaemenids

Of the many nomadic Persian tribes who roamed the Iranian Plateau, one tribe rose to greatness, the Achaemenids. They gained control of the Elamite city of Anshan, and there they began a dynasty of kings, the most famous of whom was Cyrus II, known to history as Cyrus the Great. Cyrus was the grandson of a Median king, and he founded the Achaemenid Empire, known in history as the First Persian Empire (559–330 BCE).

With all their magic, the Medes could not stave off the incursions of Cyrus II.[7] In 549 BCE, Cyrus and his Persians conquered the Medes, and the unpronounceable city Pasargadae became the political and economic center of an empire that reached from the Persian Gulf to India. But before we describe his empire, we need to take a break from Persian history and bring ourselves up to date on the history of Israel, because Israel's fate was inextricably connected to Cyrus.

Toynbee[8] notes "the legendary story of the hero's miraculous escape in infancy from an exceptionally dangerous threat to his life has attached itself to the traditional accounts of Cyrus II's infancy and of Moses' infancy alike." Toynbee cites this tale as an example of how Cyrus was identified in folklore with Moses. We will see why one might make the comparison.

---

[7] Home, Charles F., 'The Kurash Prism: Cyrus the Great; The decree of return for the Jews, 539 BCE,' *Iran Chamber Society*, April 7, 2016, accessed July 2016, https://tinyurl.com/ycskksrg. Note that this article comes from a journal published in contemporary Iran, no friend of Israel at the moment.
[8] Toynbee, Arnold, *Mankind and Mother Earth*, (New York: Oxford University Press, 1976) p. 110.

In the land of Israel,[9] the period of 1800–1701 BCE is known as the Patriarchal Age, the time of Abraham, Isaac and Jacob. In around 1020 BCE, it became a country with a king, and Jerusalem was the capital, graced by a stately Temple that King Solomon built on top of Mt. Moriah. This is the hallowed mountain on which – according to the bible – Abraham had almost sacrificed Isaac. After King Solomon died around 930 BCE, the Jewish kingdom split into a northern kingdom, called Israel, and a southern one, called Judah. This division lasted for 200 years.

Next the great imperial forces of Mesopotamia invaded, perhaps attracted by the riches of the Temple, perhaps because conquest was just what they did. The Assyrians came first. In 722 BCE they conquered Jerusalem. The Assyrian King Sargon II bragged after his conquest that he deported 27,290 people.

This was the Assyrian Exile, and the tribes had been taken from the northern Kingdom of Israel, the area now called Samaria, on the West Bank of the Jordan River. After this, these ten tribes seemed to vanish, memorialized in history as the Ten Lost Tribes. There has been endless speculation about where they went and who they became. Given all this uncertainty, the Jews of Kurdistan probably have the best claim. They have lived for millennia along the Khabur River, a tributary of the Euphrates, in Nineveh Province, Iraq. And the bible recounts that the Israelites were taken to live in Halah, Habor and Hala, names remarkably similar to Khabur. Still, we will talk about other claimants to the role of lost tribes in later chapters.

Yigal Levin[10] writes that the Assyrians took the elites of Israel to enrich their empire, leaving behind the rural people of Judah, and they dispersed these higher-class deportees widely within the

---

[9] Foltz, Richard, *Religions of Iran – from prehistory to the present,* (London: Oneworld Publications, 2013).

[10] Yigal Levin, Judea, 'Samaria and Idumea: Three Models of Ethnicity and Administration in the Persian Period', 2012, in Johannes Unsok Ro (ed.), *From Judah to Judaea: Socio-economic Structures and Processes in the Persian Period,* (Sheffield, Sheffield Phoenix Press, 2012), https://www.academia.edu/38554916/Judea_Samaria_and_Idumea_Thr ee_Models_of_Ethnicity_and_Administration_in_the_Persian_Period?overvi ew=true#

Assyrian Empire, according to local needs for scribes, craftsmen, military or other educated men. This would imply that the legendary lost tribes may not have remained in one place, that perhaps they simply dissolved into the populace of Assyria. The Assyrians replaced them too, in whole or in part, by sending back to the land of Israel a disparate population of Jews, Persians, Phoenicians, Ammonites and Edomites.

In this small land, these populations could not have moved too far from the people who had never left the Kingdom of Israel, now called Samaritans (Samarians), who already lived next door to Judeans and Edomites (Edumeans). Surely all these diverse people came into contact, not only in Assyria, but also in the kingdoms of Israel, Judah and Edom. Later, more deportations would take place in the time of the Babylonians.

But deportations and importations of people never stopped. In the time of Alexander the Great, this area became Hellenized, adding in a Greek element. Later the Arabs moved in, but we are getting ahead of ourselves.

In 586 BCE, the Babylonians conquered Jerusalem, destroyed the First Temple, and exiled an estimated 20,000 Judeans to Babylonia, a catastrophe called the Babylonian Exile.[11] This caused a dramatic shift in the center of gravity of Judaism. While small communities of Jews remained in the Galilee and in other scattered areas of the land, the major institutions of learning and worship now moved to Babylon, where they would remain for centuries.

Here is where we return to the story of Cyrus. In 539 BCE, a miracle occurred. Cyrus conquered Babylonia. And, in a surprising move, he immediately liberated all of Babylon's captive people. This included the Jews, who became full-fledged citizens of his empire. Moreover, the Jewish-Roman historian Josephus wrote that Cyrus was moved by God to encourage the Jews to return home and rebuild the temple that the Babylonians had destroyed. As a result, Cyrus is revered as a great hero, and

---

[11] Many books recount this history. I will not footnote everything, but I do recommend consulting a standard reference, one of which might be Ben-Sasson, H.H., *A History of the Jewish People*, (Cambridge: Harvard University Press, 1969).

he is portrayed glowingly in the Jewish bible. Some suggest that Deutero-Isaiah calls Cyrus the Messiah. Well maybe. Verse 45:1 says, "Thus says the Lord to his anointed, Cyrus, whose right hand I grasp."

When Cyrus encouraged the Jews to return and rebuild, many did, taking home precious artifacts of the First Temple that the Babylonians had stolen. Remarkably, Cyrus had given them back. By 516 BCE the Jews had rebuilt the temple, now called the Second Temple. It was smaller than the First, but it still was on the sacred Temple Mount, Mt. Moriah. Later, under Roman rule, the Roman vassal king Herod built a broad platform around the Temple, with monumental retaining walls that we still see today. And on the platform, Herod rebuilt the Temple, lavishly. For Jews today, the holiest site in Jerusalem is the western wall of Herod's great platform. Here the Jews pray, and over the centuries, here they cried for their destroyed Temple. They called it the Wailing Wall.

Just to complete this part of the story, the rebuilt Temple did not last. The Romans arrived in 63 BCE, and they pressured the Jews to follow Roman religious practices, making it impossible for the Jews to follow their own religion. The Jews rebelled in 66 CE. It did not go well. The Romans destroyed the Second Temple in 70 CE, and they planned to erect a temple to Jupiter in its place on the Temple Mount. As a result, the Judean leader Simon Bar Kokhba led a new rebellion. That did not go well either. In 132 CE, the Romans reportedly killed over 500,000 Jews, sold unknown numbers of Jewish war captives into slavery, and expelled as many Jews as they could from Jerusalem. This expulsion would last for two thousand years.

Revered by the Jews, Cyrus was an extraordinary figure, and his conquest of Babylon was a turning point in Middle Eastern history. The Achaemenid Empire that he founded ultimately extended from the Mediterranean through Asia Minor, across the Middle East, and as far as the Indus River on the western border of present-day India. He also conquered the Balkans, Macedonia, Greece and portions of Central Asia. In addition, he conquered the shores of the Persian Gulf and the Red Sea. It was an empire greater than any the world had ever seen. According to Jewish

lore, this covered 127 countries, though, according to one translator, more likely provinces.[12]

It is hard to imagine what this would look like today if all
these lands were under one rule, dominating the crossroads of
Europe, the Middle East, Africa and Asia, and it is difficult to
imagine the importance of these population exchanges. We
already have seen that every time a great king conquered a new
territory, he would uproot a new batch of captives and send them
to another part of the empire. Both the Assyrian and the
Babylonian Exiles exiled at least 20,000 each, surely exposing
people of many different cultures to each other's ideas, beliefs and
customs. No wonder the Jews, Persians, Arabs and the inhabitants
of the Indian subcontinent have had some surprisingly similar
myths and legends.

Remember too that this technique of population transfer was
not only used by the ancient empires of the Middle East, it continued through the twentieth and twenty-first centuries. When
Constantinople fell in 1453, the Ottomans' forced the Jews of the
Balkans and Asia Minor (Anatolia) to relocate to Thessaloniki,
now in Greece. In 1915–22, the Turks not only perpetrated
genocide against the Armenians, they also moved thousands of
hapless people of Greek origin to a Greece they never knew and
moved thousands of Greek Muslims from Greece into Turkey, a
land whose language they did not speak.[13] When the Chinese took
control of Tibet, they transported thousands of Han Chinese into
Tibet to dilute the indigenous population of devout Buddhists.

In his day, Stalin moved large numbers of ethnic Russians
into the Baltic countries, where he left them as Trojan horses,
poised to complain of mistreatment and to "request" that the
Russians come and save them. On a trip to Latvia and Estonia, we
met two of these ethnic Russians, lawyers, who told us they felt
Estonian, hated Russia, and they were prepared to fight to prevent
the Russians from coming back. Not everyone is willing to be used
as a tool.

---

[12] Gindin, Thamar, *The Book of Esther Unmasked*, (Zeresh Books, 2016), p. 33.
[13] Gaunt, David, *Massacres, Resistance, Protectors: Muslim-Christian Relations in Eastern Anatolia During World War I*, (Piscataway: Gorgias Press, 2008).

Given this conglomeration of lands and peoples, Cyrus needed an efficient government. For that purpose, he adapted the administrative systems of the Medes, and the Akkadians before them. They divided the land into provinces and set up satraps (governors) to rule each province. This system lasted into the Islamic period, becoming the governing structure of the Ottoman Empire. After the Ottoman Empire broke up, this became the basis of the bureaucratic system employed by its successor Arab states. Israel and Jordan today still have vestiges of Ottoman land law.

Though Cyrus was a devoted Zoroastrian, he showed respect for the religions of his conquered nations and peoples. A small cylinder covered with Akkadian cuneiform writing sits in the British Museum. Found during a British Museum-sponsored dig in the ruins of Babylon, it is known as the Cyrus Cylinder.[14] The former Shah of Iran proclaimed this to be the oldest known charter of human rights. This is open to dispute, but surely it is the oldest known written expression of religious tolerance attributed to any empire. Some biblical scholars also believe the text confirms that Cyrus sent the Jews back home to repatriate their land.

Cyrus died in 530 BCE while fighting Scythian nomads who had migrated down from north of the Caspian Sea. This was only nine years after he conquered Babylon. In the end, his life and accomplishments were the stuff of legend, and a major inspiration for Alexander the Great, whose own empire lasted for only 13 years (336–323).

After short reigns by two ill-fated successors, in 522 BCE Darius I came to power, and he became known as Darius the Great.[15] It is easy to see why. He extended Persian rule west into Egypt, through Macedonia and Turkey into Afghanistan, and far enough east as the Indus Valley of India, now part of Pakistan. In

---

[14] Antoine Simonin, 'The Cyrus Cylinder', *Ancient History Encyclopedia*, Jan. 18, 2012, https://www.ancient.eu/article/166/the-cyrus-cylinder/

[15] Toynbee, Arnold, *Mankind and Mother Earth*, (New York: Oxford University Press, 1976). The history of the Persian Empires is given in many standard reference books. Toynbee is one of the most famous classic historians, and this last book summarizes the rest.

short, his empire covered most of the known world between the Mediterranean and India.

On a map, the Achaemenid Empire looks like a legless dragon with its mouth open, holding the entire eastern half of the Mediterranean between its jaws. Toynbee calls it "the biggest, and also the least oppressive, empire that had yet been built." The Achaemenid Empire has been called second only to the far-flung British Empire, and one of the largest empires in the history of the world.

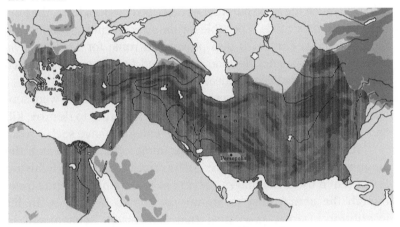

Map of the Achaemenid Empire
By Jona Lendering, Livius.org (CC0 1.0 Universal)

The Royal Road is credited to Darius. This was created out of an ancient trade route that Iranian Chamber Society publications refer to as the Persian Silk Road.[16] Historians believe this route first was traveled in the time of the Medes, long before silk ever was imported into Persia, but in time it did serve as the westward extension of the Chinese Silk Road into the Middle East. Darius was the one who built up this road, fortified it with military check points and used it as an instrument of empire, since it stretched from Susa, Iran all the way to Smyrna (Izmir) on the Turkish coast of the

---

[16] 'The contribution of ancient Iranian civilization to the Silk-Road', *Iran Chamber Society: History of Iran: The contribution of ancient Iranian civilization to the Silk-Road.*

Mediterranean Sea. On it, Persian couriers used the technique of traveling in relays, covering the entire distance in seven to nine days.[17] Later, the Romans used the same Royal Road, and from its Mediterranean terminus Roman ships found their way to India via the Red Sea, some of the ships apparently operated by Jewish shipping agencies, according to the receipts found in one archive. The Jews themselves were the clients for some Indian spices, which were used in preparing the incense used in the Temple.

This anticipated the Chinese Silk Road by 300 years,[18] but it achieved much the same purpose. As described by Herodotus, the Royal Road not only made it possible for the Achaemenids to administer their enormous empire, it also provided a route for sending royal decrees and dispatches, for commerce, and for travel, all of which facilitated the movement of ideas through the heart of the empire.

In the Book of Esther, verse 3:13 begins "Dispatches were sent by couriers to all the king's provinces with the order to destroy, kill and annihilate all the Jews–" How convenient to have such a road.

It was under Darius too that Aramaic officially became the language of the Persian Empire. An inscription on Mount Behistun is written in three languages, serving as a veritable Rosetta Stone, though the actual Rosetta Stone was in two languages. In his inscription, Darius proclaims that he is 'an Achaemenid, a Persian, son of a Persian, an Aryan, having Aryan lineage.'

And who was a Persian exactly? According to Darius, the Persian people included people of the Iranian Peninsula, Medes and Bactrians, whose land now is divided between Afghanistan, Uzbekistan and Tajikistan. It should be apparent by now that when we write of a Persian Empire, we visualize an entity far larger than the Iran of today. And it is becoming apparent that the Iran of today visualizes something like that too.

Xerxes[19] was the son of Darius, and, if this could be possible, he was even more ambitious. In 480 BCE, he invaded Athens, and he burned down the Parthenon. Under Xerxes, the Achaemenid Empire extended along the eastern and southern Mediterranean coasts, co-

---

[17] 'Darius the Great Builds the Royal Road,' *History of Information.com.*

[18] 'Royal Road', *Livius.org,* Dec. 16, 2019, *Articles on ancient history.*

[19] Mark, Joshua J., 'Xerxes I,' *Ancient History Encyclopedia,* https://www.ancient.eu/Xerxes_I/

vered much of Egypt, most of Asia Minor and spread east to the Indus River valley. But it also extended south to the Arabian Sea, included Armenia and covered Sogdiana. Sogdiana? This large area straddled the Silk Road, and its territory is now in Uzbekistan, also partially overlapping adjacent parts of Tajikistan, Kazakhstan, and Kyrgystan. The holdings of the Achaemenids were nothing if not eclectic.

But let us stop for a moment and look at a map. The Achaemenid empire swallowed up land that now belongs to Egypt, Greece, most of Turkey, Israel, the Arab countries of the Middle East, the Caucasus, Pakistan, and the "stans" of central Asia. How could that be? Well, we do not know how they did it, but they set the pattern for all the empires that followed.

Jewish history is relevant here again. Xerxes is believed to have been the fabled King Ahasuerus of the Book of Esther. This book, called the Megillah, is read every year in synagogues across the world during the holiday of Purim. Set in the Persian city of Susa, probably at a time between 480 and 470 BCE, it tells of a lovely Jewish girl who was chosen in a beauty contest to become a wife of King Ahasuerus. As she was greatly beloved by the king, all was well at first, but then she is warned by her cousin Mordecai that the king's viceroy, the evil Haman, is plotting to massacre all the Jews in the kingdom. Urged by Mordecai, Esther discloses the plot to the king, making it clear it was her kinsmen that Haman wanted to kill.

Through subterfuge, Esther engineers a confrontation between Ahasuerus and Haman, after which the king orders Haman to be hanged and thousands of his relatives and supporters killed. Whether this really happened or not we do not know, but, in any event, Iranians to this day still have not forgiven the Jews. According to legend, the tombs of Esther and Mordecai are in Hamadan, Iran. They were set on fire in May 2020, but allegedly, the damage was minor.

These names have meaning too. The name Esther may be derived from the Persian name for the goddess Ishtar, whose name is related to star. The name Mordecai may be derived from the Mesopotamian god Marduk. Gindin[20] even cites a theory that

---

[20] Gindin, *The Book of Esther*, p. 90.

"the Book of Esther is a Judaization of a story about the wars of the gods, where the Babylonian gods Marduk and Ishtar prevail over gods of other cultures."

The Jewish spring festival that celebrates the story is called Purim and it is held in March or April. The Septuagint refers to it by the Greek term *Phrouraia*, which comes from *phroura*, meaning vigil. This is etymologically close to *Fravardigan*, the Iranian spring festival. In the Book of Esther, the two Jewish protagonists have names that hark back to Mesopotamian deities. Esther, as we said, came from Ishtar, while the name also has a Hebrew root that means 'hidden,' and in the story, Esther's Jewish background initially was hidden from her husband, the king.

All within the same Persian Empire, Assyrian traders from as far away as Syria could barter with Sogdian traders in Central Asia. That was one advantage of the empire's massive size. A disadvantage was that the legal, governmental and bureaucratic systems of all these conquered kingdoms must have come in conflict at their borders. In 519 BCE,[21] king Artaxerxes I, the son of Xerxes I, called for all the laws in his empire to be codified, and "Artaxerxes is said to have called upon Ezra, 'a priest and expert in Torah', to regulate Jews living in Judah and the Trans-Euphrates province 'according to the law of your God.'

It says in the Jewish Book of Ezra 11:25–26, "And you, Ezra, in accordance with the wisdom of your God, which you possess, appoint magistrates and judges to administer justice to all the people of Trans-Euphrates – all who know the laws of your God. And you are to teach any who do not know them. Whoever does not obey the law of your God and the law of the king must surely be punished..." Commentators have interpreted this verse as meaning that the king established Mosaic law in the Persian Empire.

ALEXANDER THE GREAT

Not all the great empires of the Middle East were Persian. One of the most important was Macedonian. Never mind the high school

---

[21] Rose, Jenny, *Zoroastrianism: An Introduction,* (I.B. Tauris Introductions into Religion ebook).

teacher who told you it was Greek. In the last third of the 4th century BCE, Alexander the Great[22] of Macedonia took center stage. He overthrew the Achaemenian Empire, conquered Babylon, burned libraries, murdered priests and tried to eradicate all signs of the official Zoroastrian religion. Alexander created one of the largest of all the ancient empires, even though it only lasted from 336 to 323 BCE, when he died.

Historians relate how Alexander crossed the Hellespont (the Dardanelles) with no opposition, met Darius III in battle, and with vastly fewer troops, he slaughtered the Persian army. When he reached Babylon, he was greeted enthusiastically. He conquered Tyre, annexed Egypt and advanced to Persepolis. After burning its palaces to the ground, he proceeded to destroy an army of over a million that Darius had assembled in a last-ditch effort to defend himself.[23]

During his short reign, Alexander stormed across enormous territories. The empire that he created went from Egypt east across Babylonia to Persia. Its northernmost reaches stretched up to the Caspian Sea and the Himalayas, and the southernmost bordered the Persian Gulf and the Arabian Sea. It was similar in extent to that of Darius, but of course it covered Greece and Macedonia. After years of nonstop campaigning, Alexander reached northern India. By then, his troops were exhausted and rebellious, and he was forced to turn toward home. In the end, he died in Babylon, leaving the Greek culture implanted from the Mediterranean to the Indus River. This began the Hellenistic Period, which lasted for over 300 years.

Alexander's impact was inestimable. Among the many cities named for him was his namesake in Egypt, Alexandria. In its day, the great Lighthouse of Alexandria was one of the Seven Wonders of the World. Though little was left of it, 20 years ago my husband and I walked out to its former site on a rocky peninsula that jutted out into the Mediterranean. According to the locals, the site of the

---

[22] Toynbee, Arnold, *Mankind and Mother Earth*, (New York: Oxford University Press, 1976). References to Toynbee are in all standard history texts, and I refer to him in several places in this chapter.

[23] Durant, Will, *Our Oriental Heritage*, (New York: Simon and Schuster, 1954), pp. 383–84.

great library of Alexandria was just up the beach. It once held the largest collection of ancient papyri in the world, but it either had burned, fallen into disrepair, or both. On our trip, when we stood on Alexandria's beach promenade, overlooking a rocky beach littered with rubbish, our Alexandrian hosts pointed to where they believe its remains are – under the sea.

In its heyday, Alexandria was an intellectual and cultural hub. It also was the location of the Patriarchate of Alexandria, a patriarchate of the Eastern Orthodox Church. Thanks to Alexander, Greek became the language of the entire Mediterranean world. It must have been quite natural for the early Christians to have used Greek when they wrote the New Testament, and the first official list of its contents came in a letter sent by a bishop of Alexandria.

But the influence of Alexander went far beyond Greece and Egypt. In northwest India, Greek artists who had accompanied Alexander's troops stayed on to work with local sculptors, and together they created the exceptional Gandhara art, a fusion of Greek and Buddhist styles that blended with the iconography of Iranian gods.

Following Alexander's death, his empire fell into pieces, and warring generals vied for control. One general, Seleucus Nicator, founded a dynasty that took his name. Though it only was a portion of Alexander's empire, the Seleucid dynasty alone stretched across Babylonia, Asia Minor, the Caucasus, Central Asia and the Indus Valley. Then in 250 BCE, the Arsacid Dynasty overthrew the Seleucids. The empire they created, better known as the Parthian Empire, was to last for almost four centuries.

THE PARTHIAN EMPIRE

The Parthian Empire was also known as the Arsacid Empire, first named after its founder, Arsaces, a tribal leader whose tribe conquered the northeast Iranian land of Parthia. From 247 BCE to 224 CE, the empire, located on the Silk Road to China, was a thriving conduit for commerce and trade. The Parthians were strongly influenced by Persian and Greek culture, and they fought repeatedly with the Romans for land and power.

In many ways, the Parthian Empire was a throwback to the Achaemenids, and we might argue that it was even more important in the story of Persian religion, in particular Zoroastrianism, which we will discuss in another chapter. After he supplanted the Achaemenids, Alexander abolished the Zoroastrian religion, and it was the Arsacid Parthian Empire that restored it. The Parthian King Vologeses (Valakhsh)[24] had his people bring to court all the scattered fragmentary manuscripts that still survived after most of the originals were lost in the time of Alexander. Specifically, referring to the foundational literature of Zoroastrianism, he ordered his subjects to preserve and safeguard "in each province whatever had survived in purity of the Avesta and Zand, as well as every teaching derived from it... whether written or in oral transmission"[25]

Later it was King Ardashir, the founder of the Sassanian Empire, who ordered that these manuscripts be compiled into an official compendium of the Zoroastrian literature. This became the accepted version of the legendary Avesta until its final redaction in the ninth century.

The Jewish philosopher Philo (c. 20 BCE-50 CE) and the historian Josephus (c. 37–100 CE) document the life of Jews under the Parthians. In *Antiquities* 20.17–96, Josephus writes of the Parthian Queen Helena and her son, Prince Izad of Adiabene (Erbil), in Iraq. They both converted to Judaism in 30 C.E., and Helena became known for her extreme piousness and generosity.[26] From 45 to 46 CE, Helena donated grain from Alexandria and figs from Cyprus to Jerusalem to help the inhabitants through a famine. She finally moved to Jerusalem, where she took vows as an ascetic, a female Nazarite. She also donated golden gifts to the Temple, and she built a palace whose foundations are in the City of David. Finally, she commissioned her own tomb, had it inscribed in Aramaic, and was buried in it.[27] Or perhaps only some of this is true. It is a legend, you know.

---

[24] Boyce, *Zoroastrians*, p. 94.
[25] 'Arsacids iv. Arsacid religion,'Encyclopaedia Iranica, July 1, 2016, *ARSACIDS iv. Arsacid religion – Encyclopaedia Iranica* (iranicaonline.org)
[26] Richard Gottheil and M. Seligsohn, 'Helena,' *Jewish Encyclopedia*, 1906, accessed in July 2016,
http://www.jewishencyclopedia.com/articles/7525-helena
[27] Ben-Sasson, pp. 288–89.

Buddhism, Judaism and Christianity all were undisturbed during Arsacid (Parthian) rule. The early Christians in Parthia were able to establish hundreds of churches and over 30 bishoprics. A tolerant empire, the Parthians adapted to the Zoroastrian traditions that they had inherited. They used the word magus for priest, and they adopted the cult of the temple fire.[28]

One book, *Tales from Parthia*, is purported to be an ancient Persian prophecy of impending apocalypse, and, according to some German scholars, it shows the influence of Jewish traditions. The original text has disappeared, but it was rewritten in Greek by a writer who may have been Jewish. His version, *The Oracles of Hystaspes*, is believed to have influenced the Christian *Book of Revelation*.[29] There are many other examples of Parthian influence on other cultures and religions. For instance, the Parthians used jewel and flower metaphors profusely in their poetry, which ornamental style was widely emulated in the Greek and Latin literature of the time.

Flowery imagery notwithstanding, the Parthians were fatally weakened by constant wars with the Romans, and they ultimately gave way to the next great Persian empire, the Sassanians. This was an empire under which both Zoroastrian and Jewish literature flowered.

THE SASSANIAN EMPIRE

Ardashir was the grandson, or perhaps the son, of a pious man named Sasan, who was born in the Pars region of Persia. In 224

---

[28] 'Arsacids iv. Arsacid religion,'*Encyclopaedia Iranica*, July 1, 2016, ARSACIDS iv. Arsacid religion – Encyclopaedia Iranica (iranicaonline.org)
[29] Werman, Cana, 'A Messiah in Heaven? A Re-evaluation of Jewish and Christian Apocalyptic Traditions'. In footnote 6, Cana writes: "To cite Flusser: "To save the Persian character of the Oracle, scholars had to disregard the Jewish elements... So they were obliged to perform a dangerous operation and cut off the Jewish elements from the story although they are an organic part of it" (398). Aune accepts Flusser's position regarding the relationship between the Oracle and Revelation." http://orion.mscc.huji.ac.il/symposiums/9th/papers/WermanAbstract.html

CE, touting himself as a faithful worshipper of the Persian god Mazda, Ardashir rose to power, creating the Sassanian Empire. This empire lasted until the advent of Islam in 651.

It was Ardashir who first called his land Iran, giving the term a political meaning for the first time. At its greatest extent, the Sassanian Empire stretched from the Nile through Turkey; surrounded the eastern Mediterranean and the Persian Gulf, blanketed the upper Arabian Peninsula and extended all the way to Pakistan. In Europe, the Sassanians took more land than Alexander the Macedonian did. Again, Israel and the western bank of the Indus River (now in Pakistan) found themselves within one administrative entity, with one bureaucratic system.

The reader may find the descriptions of all these empires mind-numbing, but certain things stand out. One is how large they were, long before modern forms of transportation or warfare existed. Another is how similar their eastern borders were. An Indian friend reminds me that – at least until the rise of Islam – these conquerors all stopped at the Indus River. Thus, while people and ideas moved freely within these empires, the Hindu Kush to the north and the Indus River to the west provided some insulation for India, allowing it to develop its own unique culture.

The Sassanians sheltered the first Christians who were oppressed by the Roman Empire, but when Constantine legalized Christianity in 313, and when Christian missionaries came to Mesopotamia, they were perceived as a threat. King Shapur I (Shahpuhr), struck back at the Romans[30] in three wars. In 244, during his first war against the Romans, he seized the important Turkish city of Nisibis (Nusaybin). Ten years later, he followed this up with a stunning victory. He captured the entire Roman army, and the Roman Emperor Valerian! Following the time-honored imperial tradition, he deported large numbers of Christians from Syria, Cilicia and Cappadocia (Asia Minor) to Mesopotamia, Persia and Parthia,[31] and among them were many artisans and skilled workers.

---

[30] Toynbee, *Mankind and Mother Earth*, p. 307.
[31] Kalmin, Richard, *Jewish Babylonia between Persia and Roman Palestine* (Oxford: Oxford University Press, 2006), p. 7.

The empire was majority Zoroastrian, and Shapur left many coins and inscriptions that proclaimed he worshipped Mazda, the chief god of the Zoroastrians. Yet there was an early period of religious tolerance. At its tolerant height, the empire was a benign host to Jews, Christians, Manicheans and Mandeans. These minorities were permitted to have their own courts, raise their own taxes and to worship freely. Scholars call it the period of "legal pluralism." With burgeoning numbers, the Syriac Christians established important centers of learning. The most famous one was in Nisibis, now Nusaybin, Turkey. Another started as a Nestorian Christian seminary in Gundishapur, in the Persian province of Khuzestan. This later became a renowned medical center.

But things never stay the same in the Middle East. After Shapur I died, the Sassanians began persecuting Jews, Christians, Manicheans, Buddhists and Brahmins. Jewish views of his dynasty are mixed. Shapur I transplanted thousands of captives from the eastern Roman Empire to Mesopotamia, Syria and western Persia.[32] In Cappadocia he murdered 12,000 Jews,[33] yet at one time his son Shapur II had close relations with the Jewish sage Samuel and his disciple R. Judah.

It was complicated. King Yazdgird I married the daughter of the Jewish *resh galuta*, and Yazdgird II and his son Peroz persecuted the Jews vigorously.

Sassanian conflicts with the Romans resulted in the death of an estimated 35,000 Christians. Starting in 340, over a period of 80 years, Shapur II is said to have killed some 150,000 Christians. He became suspicious of Buddhists and Brahmans to the east, and he even saw the indigenous Iranian Mandaeans as a threat to Zoroastrianism, the state religion. Little wonder, with that background, that so many Iranians today continue a long national tradition of antipathy toward state religion.

With all this, Jewish scholarship flourished under the Sassanians. Somehow in the midst of all this turmoil, the Jews managed to study, to debate, and to record their debates in formidable works of scholarship. Let us stop and look at the timing.

---

[32] Kalmin, p. 4.
[33] Ben-Sasson, pp. 348, 376.

Once the scattered vestiges of ancient Zoroastrian writings were gathered up and brought to court, then under the Sassanians they were collated and assembled into the reconstituted Avesta,[34] the foundational work of Zoroastrianism. The bulk of this work was done in the Sassanian capital, Ctesiphon, essentially Baghdad, between the third and sixth centuries CE, and the final editing was in the ninth century.

At nearly the same time, the Jewish scholars who had been debating points of law in the Torah for centuries collected all this material, arranged it, edited it and created the Babylonian Talmud, the foundational literature of the Jews. And this work was done in Baghdad in the first five centuries of the Common Era,[35] with subsequent editing over the next few centuries.

What does this tell us about the potential for cross-over influences? We will talk more about this. A lot more.

The last major Sassanian king was Khostrow I, whose religious interests seem to have been eclectic. Early in his reign, his armies captured much of the Levant and North Africa, and when his troops captured Jerusalem in 614 CE, they are said to have taken a portion of the 'True Cross' back to Iran. Khostrow also married a Christian, and he was a patron of the Nestorian academy at Gundeshapur.

At the same time, he was a Zoroastrian, cosseted the Zoroastrian clergy, and he supported the ongoing work of committing the Avestas to writing. He also put down a revolution started by Mazdak, the head of the Manicheans. As we will see when we come to them, adherents of this religion advocated many Communist ideas, even going as far as sharing wives. As we might imagine, this was popular with the masses, but it shocked both the Zoroastrian and the Nestorian Christian establishments.[36]

Khostrow was a reformer, and he was a patron of the arts, a highly accomplished man. His ministers brought chess from India,

---

[34] Boyce, Mary, Zoroastrians – *Their Religious Beliefs and Practices* (London: Routledge, 1979). This subject appears in several different chapters of this book.

[35] Ben-Sasson, H.H., *A History of the Jewish People*, (Cambridge: Harvard University Press, 1969), pp. 307ff.

[36] Toynbee, pp. 330–31.

and they sent backgammon and polo back to India. The court musicians of Khostrow formalized Iranian music, and this is the music that court musicians have played in the perfumed evenings of the Middle East and India ever since.

One of the great classic works of Persian literature is the *Shahnameh, The Book of Kings*. This is the epic poem of Iran, written in the end of the tenth or the beginning of the eleventh century, CE. The verses about Khostrow portray a highly romanticized tale of his life in which he is lauded as a hero and a great lover. Between this poem and another popular tale of love, that is how he is remembered.

The Greeks regarded Khostrow as a philosopher king. Perhaps the most distinguished of the Sassanian kings, he was considered by many to have been as great as Cyrus. Adding to his accomplishments, he had the wisdom to promote the Silk Route.[37]

Khostrow's empire finally fell apart in 628 when his son perpetrated a coup in an orgy of regicide and fratricide. At the end of it, only Khostrow's eight-year-old grandson was left to inherit the throne, and he was in no position to defend his regime against muscular outside forces. Neither love nor poetry, court music or chess would help him. Unfortunately for the diminished remains of the last Persian Empire, a vigorous new religion had emerged in Arabia.

Much of the history of this religion is well known, so in the next chapter we will start by reviewing just a few of the salient events and dates. We also will review something about the religion, concentrating on intriguing parallels and contrasts with the other religions of the Middle East. While this discussion will not be comprehensive, the hope is that it will help the reader to better understand the subsequent history in which Islam plays such an important role.

Coming back to our story, as Khostrow's little grandson struggled to stay alive amid the jealousies of the Persian Court, the Arabian Peninsula held even more danger for him. A man named Mohammad had reached full maturity.

---

[37] Mark, Joshua, 'Kosrau I', *Ancient History Encyclopedia*, Feb. 2020, https://www.ancient.eu/Kosrau_I/

CHAPTER SEVEN.
ISLAM ARRIVES

Mohammad was born in Mecca, in 571 CE, to the Quraysh tribe. He was brought up by his grandfather and uncle after he was orphaned at age six. At age 40, he received Divine messages, and he began preaching to those around him. In 622, he and his followers migrated to Medina, an Arabic word that means city. This migration was called the Hijira, and it is commemorated every year with a mass assembly of the faithful in Mecca, an event called the Hajj. After spending some time in Medina, Mohammad acquired an army of followers, and they began to seek converts. By the time he died in 632 CE, the entire known world was about to change.

Soon, Arab armies would sweep through Syria, Persia, Mesopotamia, the land of Israel, Egypt and beyond. They took many lands that bordered the Mediterranean, and among them was Spain. Things started out well. Jews who had been converted to Christianity were permitted to return to Judaism. The Arabs had big plans for Spain. They even gave it an Arabic name, Al-Andalus. And they still want it back. A restaurant in the Lebanese community of Dearborn Michigan is nostalgically named Andalus.

Jews who had been relatively oppressed under the Sassanids initially welcomed the Arabs, but soon they learned how life would be under them.[1] And it would affect almost everyone. After the Arab conquest, as Ben-Sasson writes, "Almost all the Jewish

---

[1] Lewis, Bernard, *The Middle East: A brief history of the last 2,000 years*, (New York: Scribner, 1995), p. 56.

people dwelt in the areas conquered between 632 and 711; more than 90% of Jewry now lived within a single empire."

Once the soldiers of Islam had taken over the Arabian Peninsula, that gave them control of the Gulf trading posts that once had been dominated by Persia. This was their first contact with Persia. The next would be far more significant. They progressed through Asia Minor, on to Afghanistan, through the "stans" of Central Asia, and reached China. In time, many nations of North Africa, the Middle East and Central Asia converted to Islam, and they found themselves ruled by the same caliphate. Within this caliphate were established a whole network of trade connections between major commercial centers. In most of these centers, the functions of commerce, diplomacy and administration were dominated by Aramaic speaking Christians, along with Jews and Greeks. As recently as the early twentieth century, Baghdad was 30% Jewish.

When Muslims conquered the Sassanian capital Ctesiphon – 20 miles from Baghdad – it gave them control of a massive treasury. After that it was easy for them to take Damascus, the most prestigious city of the Byzantine world, and that became their capital. In the eighth century, they moved their capital back to Baghdad, the former capital of the Sassanid Empire. Since that city still was dominated by Persia, Persians and Persian scholars came to play an important role in developing the language and ideas of Islam.

A Persian linguist wrote the first systematic grammar of Arabic. This was necessary because, now that the Persians had to learn Arabic, they needed comprehensible rules of grammar. They also needed to enlarge the basic Arabic vocabulary in order to express many sophisticated Persian concepts. Thus, many Persian words appeared in Islamic writings. As Islam became urbanized in Baghdad, Persian experts helped shape much of Islamic culture, law, theology, science, philosophy, history, geography, arts and literature. This may explain why Islam adopted some of its stories from the Zoroastrians. For instance, Mohammad's miraculous night journey to heaven parallels a Zoroastrian tale told in the

Persian *Book of Righteous Virtue.* The Islamic version of this tale may have been the original source of Dante's Inferno.[2]

By 1000 CE, about 80% of all urban Persians had become Muslim. In order to understand this new religion, Persian scholars translated the six Hadiths (collections of sayings), and they played an important role in codifying Sharia law. Much of this was done by members of the Persian elite who had converted to Islam, even though some still secretly practiced some form of an esoteric Persian religion, often Manichaeism. This was perfectly consistent with the time-honored Persian/Iranian tradition of covert resistance to any official state religion. Even today, Christianity is the fastest growing religion in Iran, of necessity practiced by small groups in secret rooms.

When Arab armies conquered the Sassanian empire in the 640s, Jews were in the majority in parts of Mesopotamia, so it should not be surprising that Islamic legal code, *sharia*, came to acquire a certain resemblance to Jewish legal teachings.[3] Scholars also write that many of the lawyers who codified the sharia were the descendants of converted Jews. A major Jewish Talmudic scholar, Rav Nahman, lived in Ctesiphon, and another, Rav Yehuda, lived near modern day Fallujah, about 60 miles away.[4]

Scholarship was hardly limited to Jews though. Working in or near Ctesiphon were Muslim, Christian, Manichaean, Mandaean, Elchasite and Zoroastrian scholars. We know that Arab, Persian and Jewish theologians used similar techniques of debate and scholarship. Secunda writes that "renewed interest in the Bavli's Iranian context stems from the almost tangibly rabbinic "feel" of the discursive [Persian] Zand." The Bavli was the Babylonian Talmud. We will come back to that.

Over the years, Islam split into various divisions, based on theological considerations, geography, different schools of

---

[2] Foltz, Richard, *Religions of Iran – from prehistory to the present,* (London: Oneworld Publications, 2013).

[3] Lewis, Bernard, *The Jews of Islam,* (Princeton: Princeton University Press, 1984), pp. 68–74. Lewis offers a critical discussion of this possibility, giving both the pro and con points of view.

[4] Secunda, Shai, *The Iranian Talmud,* (Philadelphia, University of Pennsylvania Press, 2014) pp. 4, 21, 24.

jurisprudence, and differences between ethnic communities. Among the most problematic were disputes over the proper succession of leadership following the death of Mohammad. Another point of disagreement concerned the Hidden Imam, the Mahdi. This is Islam's version of the Messiah. He is believed to be a holy figure from the family of Mohammad who will remain hidden from view until the designated moment when he comes out of hiding, and he appears to the world, filling it with justice and righteousness. The big question is which imam is the real Mahdi in the line of succession from Mohammad. This we may never know until his time comes. Until then, he remains hidden. This concept strongly resembles the Jewish idea of 36 hidden *tsaddikim* – righteous men – who Jews believe are personally responsible for sustaining the world.

The largest branch of Islam is called Sunni, but there are other branches. Among the largest are Shi'ism and Sufism.[5] Shi'ism also is divided into Twelvers, Ismaili, Zaidiyyah and Alawites.

It is outside of our purview to provide a comprehensive discussion of Islam, but it is relevant to our discussion to realize how closely the traditions and literature of Islam correspond to those of Judaism. In the Koran, one finds many stories from the Hebrew bible, perhaps modified, but clearly recognizable. Much of the underlying theology is recognizable too. The persuasive arguments are familiar. The injunction to follow the law or suffer consequences is the same. The promise of reward for compliance is the same.

The uncompromising monotheism and the strict prohibition against graven images are exactly the same as they are in Judaism. The laws that concern killing animals for food are the same. Dietary laws? The Koran says that the Muslim may eat anything that the Jews can eat. Before Dearborn Michigan became the center of the largest Lebanese community in the U.S., and before they had hallal butchers, the Muslims patronized

---

[5] Mortimer, Edward, *Faith and Power: The Politics of Islam*, (New York: Vintage Books, a division of Random House, 1982). This is only one of many sources for this discussion.

kosher butchers. By the time I set up my surgical practice there, the city was awash in Lebanese restaurants, and the Jewish doctors who had a more casual relationship with their dietary laws could happily eat hallal take-out in the surgical lounge.

Moreover, as we will see later, some Jewish ideas may have come from Islam, through the Sufis. From there they passed to other, younger faiths, such as the Sikh religion in India. We will learn more about that when we come to India.

Anyhow It is difficult to recount the historical relationships between the countries and people of the Middle East without discussing Islam. Let us introduce some brief summaries.

SUNNIS

The first schism in the Islamic *ummah* (people) came with a battle over succession when Mohammad died. The tribal leaders of Mecca had agreed to designate a man named Abu Bakr as the first caliph of Islam, but a group of Mohammad's closest followers contended that Mohammad had designated Ali, his cousin and his son-in-law. A majority of his followers supported Abu Bakr, and they became known as Sunni. A minority supported Ali, and they came to be called Shia, or Shi'ites. This division became permanent after a civil war that began in 680 CE with a momentous battle In Karbala, Iraq. This battle still remains the cause of intense acrimony.

From the beginning, the Sunni looked to a caliph as their supreme authority, as contrasted with Shiites, who look to a series of Imams. In modern times, this difference has come to the fore as a Turkey newly rededicated to religion seems to be trying to bring back the Ottoman Empire, and many modern-day Sunnis are dreaming of reestablishing the caliphate that was at the center of that empire. In contrast, a resurgent Iran has given religious and political power to the highest Shiite authorities in their country. All this has a geopolitical impact.

After Mohammad, from 632 to 661, came a series of four major caliphates of Islam, presided over by the patriarchal caliphs, who the Sunnis consider to be the 'rightly guided' caliphs. During this time Islam began its period of rapid military expansion. Islam developed its own calendar, a judicial administration, and, in time, four major schools of jurisprudence. Since those early days it also has given rise to several religious subgroups. Among them are the fundamentalist Salafis, Wahhabis, and, more recently, the Taliban in Afghanistan. In Pakistan, India, Indonesia, the Philippines and many other countries, there are still more.

Sunnis profess six pillars of faith, believing in the oneness of God, the angels of God, divine revelations, the prophets of God, resurrection and day of judgement, and preordainment. This means that everything that happens must be by the will and decree of God. While their interpretations may vary, the essence of these pillars are concepts they hold in common with Judaism, Christianity, and Zoroastrianism.

Today Saudi Arabia is the center of Sunni Islam, and it sponsors mosques and madrassas (religious schools) that teach Sunni Islam in many countries. The Muslim community of India is about 85% Sunni, but the major religious distinction in India is between Muslims and Hindus, not the difference between Sunni and Shia. Sunni Islam is in the majority today in Asia east of India, and it dominates in Turkey, Saudi Arabia, Jordan, Egypt and Syria. Sunni Muslims today number over a billion people, perhaps close to two billion. Taking all the subgroups together, today close to 90% of all Muslims are Sunni.

In contrast, Shiites represent between ten and twenty percent of all Muslims, or between 150 and 200 million people.[6] Most Shiites live in Iran, Pakistan, India and Iraq, but Shiites also are in the majority in Azerbaijan and Bahrain.

Thus, Sunni and Shia have been the dominant branches of Islam throughout the world. We now will meet the Shia.

SHIA

The key distinction of the Shiite branch of Islam is that Shiites believe that Ali ibn Ali Talib, Mohammad's cousin and son-in-law, was the rightful successor of Mohammad, and that he was vested

---

[6] 'Mapping the World Muslim Population', *The Pew Research Center*, October 2009, Mapping the Global Muslim Population | Pew Research Center (pewforum.org)

with the political and religious leadership of Islam. They regard him as divinely appointed and as the first Imam of Islam, and they believe that this authority was extended to his descendants. They further believe that only God can appoint prophets.

The position of Shi'ism in the Muslim world has varied according to the times. Early on, Shi'ism became a persecuted underground religion in the Umayyad and Abbasid Empires – which we will come to shortly – and many Shi'ites professed Sunni Islam while privately following their own Imams. But things change. As time went on, a whole succession of Shiite dynasties arose across North Africa and the Middle East. Even the Fatimid Caliphate and the Safavid Empire were Shiite. We will come to this too.

Shi'ism too split into sects, and each sect considers a different Imam to be the rightful successor of Ali. Before the sixteenth century, the most popular sects of Iranian Shi'ism were either the mystical Isma'ilis (Seveners) or the Zaydis (Fivers). From the sixteenth century on, Iranians have followed Twelver Shi'ism, which teaches that the number of hidden Imams is divinely designated; the final hidden Imam is yet to appear, and the last hidden Imam, called the Mahdi, will be the twelfth. This too is a Messianic idea, but in Islam.

The Twelver school of Shiite Islam expanded during the Safavid Empire, an empire which forcibly converted the Persians to Shi'ism, persecuted Zoroastrians, marginalized Jews and other non-Muslims, and created a climate of fear.

Here the history books tell a peculiar story. In this atmosphere of extreme repression, the terrified Jews were hungry for a savior, and in the 1660s one seemed to appear. A rabbi from Ottoman Turkey, Sabbatai Zevi, held himself out as the long-awaited Messiah.[7] He acquired many followers; however, when he arrived in Constantinople, the Muslims caught him and threw him in jail for fomenting sedition. While in jail, he was given a choice, conversion or death. Bizarrely, the self-designated savior chose conversion to Islam. Then, perhaps to save face, he urged

---

[7] Raphael, Chaim, *The Road from Babylon – The story of Sephardi and Oriental Jews* (New York: Harper and Row, 1985), p. 143.

his followers to do the same, but secretly. These followers became known as *Donmeh*, meaning renegades, but essentially signifying converts or crypto-Jews. While they outwardly are Muslim, their liturgy continues to be in Judeo-Spanish. Many of them lived in successful communities in Constantinople and in Thessaloniki, where my husband and I heard this story from the Jewish community. In fact, we learned that in the twentieth century, *Donmeh* were among the Young Turks who started a revolution against the Ottoman Empire

All the countries surrounding Israel are Muslim. Some have Sunni majorities; others have Shi'ite majorities. Regardless, the survival of Israel as a modern country has depended on its ability to fend off continuing attacks from these neighbors. India has a large Sunni population within, and Pakistan is a Muslim nation next-door, with the result that India has experienced sectarian violence periodically throughout its history.

On this point, Israelis and Indians have had much in common, but there is another branch of Islam that seems to love everybody.

SUFIS

This other branch of Islam is Sufism,[8] a form of Islamic mysticism that arose in the eleventh century. According to most academics, the first Sufi brotherhoods were founded in eastern Iran, and from there they spread into India, China and Southeast Asia. Our friend Ram Jethmalani was born in Sindh, now in Pakistan, and he always insisted that the Sufi movement started in Sindh, where Sufis had a harmonious relationship with the Hindu community, exchanging gifts and food every year on both the Sufi and the Hindu holidays.

The Sufi immerses himself in God, much like the Buddhist who seeks Nirvana. Sufi spiritual techniques employ a mantra-like repetition of Divine names or of verses from the Koran. Sufi poetry and painted miniatures draw on Buddhist inspiration. The Sufi mystical experience is described as one of love, and Sufi mystics work themselves into ecstatic trances in order to feel a

---

[8] Lewis, Bernard, *The Middle East*, pp. 238–41.

union with the divine. Jewish ecstatic mysticism resembles the ecstatic trances of Sufism.

Sufic elements could have influenced Jewish mystics[9] in the important Galilee city of Safed as early as the thirteenth century. It was not that far from a major center of Sufism. From the nearby Golan Heights, one can see the outskirts of Damascus.

Eleventh century Sufi poetry used symbols and metaphors borrowed from Persian poetry, describing romantic love as a metaphor for God's love of His creation. These are the very same images and metaphors that we see in the biblical psalms attributed to King David. Among the poems and songs that the Sufis love so much are ghazals – the romantic, nostalgic poetry of Persia that originated in the Umayyad and early Abbasid years. These became the Urdu poetry of South Asia, often about unrequited love. I can still see our friend Ram on his old porch swing, sitting dreamily, eyes half closed, listening to ghazals on a sultry night in Delhi.

Four years after Mohammad died, his followers attacked the Sassanians, and they completed their conquest within a decade. With the Muslim invasion came massacres, enslavement, and attacks on libraries, schools and universities. All public manifestations of Zoroastrianism were ended. The Arabs became dominant, and they subjugated all others to their religion. This was the new Middle East.

Muslim caliphates took over. In many senses they adopted the forms and governmental systems of their predecessors, but in other ways they put their own stamp on them. We will look at some of their most significant empires.

THE UMAYYAD CALIPHATE

The Umayyad Caliphate, lasting from 661 to 750 CE, was the second of the four major Muslim caliphates that followed the death of Muhammad, and it was one of the largest. In the time-honored tradition of Middle Eastern empires, its size is almost unimaginable. Early Muslim caliphates spread rapidly along the

---

[9] Idel, Moshe, *Kabbalah, New Perspectives*, (New Haven: Yale University Press, 1988), pp. 15–16.

shores of the Arabian Sea, across the Arabian Peninsula and North Africa to the Iberian Peninsula, which they called Al Andalus. Umayyad armies conquered Babylonia, Persia, Asia Minor, half of the Caucasus, the "stans" of central Asia, the legendary Silk Road cities Kabul, Bukhara and Samarkand. Then they went on to Sindh, and part of the Punjab, now divided between Pakistan and India. Extending from Israel to India, this empire was another one of the largest in history, with 33 million people, one capital in Damascus and another in Cordoba, Spain. And the Umayyads built the Dome of the Rock in Jerusalem.

Prof. Miriam Goldstein emphasizes that, at its largest extent, this caliphate itself contained 90% of all the Jews in the world.[10] By now, most Jews were making the transition to using Arabic as their native tongue and to writing in Judeo-Arabic. This was a transcription of their spoken Arabic, written in Hebrew letters.

In Christian and Jewish history, the Umayyad Caliphate is notorious for the Pact of Omar. This supposedly was written by Christians at the behest of Caliph Omar I (or Umar) in 637. Or, it may have been under Caliph Omar II a hundred years later. Or it may be apocryphal. It does not matter. The Arab world has believed in it and made use of it, for centuries. Its importance resides in a list of conditions under which the Muslims promised to protect Christians. This later came to include Jews and, in certain periods of time, also Zoroastrians. Significantly, if the minorities did not comply with these harsh conditions, they relinquished any right to be protected, assuming the promised protections ever were implemented.

Protected minorities were called *dhimmis*.[11] These were defined as 'People of the Book', second class citizens with limited rights. Their treatment was meant to be both demeaning and debasing. Among other insults, the Muslims sought to humiliate them by forcing them to pay a special tax, the *jizya*, a payment

---

[10] Goldstein, Miriam, 'How Judeo-Arabic Literature and Culture Shaped Judaism as We Know It', Webinar, Nov. 4, 2020. Prof. Goldstein is the Chair of the Department of Arabic Language and Literature at Hebrew University in Jerusalem.

[11] Bar Ye'or, *The Dhimmi: Jews and Christians under Islam*, rev. ed., trans. David Maisel (London: Associated University Press, 1985).

often deliberately accompanied by a slap in the face. In all, over 20 restrictions were placed on the rights of *dhimmis,* who, in return, were promised a limited amount of respite from overt persecution.

This putative pact has shaped the way that Muslims have treated minorities in most Middle Eastern countries ever since. Bernard Lewis[12] argues that the story of this pact must be fiction, but it is regarded by Arabs everywhere as real. And it continues to be the reason why so many Arab countries still bar Jews from building a synagogue higher than a mosque, from repairing one, or in some cases from building one at all.

Islam pushed non-Arabs to convert, but these new converts felt marginalized. As a result, a militant group of slaves, led by a freed Persian slave, rebelled, and they overthrew the Umayyads in 750 CE. This became the Abbasid movement. Once in power, the Abbasids built a new capital just north of Ctesiphon, and they called it Baghdad, a Persian word meaning given by God. Here Islam enjoyed a Golden Age. But the Jews, Christians and Zoroastrians still were *dhimmis.*

THE ABBASID CALIPHATE AND THE FATIMIDS

The Abbasid family that seized power were Iranians from central Asia. Though they claimed descent from the family of Mohammad, some speculate that they were descendants of Buddhist priests.[13] The Abbasid Caliphate has been called a Persian government. The Arabs of the caliphate married Persian women, formed alliances with prestigious Persian families and became Persianized, especially after their capital was moved back to Iraq, the stronghold of the former Persian empire. There, Abbasid caliphs ruled for almost five centuries, and there the Abbasid court maintained the governmental administrative departments of the Sassanians. They continued the same court system too, the solar calendar and the same equinox festivals, some of which resembled the spring and harvest holidays of the Jewish year.

---

[12] Bernard Lewis, *The Jews of Islam,* p. 25.
[13] Bernard Lewis, *The Middle East,* p. 77.

It should be clear that the Abbasids were not angels. Tales of their massacres, assassinations and atrocities in the early years of their regime are legend. After all that, Caliph Harun al-Rashid became a patron of the arts, and he ushered in a golden age of learning on the ashes of his predecessors.

The Abbasids ruled Iran, Arabia, Anatolia and half of North Africa, in effect an Islamic version of the Sassanid Empire. They also invaded parts of India. On our travels, we have seen some of their legacy there.

The Islamic garden embodied the ideal aesthetic of the caliphate's golden age. This garden consisted of a quadrangle crossed by two perpendicular intersecting water channels, replete with shrubs and flowers, with a fountain in the middle. This is the Persian model of paradise.[14] My husband and I saw this pattern in several of the famous Mughal gardens of India, especially the gardens of the Taj Mahal and the famed Shalimar Gardens of Srinagar, Kashmir.

In the Persian old Avestan language, *pairi daeza* or *paradeisos*, meant a walled garden, enclosure or a final place of happiness. The Elamite word *partetash* means orchard, and so does the Hebrew *pardes*. By the late third century BCE, the Greeks had modified the Persian word to *paradeisos*, and this is how it entered the Greek spoken by the Jews in Alexandria. The Septuagint used the same word for a garden, an orchard, or the Garden of Eden.

While it may not have been a paradise, the Jews of the caliphate benefited when the capital moved from Damascus to Baghdad. That was a time when they built great Jewish institutions of learning. In the ninth and tenth centuries, "The Arabic world was then an arena where the rival religions and philosophies and East and West crossed swords."[15] Weinstein adds that Muslims and Jews in Baghdad "participated in the discussions and debates, and they may have influenced Jewish and Islamic thoughts about the stars." Some of these debates were

---

[14] Hobhouse, Penelope, *The Gardens of Persia*, Kales Press, 2004.
[15] Weinstein, Brian, 'Traders and Ideas,' Chap. 2, in Katz et al, quoting Rabbi Abraham Heschel, p. 47.

over Sanskrit works that had brought by an Indian and translated into Arabic in Baghdad.

It would not have been difficult to conduct debates. The Jews in the Caliphate now spoke Arabic everywhere but in their religious schools, and they wrote in Judeo-Arabic. The Persians too used Arabic script, even as many continued to speak Persian. In this eclectic environment, vocabulary surely migrated back and forth between languages.

Eventually the empire fragmented with a civil war and under pressure from vigorous new ethnic groups who came from north Africa and from Central Asia. In 969 it yielded its Egyptian holdings to the Isma'ili Shi'ite Fatimid Dynasty, whose capital was the ancient city of Fustat. When that became too small, a new capital, Cairo, was built next to it.

AFTER THE ABBASIDS

As the Abbasid Caliphate declined, the Seljuk Turks[16] were on the move out of Central Asia. They came to Asia Minor, spread across most of the Middle East, worked their way along the eastern Mediterranean shore, and continued down to the Persian Gulf. They reached India too, bringing the Turko-Persian culture and language. One of the most famous poets was Omar Khayyam, born in Nishapur, Iran, whose most iconic work is the *Rubayait*, though experts have questioned whether he really wrote it.

By 998 a Shi'ite Fatimid ruler controlled the western Punjab, introducing Jewish and Persian influences to the region. It is no accident that the Sikh religion that began in the Punjab in the 1400s bears so much resemblance to Islam, and to Judaism. We will come back to that.

Now other powerful conquerors appeared in both the Middle East and South Asia, but in the end, they too were conquered by Islam.

---

[16] 'Seljuks', *The Middle Ages.net* (this is part of a series), https://www.themiddleages.net/people/seljuks.html

GENGHIS KHAN AND THE MONGOLS

In the thirteenth century, the Mongols came raging out of Central Asia. Completely uneducated, they not only burned precious books of Muslim learning – a loss from which Islam never recovered – they also destroyed the last remaining collections of Zoroastrian holy books, including every copy of the Sassanid Avesta that they could find. To boot, they slaughtered Muslims, Zoroastrians, Jews and Christians.

The Mongol Il-Khan dynasty conquered Baghdad in 1258, and it ruled Iran until 1336. In time, following the pattern of the Muslims before them, the Mongols quietly assimilated into Persian culture and converted to Islam.[17]

The most famous, or perhaps infamous, Mongol leader was Genghis Khan. In Europe, his armies were known as the Golden Order. By reputation, they were a bloodthirsty mob. Galloping and plundering their way through much of the known world, they came to dominate a mammoth territory that included upper Egypt, much of Anatolia, Iraq, Iran, Russia, Afghanistan, Azerbaijan, Armenia, Georgia, Turkmenistan, northwestern India, and the Silk Road through China, up to the Korean peninsula. Though historians call the Achaemenid Empire the largest empire of the premodern world, a map of Mongol conquests shows them to have been the most extensive by far.

Ghengis Khan needed to govern all these disparate territories, and he demonstrated himself to be an administrative genius.[18] He adopted and adapted Persian bureaucratic systems, ruling it all with remarkable uniformity. Using his model, Russian krais and oblasts today are organized like the provinces and vilayets of the Ottoman Empire, a structure that went back to Genghis Khan, before him to ancient Persian empires and before that even further back in antiquity. Even today, a traveler will

---

[17] Weatherford, Jack, *Genghis Khan and the Making of the Modern World*, (New York: Crown Publishers, 2004).

[18] Fitzhugh, William W., Rossabi, Morris, Honeychurch, William, *Genghis Khan and the Mongol Empire*, (Washington: Artic Studies Center Smithsonian Institution, 2013) .

find something familiar sounding about the political organization of countries from the Middle East to East Asia.

During the Mongol period, the Silk Road cities of Samarkand and Bukhara had large Jewish populations. In the early Islamic period, Jewish traders traveled from Europe to the Middle East, India and China. They also played an important role as bankers and entrepreneurs in the trade. Along these same routes came Christian traders, carrying their languages, their religions, and their sacred manuscripts. In 2011, a 1000-year-old cache containing 150 Judeo-Persian fragments was discovered in Samangan, Afghanistan.[19] Other artifacts have been found along the route too, such as a letter in Judeo-Persian dating from 718 CE.

Tamerlane followed Genghis Khan, and he did everything he could to deserve a bad reputation.[20] To start, he married Khan's daughter in order to trade on his name. In his own name – Timur the Lame – he founded the Timurid Empire in 1370. The empire he created also was immense, but it did not extend to Turkey or to the Mediterranean coast. It did include Central Asia, including Uzbekistan, where he is revered today for building their capital, the famous Silk Road city of Samarkand.

Be that as it may, Tamerlane was a cruel and murderous despot. He was no Genghis Khan. The history books are filled with tales of his bloody massacres as he conquered the greatest cities of the time, leaving mountains of skulls. In the end a Timurid governor, Babur, built Kabul, conquered Delhi and founded the jewel-encrusted Mughal dynasty of India.

THE MUGHALS

The Mughal Empire was founded in 1526 by Babur, a warrior from Uzbekistan. The most celebrated king of the Mughal Dynasty

---

[19] Harris, Ben, 'Mystery Swirls around Judaic Manuscripts Discovered in Afghanistan', Jan. 24, 2012, *Jewish Telegraphic Agency*,
https://www.jta.org/2012/01/24/global/mystery-swirls-around-judaic-manuscripts-discovered-in-afghanistan
[20] Weatherford, Jack, *Genghis Khan and the Making of the Modern World*, (New York, Crown Publishers, 2004), pp. 252–53.

was Babur's grandson, Akbar the Great,[21] and under him India became the richest land in the world. And it was very Persian. Most Mughal administrators were ethnic Iranians; the culture of the court was Persian. They had Persian governmental systems, renowned Persian court poets, Persian musicians and skilled Persian miniature painters. In all, this represented the greatest expansion of Persian culture in all of history. Unfortunately, what was good for Persian culture and for Islam was bad for Hinduism.

Except for a few that escaped, the Mughals destroyed all the Hindu temples and monuments of northern India. Today, almost all the architecture that we see in the north is in Persian style. The tourist visiting the Taj Mahal in Agra or the Red Fort in Delhi is taking selfies in front of Islamic architecture, because that is all there is left.

This is a shame. The differences between Mughal monuments and elaborate Hindu temples are profound. The visitor can see it when she travels from north to south India. Think high Lutheran versus Baroque.

Fortunately, one notable Hindu site survived, Khajuraho, a trove of Hindu masterpieces that remained hidden in the jungle while the canny locals diverted the Mughal destroyers away from them. Of the original 94 temples, some 19 remain, and they serve as reminders of those the world has lost.

One year we visited Khajuraho, and we were amazed to find such an extraordinary complex of ornately carved Hindu temples. It seemed like a miracle that they could have escaped destruction when the Mughals razed the bulk of the temples in north India. Fortunately, the temples had been overgrown by thick jungle that served as camouflage. Despite the impressive beauty of its workmanship, Khajuraho is best known for the sculpted friezes of erotic art that cover the exteriors, with images of gods copulating in the most extravagant positions the artists could imagine. Our tour guide explained the religious meaning of all this athleticism with a completely straight face, and giggling seemed impolite. In front of one temple, we spotted two

---

[21]Metcalf, Barbara D., and Thomas R. Metcalf, *A Concise History of Modern India*, (Cambridge: Cambridge University Press, 2001).

white-haired French ladies politely inspecting the sculptures, and we asked what they thought. They answered calmly, "It is all very interesting, but unfortunately it is too late for us."

South Indian temples did survive. Some have been renovated, some repainted, some allowed to weather into ruins. Routes to functioning temples are lined with rows of shops that sell trinkets, clothes, images of gods, and overpriced jewelry. In the temples, bare-chested priests wearing sarong-like white *dhotis* conduct their puja ceremonies as they have for thousands of years. Temples that have crumbled enchant the imagination as noble ruins.

In south India too, temples have been lost, but you still can see the vision of their creators, even if the strongest conqueror of all – time – has destroyed many of the most beautiful. In 1974, we first visited Mahabalipuram, located on the Bay of Bengal, near Chennai, formerly Madras. At that time, we could walk undisturbed along the beach, stumbling occasionally across forgotten ruins. Only a few had been excavated. The others just sat there, half-buried in sand, as they had since the eighth century. You could walk right up to them, peer in, and enjoy their spectacular carvings. Then, you might see another in the distance, and you would swish through the sand toward it. By our next trip, the locals had excavated the most spectacular temples, built walls around them and were charging admission. We could see the temples completely, but the magic of discovering them partially submerged in the beach was lost.

The period of Mughal rule in India created an environment that permitted the lavish expenditures of Shah Jehan when he built the Taj Mahal. This prodigal outpouring of money lasted until Aurangzeb imprisoned his father in order to prevent further extravagance. There the shah stayed, locked in a cell from which he could see his masterpiece only through a barred window, across a river. From there the regime went into a slow decline. Under pressure from the British, it finally collapsed in 1857.

THE SAFAVID EMPIRE, AND THE IRANIAN REVOLUTION

The Safavid Empire began in Iran in the early sixteenth century, founded by Shah Ismail I, a member of a Kurdish family from the

Safavid Order of Sufism. Their home was in Ardabil, a city now in Iran. This empire grew into the largest Persian empire since the Sassanian Empire. It extended from Turkey through Syria, Iraq, Persia, Azerbaijan, Afghanistan, and parts of Russia. It incorporated Uzbekistan, Turkmenistan and Pakistan, took most of the Caucasus, and it stretched south from the Caspian Sea to the Persian Gulf and the Arabian Sea. It did stop short of the land of Israel and of India.

Since then, all these lands have been Muslim, either Shiite, or Shiite-majority. The Safavids supported Persian arts, especially the architecture and literature, and this was when the famed Persian carpet industry came into its own, centered in Tabriz. Historians call the Safavid period the Golden Age of Persia. Historians love to proclaim golden ages.

This empire is considered the beginning of modern Iran. It made the Twelver school of Islam its official religion, which ensured that this branch of Islam was dominant throughout all its lands, even though the Safavids originated as Sufis. Shah Abbas the Great (1587–1628), one of the greatest Safavid kings, moved his capital to Isfahan, and this grew to become a magical city with blue tile architecture that has drawn generations of visitors ever since.

The Afsharid Dynasty came next, after a blaze of border wars that culminated with the military commander Nader Shah deposing the last Safavid king and announcing he was the Shah of Iran. A cruel Middle Eastern Napoleon, he grew his empire to even exceed the size of the Safavid Empire. Early in his career, he was quite tolerant of his Christian and Jewish minorities, but he became increasingly despotic near the end of his rule, committing mass murders and building towers of skulls, imitating the Mongols.

While he never established lasting control over India, in 1739 Nader Shah attacked the Mughal Empire and sacked Delhi, killing thousands. Finally, as Dalrymple writes, he left with "700 elephants, 4000 camels, and 12,000 horses carrying wagons all laden with gold, silver and precious stones."[22] Among his spoils

---

[22] Dalrymple, William and Anand, Anita, *Koh-i-nor, The history of the world's most infamous diamond*, (New York and London: Bloomsbury, 2017) p. 81.

from India were the Peacock Throne[23] and the Koh-i-Noor Diamond, both of inestimable value, taken away to enhance the glory of Iran. And India has never forgotten them.

The last of this sequence was the Qajar Dynasty, and then the Iranians succumbed to the siren call for a nationalist revival. This came in 1925 with the Pahlavi dynasty. The Pahlavis wanted to bring back the ancient Iranian heritage and its respect for Zoroastrians. They opened new fire temples, and they established Zoroastrian schools, but they were too late and too profligate. In October 1971, supposedly in honor of the 2,500-year anniversary of the founding of the Persian Empire by Cyrus the Great, they staged a multimillion-dollar birthday bash in the desert, and they invited heads of state from all over the world to eat and drink to their hearts' content under lavish versions of traditional tents.

That was the last straw. In part because of this conspicuous excess, the regime ended with the 1979 Iranian revolution, and Ayatollah Ruhollah Khomeini came to power. Discrimination against Zoroastrians returned. Rich Iranians, if they could, decamped to Switzerland, and the population of Iran went into a sharp decline.

After all this time travel, what have we learned? And what does it all have to do with the Jews, Israel and India? Most recently, both the land of Israel and India were subjects of the British Empire, and they have had much in common since that period, but we have started as far back as our common Aryan roots. From Median priests and their descendants, we have tried to imagine empires of almost unbelievable size, comprising most of the known world.

The Achaemenid Empire, the First Persian Empire, was one of the largest in the history of the world, and within it were ample opportunities for Jews and Indians to trade with each other, along the Royal Road, later the Silk Route, through the Middle East and beyond. But there also were population exchanges. Over the course of many centuries, thousands of people were deported from one location to another, bringing them in contact with the

---

[23] When Nader Shah was assassinated, the Peacock Throne vanished, purportedly denuded of its enormous gems in a fit of looting by his soldiers.

myths, languages and religions of both conquerors and fellow conquered peoples. With all that, one enlightened king of Persia, Cyrus the Great, let the Jews return from Babylon to Jerusalem, to rebuild their Temple.

Cross-cultural influences have run throughout these great empires. The Jewish story of Purim and King Ahasuaris was set in Persia. The Septuagint was written in Greek, thanks to Alexander the Great. And, under the Second Persian Empire, Persian scholars reassembled remnants of their ancient Avesta while Jews compiled the massive Babylonian Talmud.

Islam conquered the Middle East, and the Muslim Umayyad Empire subjected Jews and Christians to the repressive Pact of Omar. In India, the Islamic Mughal Empire expanded the reach of Persia, spreading its religion, language, government and culture all the way across northern India. Even then, a traveler from Baghdad to Delhi would have found much that was recognizable.

For much of this time, Persia dominated the land between the Middle East and Asia, and in the eighteenth-century India, the Urdu language appeared. This is a combination of Persian and Hindi. It started as a literary language in the royal court, but now it is the main spoken language of Muslims in Pakistan and India. Of note, before it came to India, Persian adopted many words from Arabic, and Arabic has a great deal in common with Hebrew. So, it should not be surprising if an Israeli travelling in India today hears much that sounds familiar.

Other languages spoken today in the Middle East, Central Asia and northern India are derived from Persian, including Dari and Pashto in Afghanistan. In Kurdistan there is Kurmanji, and in the Caucasus, Tat, the language of the Mountain Jews. Many of these peoples continue to celebrate traditional Persian holidays, and throughout their lands, one still sees typical Persian architecture and clothing. Some of their religions too are related to ancient Persian religions.

This brings us to Persia, now called Iran, and her many daughter religions. Most of us in the west had never heard of any of them until ISIS thrust itself into the news with its vicious attacks on peaceful Middle Eastern minorities. Yezidis? Who are they? Mandaeans? Who? Well, I know about them now. And soon, so will you.

CHAPTER EIGHT.
SO MANY PERSIAN RELIGIONS

Now we come to some of the discoveries that led to this book. While working on a previous book, I kept finding religions that I had never heard of, and they had one thing in common. They all originated in Iran. I realized that I had no idea how many religions had bubbled up in Persia. My first question was to ask how all this religious ferment impacted the religions that I do know something about, ones primarily located to the east and to the west of Iran. In short, were the Judaism of the Mediterranean coast and the Hinduism of India related through the religions of Persia?

Anyone who reads the history of the Middle East cannot help being struck by the remarkable number of religions that were born in Persia. Most of us have heard of Zoroastrianism, but what on earth were Mithraism, Zurvanism, Mazdakism, or Mazdeism? Who were Mandaeans, Manichaeans, Yazidis or Yarsanis? Did Zoroastrianism or any of these other religions influence Judaism, Christianity or Islam? Do Zoroastrianism and Hinduism really have common origins? Does it matter?

Now this presents a problem. Zoroastrianism is the best known and it may have been the most influential of all these religions. So we should discuss it first. Right? Yet again, the others all have the same roots, and they share many of the same beliefs. Thus, knowing about them may give context to our discussion of Zoroastrianism. After weighing the options, I hope the reader will agree with the choice of studying the lesser-known religions first. Then, once we have seen the whole milieu of ideas that

145

surrounded Zoroastrianism, we will devote the next chapter to Zoroastrianism. This should prepare us to understand its role as a bridge between Judaism and Hinduism.

The earliest religion of ancient Persia (Iran) was polytheism, and they had three main gods. One was Anahita, a water goddess associated with fertility, healing and wisdom. When we read commentaries on the Avesta of Persia and the Vedas of India, we learn that the Persian Anahita corresponds to the Hindu goddess Sarasvati, which scholars believe signifies a common origin. Centuries later, Anahita was a beloved figure in Zoroastrianism. The next god, Mazda, was not a car. He became the most important god of Zoroastrianism, and we will discuss him in that connection. The third main god was Mithra.

The word Mithra literally means a friend, but Mithra's origin was as the Persian god of the sun. Later he became the god of truth and of faith.[1] The corresponding Hindu god is Mitra. In the Vedas of India, Mitra was the one who protected and sustained the keeper of a contract.

MITHRAISM

The worship of Mithra may have appeared first in Mesopotamia during the fourteenth century BCE. During the first four centuries CE, Mithraism spread throughout the Roman Empire as a male cult identified with warriors. One obviously masculine rite was the monthly sacrifice of a bull, an archaic Mesopotamian tradition that predated the Zoroastrians. The antecedents of this sacrifice could have been Aryan, originating far back in the backstory of the Middle East, because it was far more widespread than the confines of Iran. Of all the priestly sacrifices that were made in the Jewish Temple in Jerusalem, the most valuable of all was of a bull.

---

[1] Foltz, Richard, *Religions of Iran – from prehistory to the present* (London: Oneworld Publications, 2013), p. 622.

After the Romans converted to Christianity in the early fourth century CE, they began to persecute Mithraism.[2] It is no wonder. There are too many similarities with Christianity. The birth of Mithra is supposed to be on December 25, and it is celebrated at the time of the winter solstice. On that date, they hold a vigil, called *shab-e yalda.* Yalda is the Syriac word for birth. Mithra is supposed to be the product of a virgin birth, and "his depiction in popular stories celebrating "the infant Mithra" is remarkably Jesus-like."[3] The religion used the sign of the cross, and it depicted divine glory with a halo. Even the mitre worn by Christian bishops and abbots could be a version of the Phrygian cap worn by Mithra in sculptural representations. All these parallels with Christianity raise a question: did one influence the other?

Several Persian kings were devotees of Mithra. In Bactria, much of which now is part of modern Afghanistan, Mithra may have been the most popular male deity. A Mithra temple stood in Memphis, Egypt, and many of the Parthians who overthrew the Greeks in the second century BCE followed Mithraism. A Mithra temple has been found as far north as Northumberland, England, near Hadrian's Wall. On a trip to Dubrovnik, Croatia, my husband and I were told about two nearby archeologic digs in which researchers had found remains of Mithra temples (Mithraeums). In one article, a writer compiles a list of 73 Mithraic temples, or remains of temples, that were found before 1945 and another 54 found since then. Most were in Europe, a smaller number in the Middle East.[4]

The more one reads the history of the region, the more apparent it is that heretics, saviors, philosophers, poets, theologians, and masters of esoteric practices have always arisen to challenge the status quo. Many of the religions discussed in this chapter were started by dissenters, and that may be a reason why

---

[2] Mary Boyce and Frantz Grenet, *A History of Zoroastrianism, Vol III: Zoroastrianism under Macedonian and Roman Rule,* (Leiden: EJ Brilll, 1991), pp. 471–76 in the Handbuch der Orientalistik, C. van Dijk et al.

[3] Foltz, p. 763.

[4] 'Where did Archeologists find Mithraeums?' *Mithraism, religion,* May 7, 2007, Gangleri.nl.

there are so many of them. Today, in this tradition, the fastest growing religion in Iran is Christianity, clearly a repudiation of the prevailing orthodoxy. Not surprisingly then, Mithraism had competition, not just from Christians, but from another group of religions, the Gnostics.

THE GNOSTICS

Gnosticism really is not a religion. It is a philosophical approach that blends Greek, Semitic and Iranian elements.[5] Scholars have opined that Jewish thinkers in Alexandria and Palestine influenced the Gnostics, and early Gnostic movements had elements in common with Christianity. For example, Gnostics believe that man has fallen, and salvation can only be achieved through special knowledge. The word gnostic, derived from Greek, means knowledge. Most Gnostics revere John the Baptist, and they use baptism frequently as a means of self-purification. They also believe in a final judgment and a resurrection. There have been several gnostic religions.

MANDAEANS

Mandaeans are the only surviving Gnostics in Iran. The name comes from *manda*, the Aramaic word for knowledge. Their sacred text is called the Ginza Rba, meaning great treasure. Incidentally, the district of Tokyo where the national silver mint used to stand is named the Ginza. I am told there is no connection. Yet could there be?

Mandaeans believe that their sacred oral teachings go back 2,000 years, even though the first printed text was published in 1998. Some Mandaic texts refer to Jews and Judaism; others refer to Jewish literature, and the language they use resembles Babylonian Jewish Aramaic. One theory, contested of course, suggests that they are descended from Jews.[6] Foltz elaborates on

---

[5] Idel, Moshe, *Kabbalah, New Perspectives*, (New Haven: Yale University Press, 1988), p. 9.
[6] Secunda, Shai, *The Iranian Talmud – Reading the Bavli in its Sassanian Context* (Philadelphia: University of Pennsylvania Press, 2014), p. 22.

this, writing that they trace their origins to a pre-Christian Jewish sect that lived in the Jordan Valley.[7]

The essence of Gnostic belief is that man must strive to enter his true home, which is in the World of Light. There he will be reunited with a spiritual twin through the aid of angels or guardians. This is how man acquires the knowledge that will bring him salvation. They also believe that "an inner 'divine spark' is entrapped within a repulsive and impure material existence."[8] This exact idea is richly developed in the Jewish Kabbalah. The Gnostics taught many Kabbalistic ideas, and they may have influenced the great flowering of Kabbalah that took place in the twelfth and thirteenth centuries. However, since Kabbalah may have originated much earlier than that, Kabbalistic ideas may have influenced Gnosticism.

Mandaeans call this earthly world *Tibil*. Jews use the world *tevel*. The three most prominent supernatural figures of the Mandaeans are Hibil, Sitil and Anus. The Jews call the same figures Abel, Seth and Enos. The Mandaean religion is said to be dualistic, which means that they believe in a continuing battle between good and evil. They also believe that every human has a heavenly twin. We rarely read this, but the name of St. Thomas is derived from the Aramaic *toma* (similar to the Hebrew word *tom*) for twin, and some in the Syriac speaking community believe he was the twin of Jesus. The reader will notice, as we go through these Persian religions, how important the concept of twins is to many of them.

Mandaeans believe in an evil female spirit whose very name, *Ruha*, means spirit. The Hebrew word *ruah* also means spirit. They use ritual immersion in water even more frequently than the Jews use the mikveh or the Christians practice baptism.

Mandaeans are believed to have moved from the Jordan valley, possibly passing through the biblical city of Harran, to Parthia between the first and third centuries CE. Now most of them live in Khuzestan and Iran. Fewer than 100,000 still survive, but since they prohibit conversion to their religion, their eventual

---

[7] Foltz, p. 3184 in the Kindle edition.
[8] Foltz, p. 3162.

survival is threatened. The number of Mandaeans in the city of Ahvaz went from 70,000 to 5,000 after the Iraq War of 2003. Over 80% of the original Iranian and Iraqi Mandaeans left for the west.

MANICHAEISM

Once one of the world's major religions, Manichaeism has completely vanished, and now it is a religion that the world has forgotten. The founder, Mani, was born to Parthian parents in Mesopotamia in 216 CE, and they sent him to be educated in a religious commune of Elchasaites, a syncretic Judeo-Christian-Gnostic Baptist sect in Qumran, next to the Dead Sea.

At age 24, Mani had a revelation in which he saw himself as the twin of Jesus, and this was what inspired him to take up his mission. He even felt a special affinity with St. Thomas. Does this sound like a familiar theme? Mani insisted that all divine scriptures came from him, and this put pressure on Jews, Christians and Zoroastrians to commit their own scriptures to writing. He adopted a strategy of translating his works into local languages, and this too pressured his competitors to do the same. Manichaeans insisted that their religion was defined by 'the book,' though Muslims never accepted Manichaeans as 'people of the book.'

Fortunately, this was a period of toleration toward Judaism, Christianity and the local Persian religions, but Mani apparently presented more of a threat. When the Sassanian King Shapur I publicly granted protection to Mani, the Zoroastrian priests became jealous. Plotting revenge, they called Manichaeism *Zandika*, meaning an unauthorized commentary on the Zoroastrian Avesta. The Zoroastrian magi saw Manichaeism as their greatest threat, the ultimate heresy.

Manichaeism, as contrasted with Zoroastrianism, taught that this world and its people are basically evil. The only escape was to live an ascetic, celibate life. Marriage was forbidden. Their principal ritual was baptism. They were anti-materialist to an extreme, averse to agriculture, and depended on laymen to prepare their food. They believed in the classic Gnostic idea of salvation through special knowledge.

After the death of Shapur in 270, the Magi went after Mani. Kerdir, the chief priest, also attacked all the other religions that had gained traction in Iran – Jews, Buddhists, Brahmins, Greek and Syriac Christians, Baptists, idol worshippers and Mandaeans. They destroyed synagogues, and they persecuted the Manichaeans. Finally, they imprisoned Mani, and in 276 CE they tortured him to death.

It is no wonder that Mani ran afoul of the Magi. Mani was a charismatic figure, regarded as a miracle-worker and a healer – just as Jesus was at that time. Manichaeism was an early attempt at founding a universal religion, and they were known for proselytizing. This was in contrast with the Mandaeans, who did not even accept converts. Mani cleverly broadened his religion to incorporate aspects of Judaism, Christianity, Zoroastrianism, Buddhism and Jainism, preaching to all of them in terms as close to their own beliefs as possible. St. Augustine was a Manichaean for nine years.

Mani adopted the Hindu belief in reincarnation. He convinced a ruler in Sindh that he was an incarnation of the Buddha. His religion purported to perfect Christianity, but it perpetuated the Iranian cosmic hierarchy. Mani was a talented artist, illustrating his ideas through vivid paintings. Christian church windows may have been inspired by his art, which in turn was inspired by Buddhist art.

Even after his death, Mani's followers spread their ideas to Arabs, North Africa and the Roman Empire, despite governmental opposition. His religion traveled through Samarkand with Sogdian merchants, and it went east along the Silk Road to the Uighurs, who adopted it as a state religion in 763. The Chinese called the Manichaeans vegetarian demon-worshipers, but the religion survived in southeast China into the seventeenth century.

For a thousand years, Manichaeism was one of the world's great religions. During the Abbasid period when Muslims took over the government, Persian intellectuals were accused of practicing the Manichaean religion in secret, even into the eighth and ninth centuries, as a means of opposing Arab control. But today, nobody in the world practices it.

These were the Gnostics, although the origin of the next movement, the Mazdakites, also may have started with Mani.

MAZDAKISM

By the fifth century, the Persian nobility and priesthood held most of the power and wealth in the country, and people were ready for another reformer. In the 520s the Mazdakite religion appeared, led by Mazdak, son of Bamdad, who was a Zoroastrian priest. Mazdak retained so much Zoroastrianism symbolism that he was seen as a reformer, a heretical Zoroastrian, not the initiator of a new religion.

Mazdak was considered a *zandik*, one who claimed to find hidden inner heretical meanings in the Avesta. In Hebrew, a very pious man is called a *tzaddik*. Are the words related? Mazdak's religion was ascetic and pessimistic. He taught that salvation is by chance, not by choice. He taught that even the lowliest person could attain salvation. Unique in his teachings was a kind of proto-communism. He advocated land redistribution, shared property, grain silos, money, harems, and wives. Needless to say, the thought of a wife exchange gained the religion considerable notoriety in this conservative part of the world. And it caused his downfall.

Among his talents, he too was a miracle worker. With one of his miracles he won the support of a Sassanian emperor, Kavad I, but Kavad ultimately lost his throne over this support. His successor in 531 was his son Khostrow I. Khostrow staged a debate between Mazdak and a Zoroastrian priest, in which the priest bested Mazdak. Then a massive campaign against heresy ensued. According to legend, Khostrow commanded that 100,000 (or maybe it was 12,000) of Mazdak's followers be buried head down in a garden, with their feet sticking up. He forced Mazdak to see the scene before he executed him. An old Jewish curse says: "You should grow like an onion with your head in the ground."

Mazdak was hanged and riddled with arrows. In the end it is difficult to describe what his beliefs were, seemingly a mashup of ancient Iranian traditions of dualism, Zoroastrianism and Gnosticism. He visualized a world that was vegetarian, matriarchal in lineage, heretical and marked by an annual orgy.

The one thing that was not new was the orgy; it was a tradition in Iran since pagan times.

Now, could a religion be based on a god of time? Could the Persians have adopted such a religion? They did, and it has been an important influence on other Persian religions ever since.

ZURVANISM

Zurvanism is a mystical branch of Zoroastrianism that may have originated during the Achaemenid Empire. It was popular during the Sassanian Empire, and it largely died out at the end of the tenth century under pressure from Islam.

In ancient Persia, Zurvan had been the god of time, and now the Zurvanites worshipped him as their primordial deity. This is where Zurvanism differed from Zoroastrianism. In Zoroastrianism, Zurvan is the father of the two main gods, and these two main gods are twins: *Ahura Mazda* and *Angra Mainyu*.

Again we see this theme of twins intertwined with the dualism that runs through so many Persian religions. But Zurvanism claimed that the Zoroastrian idea of twin brothers betrayed the basic Zoroastrian concept that good and evil are entirely separate, allowing man the free will to choose between them.

Mani also used the name *Zurvan* to denote the Supreme Being. Even today the word *Zaman* is ubiquitous in the Middle East. In the language of Iran, in Arabic and in Hebrew (where it is pronounced zman), it is the word for time. As far back as a set of twelfth century BCE Akkadian tablets of Mesopotamia, the god of time was *Zaarwaan*. The Hindi word for time is *samay*. It looks different, but if you pronounce it aloud, you will see how similar it sounds.

Zurvanism in Iran expressed the Babylonian concept that time is cyclical. Anyone familiar with Hinduism and Buddhism will recognize this as the cycle of reincarnation.

Zurvanism was officially sanctioned during the Sassanian Empire. Then after the tenth century and the establishment of Islam, this religion too seems to have disappeared, although some of its ideas have persisted. Some have suggested that the description of St. Thomas as the twin of Jesus is an idea that could have come from Zurvanism.[9]

THE KURDS

Next come two Kurdish minority religions. The western world found out about the Kurdish Yezidis in the twenty-first century because ISIS tried to destroy them, chasing them up their sacred mountain, massacring men, and abducting hundreds of girls to sell into slavery. Israel has given covert support to the Kurds for decades, feeling a certain kinship with a persecuted community that has never managed to obtain the homeland that they begged for, and that they had been promised by the international community.

The Kurds are generally believed to be of Iranian origin, though some Kurds and some Jews believe that the Kurds are descendants of a group of Jews who lived in the time of King Solomon.[10] Genetic studies have shown a close relationship between Jews and Kurds, closer than that between Jews and Arabs.[11] Today the populations are linked by the presence of 200–300,000 Jewish Kurds who are living in Israel. In the 1960s when the Jews escaped Iraq, the Kurds helped them. In the late sixties and seventies when the Kurds arose against Iraq, the Israelis helped them.[12] Golda Meir, the prime minister of Israel, even gave them $100,000 in support. In 2015, reports were that the Israelis were getting 77% of their oil from the Kurds.

The Kurds speak several Iranian-derived languages, and they are spread across a large swathe of the Middle East: the high

---

[9] Mary Boyce and Frantz Grenet, 'A History of Zoroastrianism, Vol III: Zoroastrianism under Macedonian and Roman Rule', (Leiden: EJ Brill, 1991), pp 471–6 in the *Handbuch der Orientalistik*, C. van Dijk et al.

[10] Dillon, Kassy, 'The Little-Known History of Israel and the Kurds', *Providence*, Oct. 18, 2019, The Little-known History of Israel and the Kurds - Providence (providencemag.com)

[11] Nebel, Almut et al, 'The Y Chromosome Pool of Jews as Part of the Genetic Landscape of the Middle East', *American Journal of Human Genetics*, vol. 69, no. 5 (November 2001), 1095–1112.

[12] Black, Ian and Morris, Benny, *Israel's Secret Wars* (New York: Grove Press, 1991), pp. 521–52, 184.

Zagros mountains of western Iraq, the plains of the Iraqi Nineveh Province, northeastern Syria, northwestern Iran and southeastern Turkey. They are mountain people, and they are plains people, but all of them fiercely independent. Their land in Turkey represents almost a third of Turkish Asia Minor, which has put the Kurds at odds with the Turkey of Prime Minister Erdogan, despite their being, for the most part, fellow Sunni Muslims.

In Kurdish territories there also are, or used to be, significant communities of Kurdish Jews, Chaldean Christians, and Assyrian Christians. Unfortunately, the Christian heartland is in much the same area as land claimed by the Kurds: northern Iraq, northeast Syria, southeast Turkey and part of Iran. This may explain why Armenians, Assyrians and Chaldeans suffered at the hands of both Kurds and Turks in 1915. Competition for land was one of the underlying reasons for the genocide. Nevertheless, Kurds have lived in peace for millennia in close contact with pre-Islamic indigenous religions. And recently, the beleaguered Christians of the Middle East, under attack by ISIS, have found refuge among the Kurds of Iraq.

One scholar[13] proposes that there was an underlying, indigenous Kurdish religion, which he calls Yazdanism, the cult of angels. This may be more of a hypothesis than established fact. At any rate, in Kurdistan, because of their proximity for centuries, even thousands of years, the Yezidis and Yaresans of today hold Iranian beliefs mixed with elements of both Christianity and Islam.

YEZIDIS

Until the recent attacks on them, Yezidis (Yazidis) numbered over a half million, most of them living in northern Iraq. In 2014, the western news media carried horrific reports of ISIS attacks on the Yezidi city of Sinjar, showing how Yezidis were being cruelly persecuted, kidnapped and slaughtered. The motivation may have been that, though Yezidis are a pious family-oriented community, they are reviled in the Islamic world as devil worshippers,

---

[13] Foltz, p. 5128 in the Kindle edition.

probably because of the Arabic translation of the name of their supreme god.

In contrast, travelers who have visited them report that Yezidis are peaceful souls who believe in one God and seven angels, all emanations of God. They also believe in seven mysteries and seven holy beings. They believe in reincarnation, and they pray while facing the sun. These are all primordial beliefs that they share with religions from the Middle East to India, but they are especially characteristic of religions that are derived from traditional Iranian beliefs.

Their origin as a distinct religion was in the twelfth century, when a Lebanese Sufi master acquired a following in Iraq. As the religion took form, it melded Sufi elements with local pre-Islamic Iranian traditions. They speak Kurmanji, a Kurdish language which many of their Christian and Jewish neighbors also learned in order to conduct trade in the region.

One of their rituals is the annual sacrifice of a bull. This sounds like Mithraism, but the reader will remember that the practice goes back to the prehistoric proto-Indo-Iranians, and, as we have said, it also was reflected in the temple sacrifices of the priests in Jerusalem. Yezidis celebrate four seasonal holidays, and these resemble the seasonal celebrations of Jews as well as followers of other Middle Eastern religions. Interesting, they are strictly monotheistic.

YARESANS (YARSANISM)

The Yaresan are a heterodox Shi'ite sect that originated in Iran during the fourteenth century. As contrasted with Yezidis, they consider themselves to be a sect of Islam, and they have rituals that resemble those of the Sufis. Unlike Yezidis, they are egalitarian, with no class, caste or rank, though they have a hereditary priesthood. Most of them live in western Iran, but some of them live in northeast Iraq, where they are known as Kaka'i. Like the Yezidis, the Yaresan traditionally did not accept converts or allow intermarriage. Also like the Yezidis, they have a ritual of bull sacrifice.

They hold the sun and fire to be holy, and they proclaim the purity, righteousness, and the oneness of all. They too believe in dualism, reminiscent of Zurvanism and Zoroastrianism. Some of their beliefs appear to be derived from Mithraism. They believe in reincarnation, a belief they hold in common with other indigenous Iranian religions, also with Hinduism and Judaism. Many Yaresan and Yezidi beliefs appear to be continuations of ancient Persian religions.

The Yaresan have some Islamic beliefs too, and they have been called worshippers of Ali. Nevertheless, they are attacked by Islam as unbelievers, and they have been assailed in recent years by the Iranian government. Not long ago they numbered two or three million, but it is hard to know if they still do.[14]

Now with some background in the indigenous religions of Persia, we should be ready to discuss Zoroastrianism. But wait. There is more before that. For instance, in the rich religious mélange of this region, not only did new Persian religions appear, but even an old religion – Judaism – morphed into something new.

KARAITES

Persian religions were not the only ones to develop offshoots in Iran and Mesopotamia. In the early days of the Abbasid Caliphate, when Baghdad became the capital city, it was the beginning of a golden age. This was a time of great intellectual and cultural effervescence, when Persian and Islamic ideas mixed freely with each other.

It should not be surprising that Karaism arose. This was a Jewish sect founded by Anan ben David in eighth century CE Baghdad.[15] Ben David lived for some time in Persia, then returned to Baghdad, and for some reason he rebelled against the ruling Jewish exilarch. He was thrown promptly into prison, where he

---

[14] Boyce, Mary and Grenet, Frantz, A History of Zoroastrianism, Vol III: Zoroastrianism under Macedonian and Roman Rule, (Leiden: EJ Brill, 1991) pp. 471–6, and also C. van Dijk et al, The Handbuch der Orientalistik. Both have excellent discussions of Mithraism, Zurvanism, Old Iranian Religions and Zoroastrianism.

[15] Margolis, Max L., and Marx, Alexander, History of the Jewish People, (Philadelphia: The Jewish Publication Society, 1967), pp. 259–63, plus numerous other pages throughout the book.

fell under the influence of a brilliant fellow prisoner, Abu Hanifa, a man who had founded a major Islamic school of jurisprudence. Thus, it was a Muslim scholar who provided the arguments that stimulated ben David to create a new sect of Judaism.

Karaites believe only in the written law of the Five Books of Moses. They reject the oral laws of Judaism, and they reject all rabbinic writings. They mourn the loss of the temple, and they keep the Shabbat in their own way, not lighting any kind of fire on that day. Their rules for ritual slaughter of meat are more stringent than those of traditional Judaism. They portray their strict interpretation of scripture as coming from biblical times, but 20th-century scholars have suggested that many of their beliefs were reactions to the surrounding Islam. And since then, twentieth century Jews have suggested that it is no wonder their numbers have dwindled, considering the severity of some of their practices.

Multiple sects of Karaism developed, and many Karaite literary works were produced all over the world during a "Golden Age of Karaism" between 900 and 1100. Note that this was during the "Golden Age of Islam". Karaism was not a small sect. At one time, as much as 40 percent of world Jewry may have been Karaite. By the 12th century, Karaism had moved into eastern Europe. On a trip to Trakai, Lithuania, my husband and I once walked through an old Karaite village, where we saw a metal-roofed synagogue in front of little wooden houses, all empty.

After World War II, most Karaites moved to Israel. The Karaite Synagogue of Jerusalem is located up an obscure stairway in the Jewish section of the Old City, and there I once saw a fascinating poster presentation of their beliefs and history.[16]

MOUNTAIN JEWS

Yet another Jewish group came from Iran. Some believe that the Jews of the Caucasus Mountains and Azerbaijan were descended

---

[16] http://www.jewishencyclopedia.com/articles/9211-karaites-and-karaism The Kara'ite Synagogue in the old city of Jerusalem displayed an excellent presentation of world Karaite history when I visited. This synagogue was built in the ninth century, destroyed by the crusaders and rebuilt shortly after Saladin reconquered Jerusalem in 1187.

from the Ten Lost Tribes of the Assyrian Exile. While the Kurdish Jews of northern Iraq still lived in the land of ancient Assyria, other deportees spread from Assyria to Persia, becoming known as Iranian Jews, and some of them apparently migrated east from Iran to settle in southern Russia, Azerbaijan, and the Caucasus. There they are known as Mountain Jews.

An Armenian friend of mine from Baku remembers the warm relationships between Armenians and Jews in Azerbaijan. In Baku there were both Ashkenazi and Mountain Jews, and she remembers the two groups maintaining a certain separation from one another. For one thing, the Mountain Jews spoke their own language, a Hebrew-influenced dialect of Persian called Tat, or *Juhuro*. By now, more than 100,000 have moved to Israel. In addition, 30,000 live in Russia, 12,000 in Azerbaijan, and more are scattered around the world. One man once appeared in a Hebrew class I was attending in Detroit.

HOLY MEN AND MESSIAHS

Holy men, sects and diverse religions have all swirled around in the complex environment of Iran. In the 740s, a cult developed around one Abu Isa Esfahani (Abu Isa Obadih of Ispahan),[17] the leader of a radical Jewish resistance movement. His followers considered him to be the Messiah, and he said that he was one of the five heralds from on high who were supposed to announce the arrival of the Messiah. At the peak of his success, he led a vegetarian sect that had 10,000 members, possibly influenced by Manichaeism. He must have had contact with Shi'ism, which was growing in importance at that time. He also may have interacted with Karaites, since some of his ideas seem to have influenced them. In the end he escaped governmental pursuit, fled north, joined a Persian chief who was fighting the caliph, and he died in battle.

In 1121, David Alroy,[18] a Jew from Amadiya, east of Mosul, was another would-be Messiah. According to Benjamin of Tudela,

---

[17] Margolis, p. 259.
[18] Sabar, Yona, *The Folk Literature of the Kurdistani Jews: An Anthology*, (New Haven: Yale University Press, 1982), pp. 94–100.

a medieval Jewish traveler, Alroy was a Baghdad-trained scholar who claimed to speak seventy languages. He also was a magician and an expert in both Jewish and Muslim law. Known as a miracle worker, he attracted an enormous following throughout Kurdistan. Early in his career, he incited thousands of Jews to rebel against the King of Persia. Hearing of this, the king summoned him, to ask if indeed he was the Messiah. Announcing that he would only believe him if he was able to escape, the king threw David in prison, but he escaped miraculously. The king's soldiers went after him and caught him at a riverbank, whereupon he spread his shawl on the water and walked safely across the river on his shawl.

In great anger, the king insisted that the exilarch in Baghdad force the Jewish establishment to do something about him. When he was called to testify before them, David convinced them that angels from heaven were about to come for him, but they did not. A friendly king of Turkey intervened and confided in David's father-in-law that something had to be done. As a result, the father-in-law invited David to a banquet, and, in the end, David became dead.

We already have learned about the ill-fated Sabbatai Zevi who appeared in the 1660s, and there were more would-be prophets. But centuries later, a new prophet was born, and he continues to make an impact in the modern world. Today the religion that he founded has a total membership of over five million, possibly as high as seven million, and, along with Islam, it is one of the fastest growing religions in the world. For its stunning success, the Iranian government has persecuted it relentlessly, and the Bahai religion has had to make itself a new home in a country where it is warmly admired, in Israel.

BAHAIS

The newest religious movement of Iran appeared in the 1850s, and its followers are the most reviled of all in Iran – the Bahais.

The Bahai religion originated with Seyyed Ali Mohammad,[19] born in Shiraz, Iran in 1819. Known as the Bab, he claimed divine revelation, announcing that appearance of the prophet – the Shi'ite Twelfth Imam – was imminent. Initially, he said that he was the gate (*bab* in Arabic) to the Mahdi – this Hidden Imam – but while on trial in 1848 in Tabriz, he made the heretical claim that he *was* the Mahdi. This was an existential threat to the religious authorities, because the coming of the Mahdi renders the existing secular and spiritual authorities obsolete. For this heresy, he was imprisoned in Azerbaijan, and in 1850 he was executed in Tabriz.[20]

In defiance of Islamic law, the Bab taught that revelation is progressive, that salvation comes through recognizing the Bab as God's messenger, and that the Twelver Shi'ite clergy are obsolete. He also taught that his new religion superseded Islamic law, and he focused on individual, not collective, prayers. He emphasized the need for spiritual – as opposed to ritual – purity, and he told his followers that the Hajj to Mecca should be replaced by a pilgrimage to his home in Shiraz. None of this endeared him to the Muslim establishment.

The most prominent follower of the Bab was Baha'ullah. He claimed to be the long-awaited prophet, and he is seen as the founder of the religion. He was arrested by the Ottomans, taken from Baghdad to Istanbul, and finally imprisoned in Acre, Israel, where he died in 1892. Today his tomb is near Acre.

The oldest son of the Bab was Abdul-Baha, who also was imprisoned for heresy. After he was released, he continued preaching, and when he died in 1924, he was succeeded by his son. After that, the religion was directed by a nine-member governing body whose headquarters are in Haifa, Israel.

---

[19] Hassell, Graham, 'Ba'hai History in the Formative Age, The World Crusade, 1953–1963', Published in the *Journal of Bahá'í Studies* Vol. 6, number 4 (1994) © Association for Bahá'í Studies 1994,
https://web.archive.org/web/20120322081619/http://www.bahai-studies.ca/journal/files/jbs/6.4%20Hassall.pdf

[20] MacEoin, Denis, 'The Trial of the Bab', *Occasional Papers in Shaykhi, Babi and Baha'I Studies*, May 1997,
https://www.h-net.org/~bahai/bhpapers/babtrial.htm

Today, the Shrine of the Bab, a shining, temple-like tomb with a golden dome, sits in the middle of the spectacular Hanging Gardens of Haifa, amid perfectly manicured gardens that cascade in tiers down Mount Carmel to the level of the sea. These, along with the Monument Gardens and Shrine of Baha'ullah in Acre, form the Bahai World Centre. Every day this flowery Eden welcomes tour groups, like one I joined, and the temple hosts visiting Bahais from all over the world. Though this religion was born and grew up in Iran, its founders ended up with their final rest in Israel.

The Bahai religion has acquired many converts from Judaism, Islam and many other religions, and it has tailored its teachings shrewdly to appeal to communities around the world. A major Bahai temple that I visited in Delhi is shaped like a lotus with nine petals, a symbol designed to appeal to both Hindus and Buddhists.

Around 90% of Iranians are Shi'ites today. Armenian Christians in Iran have coexisted with the majority Muslims the most successfully, and the Bahais have suffered the most. With all that, there are said to be over 6 million Bahais world-wide, and they still may be Iran's largest non-Muslim minority, numbering over 300,000.

Now we are ready to learn about the Zoroastrian religion, its commonalities with Hinduism and Buddhism, its possible influence on Judaism, and the cross-relationships between all of these. To get started, we must travel more than 2,500 years back in time.

CHAPTER NINE.
ZOROASTRIANISM, PARSIS AND MORE

The Zoroastrian religion is one of the world's oldest, and it was the official religion of more than one great Persian empire. We in the west do not know much about it, but the mysterious name Zarathustra has long been part of our culture, primarily because of the celebrated novel *Thus Spoke Zarathustra,* written in the nineteenth century by the German philosopher Nietzsche. This book made Zarathustra into a near-mythical entity in the western world, but, under a different name, he already had entered European legend. More than a hundred years before Nietzsche, in 1791, the Mozart opera *The Magic Flute* had its premiere. In it, the high priest was named Sarastro, a fictionalized version of Zarathustra. Then in 1896, Richard Strauss took the theme for his tone poem, *Also Sprach Zarathuster.* From all this came exotic western fantasies of Zoroastrianism.

The Avestas are the oldest compilation of Zoroastrian teachings. Yet, it is not from Iran, but from India that we have some of the best explanations of its legends and philosophies. Are these interpretations real, or are they eastern dreams of exotic Persia? No, the oldest pre-Hindu texts, the Vedas, transcribed from ancient oral tradition, are the key to reading the Avestas, and they are the best existing commentary on it, the result of a primordial connection between the two religions, and probably a common origin. We will learn more.

ZOROASTRIANISM

Zoroaster, more correctly Zarathustra, is said to have come from eastern Iran, from the priestly class. He probably lived between 628 and 551 BCE, although these dates are controversial, as is much about his life.

We call the religion Zoroastrianism, but it also is called the Magian religion, because the priests were Magi, meaning wise men. Members of the priestly tribe of Medians, they kept the sacred fire, instructed the king's sons in religion, and made the required sacrifices to the gods. Eventually they became political figures and advisors to kings. In Jewish lore, they were diviners, astrologers and interpreters of dreams, yet in a surprising turn-around, it was the Jewish Daniel who interpreted their dreams when he encountered them in prison, and he was the one who interceded for the Magi when Nebuchadnezzar condemned them to death.

Other names for the religion are Mazdaism,[1] *Mazdayasna* (the worship of Ahura Mazda), *daema Mazdayasni* or *Zarathushti Din.* Notice the word *din.* In Middle Persian, the word *den* or *din* meant religion, and in Arabic it has the same meaning. In Hebrew it means law, which in the Middle East often is equated with religion.

Another name for the Zoroastrian religion is *daena vanguhi*, meaning the good religion. The word *daena* comes from a root that means 'to see.' Presumably, this refers to religious insight. In Sanskrit the cognate word is *Dharma.* Dharma is a complex idea that is difficult to define, but its meanings relate to duty, order, harmony, rights, laws, religion, justice, ethics, custom, the right way of living and proper conduct. More broadly, it symbolizes a duty to conform to the natural order of things. Some might say it means 'to uphold, support, nourish.'

For centuries, many sacred Zoroastrian teachings were only transmitted orally, which makes it difficult to date them or to

---

[1] Mazdaism is the title of this archival publication, which clearly is old, but very thorough.
http://opensiuc.lib.siu.edu/cgi/viewcontent.cgi?article = 5033&context = ocj

know which ones Zarathustra actually wrote. This problem is not unique to the Zoroastrian religion. Not only do the Persian Avesta and the Indian Rigveda have long oral traditions, so do a whole body of Jewish teachings that are believed to go back to Moses. In all these faiths, the priests recited precisely what they had received from their predecessors, never daring to change a single word. Generations later, when these verses finally were transcribed into written texts, the scribes again took care to avoid any error or amendment. Even so, as commentaries were written, new expositions devised, and new poetic works created on the basis of the ancient lore, many of these innovations eventually became part of the written canon.

Zoroastrianism had a complicated, intermittent history throughout the period of Persian Empire that started with Cyrus in the sixth century BCE.[2] By the time of Christ though, Zoroastrian themes had entered the Jewish literature, early Christian texts and even Buddhist iconography.

The Zoroastrian religion spread widely. It was adopted in Cappadocia, Turkey, became the majority religion in Armenia and Georgia, and it even reached parts of Central Asia. Zoroastrian fire temples appeared in China by the eighth century during the Tang Dynasty.

The first written works in the Zoroastrian tradition were in Old Avestan, a language that resembles the Sanskrit of the Indian Vedas.[3] The oldest of these works, the Avestas, have been dated between 1500 and 1100 BCE,[4] and they share many myths and gods with the Vedas, which are believed to date from 1500 BCE. Remember that these were all transmitted orally for centuries, so this dating must be understood as hypothetical.

The term *Zend-Avesta* is used for the combination of the *Avesta*, the text, and the *Zend*, the commentary. Its central five hymns, the *Gathas*, are written in the oldest dialect of all. One of the oldest parts is the *Yasna Haptanhaiti*, which may have been

---

[2] Shah, Mark, *Zoroastrianism: An introduction to Zoroastrianism.*
[3] Darmestet, James, trans., *The Zend Avesta Part I The Vendidad*, an ancient text republished.
[4] Bryant, Edwin, *The Quest for the Origins of Vedic Culture – The Indo-Aryan Migration Debate* (Oxford: Oxford University Press, 2001), p. 132.

written by Zoroaster himself. The version of the Avesta that exists today was published in 1323 CE, thousands of years after the original material was first committed to writing.[5] In the time of Alexander, invading troops burned the Archives of Istakhr. In them were 12,000 ox hides on which the sacred writings of Zoroastrianism were inscribed. Fortunately, some priests had private libraries, and one child is said to have committed this material to memory. The rest was destroyed and lost forever. Today only five books remain of the 21 volumes that reportedly once existed, and these represent the last remnant of the sacred literature of Persia.

The Avesta originally was recited by the Magi in their own language, not in Persian. Later, it was translated into Pahlavi, a language derived from ancient Persian. This translation is the Zend, which contains original verses, explanations and learned discussions by Zoroastrian authorities.[6] This format piques the interest of Jewish scholars, because it has a familiar, rabbinic feel, question and answer, question and answer.

Zoroastrians share many ideas with Judaism and the other great monotheistic religions. They believe in heaven, hell and a Judgment Day. They predict the birth of a Messiah – in this case descended from the lineage of Zoroaster. They teach respect for the living, and they promote sexual responsibility. They preach equality of genders, class and race. Remarkably, considering the times when the religion originated, they do not require devotees to believe in a deity, a Jesus or an Allah, and those who refuse to convert are not killed.[7]

According to the Gospels, wise men from the east, identified as Magi and wearing Parthian dress, are said to have brought gifts to the newborn Christ. That could be, because the three Magi, presumably Zoroastrians, had been taught that long after the death of Zoroaster there would come a savior, the *Saoshyant*, born

---

[5] Foltz, Richard, *Religions of Iran – from prehistory to the present* (London: Oneworld Publications, 2013).
[6] Secunda, Shai, *The Iranian Talmud – Reading the Bavli in its Sassanian Context* (Philadelphia: University of Pennsylvania Press, 2014), p. 23.
[7] Shah, Mark, *Zoroastrianism: An introduction to Zoroastrianism.*

of a virgin mother, who would "free the world from death and decay."

According to Zoroastrianism, the end of time will come with an epic battle between good and evil, light and darkness, and in the end, good will defeat evil. This will usher in an era of growth and prosperity and the sole sovereignty of Ahura Mazda, the god of all that is good. Finally, there will be a resurrection when the *Saoshyant* arrives, and ancient Zoroastrian prophecy predicts that this future savior will bring immortality to the righteous. Though experts may find distinctions between the concepts, to the layman this certainly sounds like the Judeo-Christian concept of a Messiah.

In the view of Zoroastrians, on Judgement Day an Account Keeper tallies up good and bad acts, assigns appropriate rewards and punishments, and God metes out Judgement. Experts argue over who originated the idea of a Judgment Day, Jews or Zoroastrians, though this may be a Mesopotamian idea that predated both religions.

The reader will recall that many Persian religions believed in the existence of a good and a bad principle and that all beings in nature are either evil or good. Zoroaster taught that the two primal spirits were[8] *Ahura Mazda*, the benevolent spirit, and *Angra Mainyu*, the malign spirit. Then in an ultimate struggle between good and evil, the evil principle will be destroyed. And since the good spirit finally will defeat the evil spirit and the good spirit will reign triumphant, Zoroastrians make the argument that their religion ultimately is monotheistic.

Zoroaster taught that in Paradise the soul must wait for his future body, and union of the two will come when the earth gives up the bones of the dead. This is the image of 'dry bones' that inspired an American spiritual, coming from Ezekiel 37:11–12, which prophesizes: "...Mortal, these bones are the whole house

---

[8] Boyce, Mary, Zoroastrians – *Their Religious Beliefs and Practices* (London: Routledge, 1979). Mary Boyce is one of the foremost experts on Zoroastrianism, and her discussion is very complete, with important points distributed throughout the book. Rather than citing individual page numbers, I refer the reader to the whole book.

of Israel. They say, 'Our bones are dried up, and our hope is lost; we are cut off completely.' [12] Therefore prophesy, and say to them, Thus says the Lord God: I am going to open your graves, and bring you up from your graves, O my people..."

The Book of Ezekiel, by the way, recorded the prophesies of Ezekiel, who lived in Babylon between 593 and 571 BCE. If Zoroaster lived in northern Iraq between 628 and 551 BCE, they would have been contemporaries. It may be no accident that those dry bones rattle with a prophecy of Zoroaster.

A Persian text teaches that each person's words and actions have profound repercussions in the wider world. Zoroastrians interpret that as meaning that human beings are "agents of healing in the world." This sounds a lot like the Hebrew concept of *tikkun olam*, which means correcting the world, an injunction that is taken very seriously in modern Judaism. Jews also are taught, especially by their mystics, that every action affects the world.

Until the Muslim conquest, the Zoroastrian religion was the official religion of Persia. Once the Arabs were in control, the persecutions began. Zoroastrians were treated as *dhimmis*. Fire temples were turned into mosques, and libraries were burned. This treatment became progressively worse under the Abbasids, and pressure to convert even increased after them.

PARSIS

In 651 CE after the death of the last Sassanian king of Iran, many Zoroastrians fled to the hills. A century later, they set sail for India. They landed first on an island off the state of Gujarat, and they stayed there for 19 years. From there they moved to the mainland, where they lived and thrived for the next 300 years. This is the legend.

Current evidence suggests that they arrived in India between the mid-seventh and the early-tenth century. These first Iranian immigrants to India were called Parsis, from the word for Persians, and they essentially became an Indian high caste of lawyers, doctors, teachers and businessmen. The community organized themselves much as Jewish communities normally do, with schools, retirement homes, charities, temples and all the accoutrements of an urban society. Preserved correspondence between Parsi priests in India and their colleagues in Iran has helped historians to reconstruct the story.

But Parsis were not the only Iranians who found their way to India. Before they came, the Achaemenids under Darius I had sailed as far as Sri Lanka, and the Sassanian military had attacked Sindh and the Punjab. Another group of Zoroastrians came to India in the late eighteenth century, and they are known as Iranis. In short, since the sixth century BCE, there has been contact between Iran and India.

During their time in Gujarat, the Parsi community preserved many of their sacred books by assiduously translating them into Sanskrit. This worked well until a Muslim sultanate was established in Delhi, and a Muslim army ravished Gujarat in 1297. After that, again *dhimmis* in their new country, the Parsis of Gujarat were forced to pay the jizya tax to Delhi. In 1572, Akbar took over Gujarat, but he at least treated the Parsis graciously. From 1600 to almost 1800, the largest concentration of Zoroastrians in the world lived in Surat, Gujarat, the very same port at which the Baghdadi Jews disembarked.

Christian missionaries challenged many Parsi beliefs in the early 19th century, forcing them to refine and reformulate many of them. As they did, they chose to emphasize the monotheist, rational elements of their religion and their individual piety. They wrote that though they believe in forces of both good and evil, they have only one supreme God, Ahura Mazda. They also explained that they believe in the original goodness of humanity and that man is created in the image of God.

Like Zoroastrians everywhere, Parsis believe that life on earth is temporary, that humans are mortal, and that death is not final. The soul always exists, but it is assigned a body at birth; the dead are impure and evil. Parsis have their own sacred chants and sacrifices, and they have their own prophets. They believe in sin, pardon, punishment and the free will of man to choose good. They anticipate a final judgment day, and it will be for all humanity. All of this is classic Zoroastrianism.

One Parsi practice sets them apart from all other communities in India. They believe that water and fire are pure, and the dead should pollute neither ground nor fire. As a result, they do not bury their dead in the ground or cremate them. Instead, Parsis build what the British have dubbed Towers of Silence. In Mumbai, the British gave the Parsi community a gift of land on Malabar Hill for a Tower of Silence. The tower remains there today, near the expensive homes of Malabar Hill and just down the elegant Peddar Road from the two-billion-dollar Ambani house. And there too, vultures pick the bones clean before they are placed in an ossuary, though many vultures in India have died of poison the farmers spread on their crops, and many of the towers of silence in India truly have fallen into silence.

Parsis have long been well integrated into the fabric of Indian life. In Kerala, a late ninth-century copper plate has an inscription bestowing privileges to Christians, and it had several Zoroastrian signatures – written in Pahlavi. Parsis once dominated the legal profession in Bombay, and to be accepted in the upper echelons of the bar a young lawyer had to pass muster with the Parsi elite. A visitor to Mumbai can see that, after partition, Parsi names predominate on a plaque that lists past presidents of the exclusive old British Willingdon Sports Club. While the Parsi community in India has been remarkably successful, today it has dwindled down to 60,000 or fewer, in part because of emigration and in part because Parsis do not accept converts.

SOME CULTURAL COMPARISONS

Many ordinary elements of Zoroastrian daily life resemble those of Judaism. Both religious Zoroastrian men and Jewish men wear skull caps. A Zoroastrian male traditionally wears a white cotton shirt, called a *sudreh,* under his clothes, and around the waist he wraps a tasseled cord, a *kusti.* Religious Jewish men wear a fringed white cotton vest, called a *tallit katan,* under their outer clothes. Zoroastrians initiate both boys and girls into adulthood at age 15. Jewish boys have their Bar Mitzvah initiation ceremony at age 13, and now many Jewish girls have a Bat Mitzvah at 13.

Both religions have had hereditary priests. In Iran, it is the Magi. In Israel, the Kohanim performed the priestly rites at the

Temple. It still is possible to identify a Kohen today, even though his ritual role is greatly reduced, because geneticists have identified a genetic marker that is specific for male Kohanim. Paradoxically, since genetic markers obviously are inherited independent of religious practice, there now are Christians with the Kohen marker, descendants of Kohanim who had converted.

Jews and Zoroastrians both forbid graven images. Though the Jews tend to be more meticulous about this. Both religions sanctify daily life, and both have special dietary laws. The Zoroastrian Zend-Avesta specifies rules of criminal law, defines the sins that require atonement and lays out other legal principles, many of which resemble principles of Jewish law in the Talmud. From the early days of both religions, lepers and others afflicted with contagious diseases were kept in isolation. In both religions, a woman who has just delivered a child is unclean. Each month after her period is over, a Zoroastrian woman must take a ritual bath, just as a Jewish woman immerses herself in a mikvah – a bath in clean flowing water – at that time. Of interest, upper caste Hindu women of South India have the same practice.

The Zoroastrian calendar year has 360 days and twelve months of 30 days each, with an intercalated month at intervals, just like the Jewish calendar. The traditional Persian New Year celebration, Nowruz, begins with the spring equinox in March, though the Sassanids changed the official new year to October. This is quite fascinating, because in a peculiarity of the Jewish calendar that school children never can understand, the bible says the new year starts in April – Nissan on the Hebrew calendar – yet the Jewish New Year, Rosh Hashanah, is officially celebrated in October.

It should not be surprising that in the bible the new year begins with the spring holiday of Passover. Nissan was the month of the New Year for Kings in Persia, and it was the traditional month of the New Year throughout the Middle East. Referring to Nissan, in Exodus 12:1–2, The Lord said to Moses and Aaron in the land of Egypt, "This month shall be for you the beginning of months. It shall be the first month of the year for you."

Today, the Iranian New Year, Nowruz, continues to be celebrated at the spring equinox in March, as it is in parts of the Balkans, Turkey, Kurdistan, the Caucasus, Afghanistan, Baluchistan, Pakistan, and Tajikistan, all the way to Uzbekistan. The lingering influence of old Persian empires is obvious.

Nowruz is a two-week celebration of life and family, the most anticipated of all the agricultural festivals. The day before Nowruz, the Parsis of India celebrate *Pateti*, meaning repentance. They also may observe ten days of prayer for their departed loved ones just before their New Year. Is it a coincidence that Jews also observe 10 days of repentance – in this case *after* their New Year – and that they too say prayers for their departed at the end of that time, on Yom Kippur, the Day of Repentance?

Zoroastrians enjoy firecrackers, and they jump over fires on Nowruz. Muslims call them fire-worshippers, perhaps because traditional homes are supposed to have a sacred fire, which the woman of the house must keep going. She even is responsible for covering it with ashes each night so the fire will not go out. An Armenian friend from Azerbaijan says that it was the custom in Baku to celebrate Nowruz with special food and also with festive fires that people would jump. This is true of Yazidis and, amazingly, Lithuanians, who share common Aryan roots with the Persians.

Lithuanians have maintained a pagan tradition of fire worship.[9] We learned about this at a wedding we attended near Vilnius, when the parents ceremonially presented gifts of bread and salt to the young couple. As we watched the little ceremony, members of the family told us that the third gift traditionally would have been an offering from the family fire. The prominent Lithuanian philosopher, Vydunas, has written, "To this very day fire is sacred to all Lithuanians. ...Only the flame turns wisdom to the path of spirituality."

---

[9] Trinkunione, Inja, 'Lithuanian Religion as a Source of Baltic Religion,' *Presented at the First International Gathering and Conference of Elders of Ancient Traditions and Cultures in Mumbay, India.*
https://www.infinityfoundation.com/mandala/h_es/h_es_trink_i_fire_fram eset.htm

During every traditional Baltic holiday, a fire (ugnis) is lit, and during ancient times, the Baltic people too were known as fire worshipers. This custom must have Indo-European roots. Even in Azerbaijan, the parents present fire from the family hearth to a newly married couple.

Whether this is related we do not know, but the Jewish temple in Jerusalem had a sacrificial fire. It also maintained a perpetually burning light that represented God's eternal presence. Even today, in every synagogue there is an eternal light. The story of Chanukah tells of persecution of the Jews by the Seleucid Antiochus IV, and it concludes with a Jewish victory – short-lived – over Antiochus. After the battle was over, the Jews returned to their temple to rededicate it and pray. To their dismay, they found that in the temple only one vial remained of the special oil needed to keep the light burning. They were almost certain that the light would go out, yet it burned miraculously for eight days while they traveled to obtain more oil. Thus, Jews celebrate Chanukah for eight days. And some scholars say that, later, the Chanukah ceremony and its candle-lighting rituals became more elaborate than ever under the influence of Sassanian fire-worship.[10]

Two texts illustrate strikingly parallel teachings about fire. One is Talmudic; the other is taken from Zoroastrian sources, the ninth century *Bundahishn* and the *Avesta Yasna*. The Hebrew text describes fire as "that which consumes but does not drink," "that which drinks but does not consume," and "that which consumes and drinks," along with other examples. The Persian verse describes several forms of fire: "one consumes both liquid and substance...one consumes liquid, but not substance...one consumes substance but not liquid," and "One consumes neither liquid nor substance." The author who discusses these comparisons does not venture to guess who copied from whom, but somebody here surely was reading somebody else's holy books.

---

[10] Koller, Aaron and Tsadik, Daniel, *Iran, Israel and the Jews: Symbiosis and Conflict from the Achaemenids to the Islamic Republic,* (Eugene: Wipf and Stock publishers, 2019), chap. 5.

Some Brahmans had the tradition of a household fire,[11] and they were supposed to perform two sacrifices a month to Agni at this fire. Historically, young Hindu householders were given elaborate instructions for how to establish a sacrificial fire.

Iranians would understand. In the fourteenth century under the Il-Khans, a group of Zoroastrians escaped to the village of Turkabad in the northwest corner of the plain of Yazd, Iran. When they fled there and to nearby Sharifabad, they brought two of the three great fires of ancient Iran, which have been burning there ever since.

Fire is hardly unique to Zoroastrians.[12] In the Book of Genesis, God spoke to Moses in Egypt from a burning bush. In Christianity, the Holy Spirit descended in tongues of fire on Pentecost. In Hinduism, Agni, the fire god, represents a full panoply of sacrificial, domestic and funeral pyres, even fire in the belly of man. But in Buddhism, it is bad for the mind to be burning with ideas. In the Buddhist view, this is the fire of lust, hate or delusion. Burning accompanies birth, aging, death, sorrows, lamentations, pains, grief and despair. Thus, fire and burning are the root of all suffering.

BACK TO THE PARSIS

Before we move on though, we cannot leave the Parsis without mentioning some who have achieved extraordinary levels of prominence. Any list of important Parsis in science and industry, law, politics, the arts and academia, among other fields, would name many of the most famous people of India. We could start with one who we know already, Zubin Mehta, the conductor so beloved in Israel. Other outstanding names are Jamsetji Tata, the founder of the entire Tata industrial complex and Ratan Tata, the founder of the Tata Group. The Tata family started in steel, and then they went into hotels, airlines, chemicals, automobiles, and

---

[11] Bettany, pp. 23–4.

[12] 'Fire Symbolism: Flames that Ignite Faiths and Inspire Minds', *Ancient Origins*,
https://www.ancient-origins.net/myths-legends/fire-symbolism-flames-ignite-faiths-and-inspire-minds-004404

many other enterprises, ultimately becoming a multinational conglomerate.

Among the lawyers, Soli Sorabjee and Fali Nariman stand out. Fali was gracious enough to invite me to his apartment and give me copies of his books a few years ago, and for that I am grateful. Feroze Gandhi was the husband of Indira Gandhi. Nusli Wadia is the chairman of the Wadia Group, an Indian conglomerate that deals in textiles and real estate.

> Years ago, my husband and I went over to visit Ram Jethmalani at his Bombay apartment, and as we arrived, Ram was getting out of a car that was driven by a tall distinguished looking man. We were introduced to him as Nusli Wadia. My husband struck up a conversation with him, and soon he impertinently invited him up to Ram's apartment. Once there, they talked law and commerce for a bit, and then Wadia excused himself. After he left, Ram's wife asked if we knew who he was. We did not.

> He was the grandson of Mohammad Ali Jinnah, the founder of Pakistan. But he had a Parsi name, not a Muslim name, we complained. She smiled and said that on his mother's side, he is the son of a Parsi businessman. Then we realized. We had just come from Hyderabad, where we toured a museum that had pictures of Jinnah, and Wadia looked just like Jinnah, but in good health. Jinnah had tuberculosis.

In short, the Parsis have lived comfortably in India for generations. This should not be surprising. Their religion has a common origin with Hinduism, as we are about to see.

Before we learn about the relationship between the Zoroastrian and the Hindu religions though, we will need to know more about Hinduism. And we will learn more about a closely related religion – Buddhism. Then, their interrelationships with Zoroastrianism and Judaism will be clearer. Of necessity though, our discussions will go beyond theology. Much of the appeal of these religions is in their rich tradition, their color, their mysticism and the stories that they tell.

CHAPTER TEN.
HINDUISM AND BUDDHISM

Hinduism is a religion, a culture, and a way of life. Its temples are covered with a profusion of carvings, and its mythology furnishes the storyline for this breathtaking artistry. I must admit that I came to Hinduism as an artist, initially as an admirer of Indian textiles, then as an ardent fan of Hindu art, especially its temple art, so in our travels, this is where we will go first.

In South India, in the state of Karnataka, near the cities of Bangalore and Mysore, are two temples covered with what I consider to be the apogee of Hindu art in India, a country that has some of the finest art in the world. In Halebid and Belur, located 16 km apart, are twelfth century confections that are not only constructed in complex shapes, but they also are ornamented all around with a series of friezes that illustrate Hindu legends. And of all the thousands of figures depicted, there seems to be no repetition. The friezes vary from an elegantly simple style near eye level to higher friezes that are baroque, almost lacey, their rhythms mesmerizing. One could dance to the music of their musicians. The temple at Halebid is dedicated to Shiva. The temple at Belur is dedicated to Vishnu, and it took 103 years to complete. One would think even longer. Anyhow, it is difficult to imagine mere humans carving anything so intricate out of stone. What inspired them? Where did they learn the technique?

HINDUISM

So far, we only have considered Hinduism[1] in connection with Zoroastrianism, but Hinduism today is the signature religion of a country with over 1.3 billion people. Zoroastrianism in Iran has had to fight for its life.

Hinduism today is the third largest religion in the world, and it is one of the oldest.[2] Its origins date back to the Iron Age (1200–1000 BCE), maybe the Bronze Age (3000–1200 BCE). Perhaps it started with the great poetry and teachings of the Vedas (500–1500 BCE). Do we not know? It all depends on how you define Hinduism, but we do know that Hinduism as a religion developed out of the Vedic literature of the Indian subcontinent. That literature finally was written down sometime between 200 BCE and 200 CE.

While Hinduism has a rich tapestry of gods and beliefs, it is nearly impossible to define. Then again, it may be one of the easiest. Ram once told me with a proud smile that he was about to take a case to court in which he would prove that Hinduism is not a religion. His argument was that Hinduism does not require its followers to believe in any god, follow any religious laws, undertake any religious conversion or even to practice it exclusively.

Two cases were involved, and the Indian Supreme Court ended up agreeing that Hinduism consists of the beliefs, traditions, culture, religious institutions and practices of those people who live in the Indian subcontinent.[3] The Court said that "the Hindu religion does not claim any one Prophet, it does not

---

[1] The reader may consult any of many references to learn more about this subject. Due to their number and diversity, I will just refer interested readers to two classics: Durant, Will, *Our Oriental Heritage*, (New York: Simon and Schuster, 1954), which is the first volume of a series, and Muller, F. Max, *The Sacred Books of the East, Parts I and II*, (Delhi, Patna, Varanasi: Motilal Banarsidass, reprinted 1973). This is one of many books in this series, many of which I have consulted.

[2] Holdrege, Barbara A., *Veda and Torah – Transcending the Textuality of Scripture* (Albany: State University of New York Press, 1996).

[3] One case was *Ramesh Yeshwant Prabhoo* and the other was *Bal Thackeray v. Shri Prabaker Kunte*, December 1995, Indian Supreme Court.

worship any one God, it does not believe in any one philosophic concept, it does not follow any one act of religious rites or performances; in fact, it does not satisfy the traditional features of a religion or creed. It is a way of life and nothing more."

In its broad tolerant way, Hinduism encompasses hundreds of regional traditions and gods, a vast amount of elaborate imagery and at least hundreds of different ceremonies. The temples covered with the antics of amorous gods in Khajuraho differ completely from the brightly painted – and more modest – *gopuram* towers of temples down in Tamil Nadu. The relative importance of the principal gods has changed over time. The gods who are the most popular today – Shiva and Vishnu – hardly appeared in the ancient Mahabharata. In fact, subsumed into the Vaishnava category of today – those who worship Vishnu – are multiple originally separate sects that once were devoted, respectively, to the gods Naharayan, Ram, Krishna and Vishnu.

Alan Brill[4] describes Hinduism as consisting of "thousands of different religious groups that have evolved in India since 1500 BCE." He also emphasizes that "Hinduism differs from Judaism and other Western religions in that it does not have: a single founder, a specific theological system, a single concept of deity, a single holy text, or a single central religious authority." Moreover, "Hinduism has been variously defined as a religion, a religious tradition, a set of religious beliefs, and as a way of life."

A good Hindu is not required to believe in any one thing or to pray to any one god. This is one of the reasons why a Jew can feel perfectly comfortable while practicing a simplified form of Hinduism. If he wishes, he may announce that he is a Hindu without feeling that he must relinquish his Judaism. Now he is a Hindu. But he still can be Jewish. No drama. From the standpoint of Hinduism, there is no conflict with his Judaism. Strict interpreters of Judaism might differ.

Christianity, Judaism and Islam are described as outer-directed, oriented toward a God that confronts man from the outside. Hinduism is inner-directed, mystic, and most sects of it

---

[4] Brill, Alan, *Rabbi on the Ganges: A Jewish-Hindu Encounter*, (Lanham: Lexington Books, 2020), p. 3.

teach that the divine can be found within the self. Rituals are not necessary. Enlightenment is the goal. Meditation is the way. Hindu friends tell me that meditation is the essence of Hinduism, that Hinduism does not prescribe a specific path, but it urges the individual to find his or her relationship with the universe. Neither Hinduism nor Buddhism need to be practiced as a religion at all.

The word Hindu comes from the name of a river. The classic Hindu literature describes seven ancient rivers of northwest India. One legendary river, the Sarasvati, no longer exists; only a few suggestions of it can be traced along its course. Another one is the Indus River, called Sindhu in Sanskrit. When the armies of Darius conquered the province of Sindh, the Persians called this river Hindu. In Greek it became *Indos*, and from *Indika*, a book written by the Greek Megasthenes, comes the word India.

It was along this river, in the Indus Valley[5], that a remarkably advanced culture appeared. This was the Harappan Civilization also known as the Indus Civilization. It may have begun at least 4,500 years ago, and it may have been even 1000 years older than that. Unique for that era, its cities were kept clean and well drained by below-ground sewage systems. They had well-designed water carriers, canals, and they had knowledge of metallurgy. Remarkably, archeologic evidence shows that Indus Valley traders engaged in commerce with Turkmenistan, Iran, Mesopotamia, ports as far away as the Persian Gulf, possibly even Egypt.

In the UNESCO World Heritage Site at Mohenjo-daro in Pakistan there are remarkable ruins of this civilization that grew, flourished, and then suddenly, inexplicably, died in 1500 BCE. It could have succumbed to droughts, maybe floods or hostile invaders. As with the vanished Sarasvati River, we really do not know what happened. We do know that the Harappan culture established the oldest known links between east and west in the history of the known world.

---

[5] Robinson, Andrew, *The Indus: Lost Civilizations*, (London: Reaktion Books, 2015).

The Sanskrit word Veda means knowledge, also wisdom. The Vedas first appeared in written form in about 1500 BCE, but the original oral tradition may predate Hinduism itself. At first it was divided into four Vedas. The oldest and best-known is the Rigveda.

The Rigveda, and originally the other Vedas, each consist of three to five parts. The Rigveda has one part (*Samhitas*) that contains mantras, verses and benedictions. A second (*Brahmanas*) has descriptions of rituals, ceremonies and sacrifices. Much like the Talmud, there also is a section (*Aranyakas*) with commentaries on the rituals, ceremonies and sacrifices. Esoteric knowledge is in the fourth, called the *Upanishads*, which set out philosophy, spirituality, and general principles that are believed to control the world.

School children in traditional Hindu schools sit in groups and practice chanting verses from these writings, and, when they get older, they learn to recite them by memory. This resembles some practices of young boys in an Orthodox Jewish yeshiva, where students study with partners and learn passages of Talmud by heart.

After the original Vedas were committed to writing, huge compendia of Hindu literature and legend were assembled. In time these became incorporated into the larger canon of the Vedas. One is the *Mahabharata,* an epic tale of war between the Pandava and the Kauraya dynasties. Assembled between 400 BCE and 40 CE, Hindus say it is the longest poem in the world. It contains poems, stories, Hindu mythology, and the entire *Bhagvad-Gita.*

The Bhagavad-Gita is a well-loved work that has a new message for the reader every time and is the best known of all the Vedas in the western world. Most of its wisdom is spoken to the warrior Arjuna by his charioteer, the god Krishna, an incarnation of Vishnu. Krishna teaches "the supremacy of the soul over the body, and in fact its eternity of existence in the supreme Being, so that death cannot harm it."[6] When Arjuna hesitates before

---

[6] Bettany, George T., *The Great Indian Religions* (New York: Cosimo Classics, 2006), first published by Ward, Lock Bowden and Co. in 1892, p. 59.

joining a battle in which he would have to kill his own kinsmen, Krishna enjoins him in poetic terms to do his duty, engage in self-renunciation, devote himself to his god, and fight. Thus, Krishna teaches that we must recognize our destiny, and we must fulfill it. Arjuna is compelled by his karma to act.

Another lesson is that "action is better than inaction," and "renunciation of all action is impossible." Krishna teaches Arjuna to "Always act with detachment to the fruits of actions. The one who is acting without attachment attains God."[7] Thus, "Do not become confused in attachment to the fruit of your actions and do not become confused in the desire for inaction."

Scholars believe that the Pandavas in the *Gita* originally were Iranian horsemen[8] who traveled through Sindh and the Rajasthan Desert to India, arriving around 800 BCE. The war between the Pandavas and Kauravas takes place in the upper valley of the Ganges, but the Pandavas eventually reach as far as Sri Lanka, which is where we find them in the *Ramayana,* an ancient work that may predate the Mahabharata, possibly going back as far as 1500–2000 BCE,[9] though some date it even before the Harappan Civilization. One reason for coming to this conclusion is that there is nothing of horses or chariots yet in this epic, while in the Bhagavad Gita, the god Krishna is the charioteer who teaches the warrior Arjuna.

The *Ramayana* is a thrilling tale of gods, abduction and miracles that starts out in the middle Ganges valley. Commentators have suggested that it is a legendary version of the first Aryan invasions of southern India. In it, the principal god Rama, an incarnation of Vishnu, fights to bring back his beloved wife Sita after she is abducted and magically flown by the demon king Ravana to a prison in Sri Lanka. Rama fights heroically to save his wife, aided by extraordinary weapons wielded by friendly gods and attacked by demonic weapons deployed by fantastical enemies. I will not tell you what happens when he

---

[7] Brill, p. 116.

[8] Parpola, Asko, *The Roots of Hinduism – The Early Aryans and the Indus Civilization* (Oxford: Oxford University Press, 2015), pp. 148ff.

[9] Venugopal, Vasuda, 'Mahabharata much older, say ASI Archeologists,' *The Economic Times,* Oct. 20, 2019.

finally rescues Sita. You must read it for yourself. Spoiler alert. I found it to be shocking and disturbing.

Other classic works of literature that joined the canon are the *Puranas,* a rambling collection of legends, royal genealogies, theology, philosophy, rituals, pilgrimages and cosmology, illustrated with symbols and folk tales. The mixture of legend and lesson is reminiscent of the Jewish Talmud. The Puranas have long been subject to learned examination and commentary; still today they are popular subjects of plays, television, movies, advertisements and children's books. We will come back to some of the symbolism.

In the Upanishads and in other post-Vedic literature, the supreme entity who created the world is *Brahman,* also known as *Sabdabrahman.* A careful reader will see that both names are related to the name of the first Jewish patriarch, Abraham. Pronounced Avraham in Hebrew, the name comes from the Hebrew word for father, *av,* plus the word for the womb, *raham.*

In the Vedas, *Yama* is the name of the first man. This name may also mean the first of the dead or the king of the dead. In the Iranian Avesta, the kingdom of the dead is ruled by *Yima,* who is called the first king. The legend of Yima comes from the Babylonian story of the flood, in which Yima, advised by Ahura, 'builds a Vara to keep there the seeds (two of every kind) of every kind of animals and plants" large enough 'to be an abode for men' and a 'fold for flocks.' Bigger than Noah's ark, this will accommodate streets, trees and houses. In it, nothing would be deformed; there would be no poverty and no meanness. It would be a sealed paradise. In this vision, Noah is completely outdone.

The flood story in the Puranas is unique, but it bears some resemblance to other ancient flood stories. In this tale, Brahma chose Manu to save the world at the time of the flood, because Manu had accumulated so much merit by meditating for thousands of years. One day Manu was bathing in a pond and he saw a little fish. He caught it, but it grew miraculously until it filled an entire ocean in just a few days. Vishnu then appeared. He commanded Manu to build an ark, fill it with pairs of all the animals and with seeds, take on board Seven Sages, tie the ark to the horn of the fish, and allow the fish to drag the ark to the top of a mountain range, which is where it was lodged when the waters subsided. Manu was then told to repopulate the earth. How does it happen that all these flood stories are similar?

Hinduism, like Judaism, places a great premium on ritual, on correct intention in performing the ritual, and attention to detail in its execution, avoiding any mistakes. The ethical Code of Manu places a high value on steadfastness, forgiveness, not being acquisitive, cleanliness, control of sensuous appetites, wisdom, learning, truthfulness, and restraint of anger. In the Bhagavad Gita, Lord Krishna says that "lust, anger and greed ruin men."[10] We also read, "Speak the truth. Be righteous. Do not neglect scriptural study. After having made a valuable gift to the teacher, do not sever family ties...Treat your mother like a god. Treat your father like a god. Treat your teacher like a god. Treat your guest like a god."

That passage could well have been written by the great Jewish scholar Maimonides, who said, "Just as a person is commanded to honor his father and hold him in awe, so, too, is he obligated to honor his teacher and hold him in awe. Indeed [the measure of honor and awe] due one's teacher exceeds that due one's father. His father brings him into the life of this world, while his teacher, who teaches him wisdom, brings him into the life of the world to come."

Hinduism has its own version of the Golden Rule: "This is the sum of duty: do not do to others what would cause pain if done to you." Hindus also prioritize charity, just as Jews do. Another highly valued virtue is hospitality, and we certainly can attest to that, having been invited to the home of many Indians on the strength of a brief introduction.

While many Indians are vegetarian, most at least refuse to eat beef. We once were at the Taj Coromandel Hotel in Madras on New Year's Eve, and the line leading to the buffet had unaccountable stops and starts. When we arrived at the point of obstruction, we saw a tempting roast beef, and before it was a whole line of Indians, stopping, hesitating, and thinking, "Can I, or shouldn't I?"

---

[10] Brill, pp. 213–5.

At meals, devout Hindus recite a blessing over their food, as do devout Jews. Laws of ritual impurity too resemble those of Jews. And in modern times, many of the rituals have softened, women have acquired new rights, and laws have been modulated, as in Judaism.

With such a long history and such an enormous geographic reach, Hinduism has developed many schools of thought, led by many revered spiritual masters. The major gurus of Hinduism, ancient and modern, are of real importance, but a proper discussion of them would require a separate book. The subject is complex, because gurus who come from different eras and lived in various locations have introduced religious innovations, heterodoxies, and, often, reinterpretations of age-old rituals, all of which would need to be explained.

To give the reader an idea of the differences among gurus, we might mention just a few examples at both ends of the spectrum of holiness. At the one end are two rather dubious gurus who were regarded as embodiments of the divine, Satya Sai Baba and Rajneesh (Osho). It would be fair to say that neither of them should be regarded as role models.

A guru may be a personal teacher and a spiritual preceptor to his disciples, or he may be the leader of a movement. Again, that may be problematic. The followers of a guru are enjoined to meditate on him, and some will pray to their guru. One of my friends told me that all his meditations were on his guru, but the guru turned out to be a grievous disappointment.

The most beloved gurus are charismatic and inspiring, and some have had enormous followings in India and abroad. One of the most influential, known from east to west, was Swami Vivekananda, born in Calcutta in 1863 to a devout Bengali family in which the father became a sannyasi. Vivekananda studied western philosophy, Sanskrit writings, and Bengali. He is known for introducing Vedanta and yoga to the western world in a spectacular speech at the Parliament of the World's Religions, on September 11, 1893 at the Art Institute of Chicago. He began with, "Sisters and brothers of America!" and an audience of seven thousand rose to a standing ovation for over two minutes.

He taught in the U.S., UK, and Europe, then returned to India, where he founded the Ramakrishna Mission in honor of his guru. Greatly revered in India and abroad, the Indian freedom fighter Subhas Chandra Bose called him "the maker of modern India," and today National Youth Day in India is celebrated on his birthday. Vivekananda died while in solitary meditation. Pathologists found a ruptured brain vessel. His followers believed that his brain was pierced when he consciously left his body at the moment of death.

> *Another aspect of Hinduism is the much-misunderstood matter of yoga. Westerners think of it as an exercise technique devoid of religious connection. I once spoke at length with the head of an ashram in Mumbai near the city airport, asking her whether she taught yoga. She smiled indulgently and told me gently that she did, but what she taught had nothing to do with contorting the body into asanas, or any other physical positions. Hers was the traditional Indian yoga, meditative and worshipful. Even the breathing techniques she taught her students were easy, not taxing. When I asked her about my breathing exercises, she agreed that I could inhale for a count of 16, but she would never teach that I should exhale for a count of 64, as was my practice. Certainly, the exhalation should be no longer than a count of 32. Softly, softly. This was not a race or a competition.*

Hinduism is a combination of traditional Indian culture, the preexisting social organization of the Indian subcontinent, ancient rituals, traditional village practices, and sophisticated metaphysics. It is an old religion, but its religious thought has never stopped evolving. The Krishna sect took on characteristics of Christianity in the late 1800s, going as far as the worship of infant Krishna on his birthday. The thuggees were a cult of murders and thieves, despised by the British. And there were many more variations of belief and practice in India.

Apart from the smaller sects though, in addition to Hinduism, three serious religions have sprung from India: Sikhism, Buddhism, and the Jain religion.

We have met the Sikhs at the Golden Temple in Amritsar, and we have learned a bit about their religion. Yet we will come back to them in this chapter, to round out the picture. Buddhism, as we have said in earlier chapters, has captured the imagination and hearts of Jews and non-Jews all over the world, and we need to study it in some depth.

But Jains have a different story, and since they are an important part of the complex tapestry of India, the reader should have a proper introduction to them. We have described their temples. Now we can look at their unique beliefs.

JAINS

The Jain religion is at least as old as Buddhism, if not older. Both are reactions against the Vedas, and they developed in parallel. Both had initial success, but Buddhism ultimately died out in India, while Jainism lived on. The Oxford Languages Dictionary says of the Jain religion that it is "A non-theistic religion founded in India in the 6th century BC by the Jina Vardhamana Mahavira as a reaction against the teachings of orthodox Brahmanism. The Jain religion teaches salvation by perfection through successive lives, and noninjury to living creatures, and is noted for its ascetics."

Brill describes the Jain concept of *Anekantavada*. This is the idea "that truth and reality are perceived differently from diverse points of view, and that no single point of view is the complete truth."[11] The long word itself means "not one ended, sided," or "many sided," signifying that truth can be expressed in many different ways. There is no one way that is absolutely right, and no statement is categorically wrong. According to Jains, truth cannot be fully expressed through language; any attempt will be incomplete. The best example of this is the classic story of a blind man who attempts to describe an elephant, based on what he perceives when he tries to feel the shape of the legs, then the trunk and finally the body.

Jains do not believe in a Supreme Divine, and they teach that the soul is independent of matter. This is a departure from Hinduism, even though the Jain religion is often lumped together with Hinduism. This difference is one of the reasons why Jains

---

[11] Brill, p. 233.

tell us that they practice a separate religion, not a breakaway sect of Hinduism.

A pious Jain is instantly recognizable because he wears a mask or a cotton wrap around his lower face, to keep from inadvertently inhaling and killing a bug. The strictest members of the sect will strain water before drinking, and they carry a brush to sweep away insects before sitting. Of course, during the Coronavirus epidemic, their mask was no longer distinctive, but that was an aberration. Religious Jains always have worn a face covering, certainly when praying. This all comes from the central Jain precept of *ahimsa*, or nonviolence, harmlessness. Of course, this is a Hindu concept too.

Jains are committed to justice, peace, freedom, nonviolence and simple living. Their most cherished guiding principle is not to kill any living thing. They do not eat onions or garlic for fear that digging them up may harm a worm or an insect. Their religion has many concepts in common with Hinduism, and they pray to some of the Hindu gods, yet Jains are more ascetic. For instance, they are enjoined to practice abstinence from sensual pleasures. They resemble Buddhists in many ways. They too are committed to non-attachment; they reject the authority of the Vedas, and they take vows.[12] They believe in transmigration of souls, an ultimate Nirvana, but not in a supreme deity. These similarities and others have led to speculation that the Buddhist religion and the Jain religion originated at roughly the same time.

Jains are obligated to take five vows. Among these are non-violence, truthfulness, sexual continence, non-possessiveness and obedience to a prohibition against theft. One can see why Orthodox Jews would feel comfortable with Jains as reliable business partners in the diamond industry.

Jain pilgrimage sites are among the most beautiful in India, some of them on forested mountains, typically built of pure white marble, all distinguished by the extreme cleanliness that Jains are sworn to maintain.

---

[12] Bettany, George T., *The Great Indian Religions* (New York: Cosimo Classics, 2006), first published by Ward, Lock Bowden and Co. in 1892, pp. 239ff.

The Jain community numbers four and a half million in India today, and successful businessmen from the Jain community are found in every part of the country. In addition, many emigres have established communities in Canada, the U.S. and Europe.

SIKHS

An imposing turbaned Indian must be the quintessential image of exotic India, and he probably is a Sikh. A traditional Sikh does not cut his beard or his hair. He simply tucks them both neatly into his turban. In addition, he wears an iron or steel bracelet and a special cotton undergarment. He carries a dagger in his belt, and he wears a wooden comb on his person. Remember that a religious Jew is obligated to wear a fringed cotton undergarment, and a pious Zoroastrian also must wear a special cotton undergarment. Why do they all wear the small cotton garment under their clothes? I cannot find an answer. Perhaps it harks back to a tradition that predates all of these religions, one more atavistic communal practice that connects them all together.

Today, as with so many ethnic communities, we can see a wide range of compliance with clothing requirements. We still see bearded grandfathers wearing *shalwar kameez* (baggy pants and a long shirt) and grand turbans, and we see clean-shaven grandsons in jeans sharing offices with American colleagues, writing software.

As one might suspect from their height and impressive turbans, Sikhs have a strong martial tradition, but their lifestyle at home is extremely peaceful. They get up in the morning, bathe and meditate. Many read a portion of their holy book each day. The traditional Sikh occupation in the Punjab is agriculture. And they do not seek converts.

The religion was established by Guru Nanak at the turn of the sixteenth century, by birth a Sindhi. The 500th anniversary of his birth was celebrated in 1969.[13] It turns out that the similarities with Judaism are no accident. Sikhism was developed in reaction

---

[13] Nagen, Yakov, *Be, Become, Bless: Jewish Spirituality between East and West*, (Jerusalem: Maggid Books, 2019), p. 161.

to the more elaborate Hinduism of the time, and it was influenced by a shift toward monotheism, as exemplified by Buddhism, Jainism, Christianity, and the Islamic regime of Aurangzeb. But it still arose under the influence of an environment that was becoming heavily Muslim. The result is a blend of Hinduism and Islam, and it was through Islam that it acquired the distaste for idols or idolatry and the concept of one God that the Sikhs share with the Jews.

Whether or not it is relevant, I do not know, but many Sindhis have emphasized to me that Sindhis are 'the Jews of India.' This could be because they are traders, thus very international in their outlook and connections, it is not clear. Certainly, after partition they became the only Indian community without a home state, as Sindh was subsumed into Pakistan, but that is long after the Sikh religion began. What I do know is that my Sindhi friends tell me that their mothers read a portion of the Sikh Granth every morning, and that they are perfectly comfortable either at a Sikh temple or at a Hindu temple. Then again, I am told that it is a Punjabi custom for the oldest son of a Punjabi family to become a Sikh. Perhaps that simply reflects the extent to which the Sikh religion is part of the Hindu environment.

Guru Nanak strongly discouraged his followers from worshiping him in any way or attributing divinity to him. Sikhs adopted the Kabbalistic idea of "Creation as an expression of God's will," emphasizing that the Creator was God, none else. They also accepted the idea of equality among all people, as contrasted with the Hindu caste system. Like Jews, Sikhs marry, work and support their families throughout life, rejecting the Hindu ideal of the householder who becomes a sanyasi and withdraws from society. The writer Nagen calls the Sikh religion the grandchild of Judaism, via Islam.

Sikhs do not have images of gods in their houses, and they are strict monotheists. Despite their striking appearance, in this restriction and in their love of their sacred book they are closer to the Jewish tradition than any other community in India. The service we attended in Amritsar made us feel completely comfortable, and on our tour of the temple we enjoyed seeing how reverently they wrapped their sacred book, the *Granth*, put it carefully in its cushioned place, and treated it just as we treat our Torah.

Today Sikhs number almost 21 million in India alone, the majority of them in the Punjab, their home state in northwest India. World-wide they number at least 25 million, many of them now living in Canada, the U.S., and the UK. And in any of these countries, as in India, if you step into a taxi and your driver is Indian, he probably is a Sikh.

BUDDHISM

The founder of Buddhism, prince Siddhartha Gautama, was born in Nepal near the Indian border between 563 and 490 BCE. To compare the ages of these traditions, Zoroaster (Zarathustra) was born around 1500 BCE, and the Vedas, the foundational teachings of Hinduism, are dated 1500 – 1000 BCE. This means that the reform movement we call Buddhism arose a thousand years after the earliest Veda, the Rigveda. Buddhism spread widely in India and even into southern China, but by the seventh century CE, Buddhism already was on the decline in India. By now it is hardly alive in India as a popularly practiced religion, though its philosophy remains very much alive. World-wide, it is the fourth-largest religion, with over half-billion devotees. Of them, 245 million are in China, and only 1.8 percent live in India.[14]

Buddhism began with one of the best recorded searches for enlightenment in history. Starting as a youth, Siddhartha studied the Vedas, and this led him to leave his comfortable home in search of further answers. He traveled widely, meeting many people along the way, and he encountered human suffering for the first time in his life. This shocked him. He studied with two renowned spiritual teachers, lived in the forest for many years and adopted increasingly ascetic practices. According to the legend, even though he exercised extreme self-discipline, he was not able to reach enlightenment before he came to Bodh Gaya, in Bihar. There, he sat down under a Bodhi tree, known as a tree of

---

[14] Taseer, Aatish, Chapter 3 in 'The Route that Made the World,' *The New York Times*, May 17, 2020.

knowledge, and he committed himself to motionless, uninterrupted meditation. And this was where he attained enlightenment. In Buddhism, this means an awakening, a liberation from all negative desires, hatred and ignorance.

At this point, he renounced the temptation of obtaining his own immediate deliverance, but instead he began preaching to a small group of ascetics. From that beginning, Gautama Buddha and his followers fanned out to spread his teachings. His followers came to be called Buddhists.[15]

The location of his first discourse now is a serene Deer Park – Sarnath, not far from Benares (Varanasi). Situated on the Ganges River, Varanasi already was one of the holiest cities of Hinduism, and that may be the reason why the Buddha went there to preach. A tour guide in Israel once told us that a site that once was holy to one religion remains holy, even when other religions replace it and build their own monuments.

When we visited the Deer Park, the scene was green and peaceful. A massive Buddhist stupa anchored the area, and small groups of people were scattered around the lawn, spinning their prayer wheels. Here and there were groups of holy men, some of them sitting on the grass, holding forth in front of rapt listeners. An Ashoka pillar once stood proudly nearby, but invading Muslims broke it. The preserved capital of this pillar is now in a museum, and an image of it is the emblem on the Indian flag. Though it is hard to imagine, at one time this site had hundreds of monuments, monasteries, and at least 3,000 monks.

In many ways, Buddhist teachings strongly resemble Hindu teachings, but the more one learns, the more one sees differences. Take temple art as an example. Hindu gods often are depicted dancing. The epitome of that style is the ubiquitous *Nataraja*, a dynamic sculpture of the god Shiva dancing the divine dance of life, one leg arising from a lotus, the other elegantly extended, the entire figure surrounded by a ring of fire. In a Hindu temple, typical images show the gods interacting, one with another, with

---

[15] Bettany, George T., *The Great Indian Religions* (New York: Cosimo Classics, 2006), first published by Ward, Lock Bowden and Co. in 1892, pp. 121–6, 159.

demons, with the observer, escorted by dancing entourages of attendants playing instruments, accompanied by elephants and other animals. We see parades, parties, love affairs, conflicts, and adventure tales.

In contrast, the Buddha normally is depicted sitting in serene meditation. When you enter a Buddhist temple in Bhutan, you see embroidered hangings and banners, prayer wheels, paintings in gold and brilliant colors, Buddhas with enigmatic smiles. On the tables and ledges, you may see precisely detailed sculptures of gods and nature, crafted out of multicolored yak butter. The stone or gilded wooden statues of Buddha that dominate the largest temples are vast, imposing, and impervious to your gaze.

The Buddhist temples of Thailand are encrusted with gold. Walking among them is like trekking through a field of gilded Christmas trees. The largest Buddhist temple in the world is the Javanese style Borobudur Temple at Yogyakarta, Indonesia, a veritable grey mountain of nine stacked platforms connected by stairways all the way around. Every wall of each platform is decorated by carved panels, with a total of 504 Buddha statues in all. We both had the flu when we climbed it, so our enthusiasm was somewhat muted, but this colossus surely was designed to evoke the awe of the Himalayas.

Japanese Buddhist temples reflect their own special culture. Guarding the gates to the temples are ferocious temple guardian figures, swollen with rage, veins of the neck distended, breathing fire, one arm raised to attack the enemy, terrifying. And temples seem to vie with one another to see which one can create the world's largest Buddha. Each of these is so humongous that the visitor only sees the feet at eye level. High up above, the eyes stare impassively out into the distance.

In contrast, the Buddhas in Bhutan never burn with excitement or rage. Of course, there were no samurai in Bhutan either. The Buddhas in Bhutan are more inclined to a Mona Lisa smile.

It is no wonder that Indians, though they admired Buddhism and gave support to Buddhist monks, found its teachings too lofty, and that they ultimately fell back to the earthy comforts of

Hinduism, leaving the austerities of Buddhism to the most committed.

Gautama Buddha taught "Right faith, right resolve, right speech, right action, right living, right effort, right thought [and] right self – concentration" as the way to avoid the endless cycle of death and rebirth, the way to attain a pure state free of suffering. This ultimate state of quietude and happiness is *Nirvana*. The concept exists in Hinduism, but it was the genius of Gautama Buddha that he taught how to achieve it.

Buddhism has a trinity, the three manifestations of Buddha. These are: the body of essence, the body of enjoyment, and the body of transformation. Hinduism has a trinity too – Brahma, the creator; Vishnu, the preserver; and Shiva, the destroyer. That trinity is what a visitor sees so beautifully carved in stone on an island near Mumbai. This monumental sculpture takes up an entire wall of the Elephanta Caves, and its execution is so pure that all sculpture in that style takes its name from this island. The best carvings at Ellora Caves are said to be in Elephanta-style. Whether this Hindu trinity or the Buddhist trinity are related to the Christian trinity is beyond the purview of this discussion, but one certainly would have a right to ask.

There are Four Noble Truths of Buddhism. The first is that everyone suffers. The second is that desire is the cause of suffering. The third truth is that suffering is stopped by stopping desire. The fourth is an Eightfold Path to overcoming desire.[16] It is just such a path, and a map for following it, that has such a powerful attraction for the western Jew. The idea of one world with one God is familiar. What most of us do not know is how to get to that understanding.

Buddhism has five prohibitions: do not kill, do not steal, live chastely, do not lie, do not drink intoxicants. Buddhist ascetics in monastic communities are required to renounce dancing, singing, music and theatrical shows. One collection of Buddhist scriptures, the Dhammapada, has a familiar teaching: "Do not speak harshly to anybody; those who are spoken to will answer thee in the same way." We in the west know this injunction as the Golden Rule.

---

[16] Lopez, Donald S., 'Eightfold Path Buddhism', *Britannica*, Eightfold Path

While the seeker of guided Buddhist practice does not need to go deeply into it, certain principles shape modern Buddhism. As Shoshanna describes them, the three pillars of Buddhism[17] are: Buddha, dharma and *sangha*. Of these, in Zen Buddhism, "Sangha is the Zen community, those who sit, work, and sometimes live together, unifying their energies, giving and receiving guidance, encouragement and support."

The primary way in which the community supports each other is through *zazen*, which means meditating, generally in the same space, guided by the same Zen master. A Zen center is called a *Zendo*.

Shoshanna, a Jewish follower of many Buddhist practices, explains that *zazen* starts with placing a cushion (a square *zabutan*, with a round *zafu* on top) on the floor, sitting with a straight back in meditation position, silently meditating side by side with the others in the room, using breathing exercises or other meditative aids, as desired. One other meditative technique she mentions is Naikan practice: write everything you have received today, write everything you gave today, write whatever trouble or pain you caused today. In all of these, be specific.

Those who write about these techniques emphasize that meditation should be a daily practice. From time to time, the meditator may participate in a *sesshin*. Buddhist sesshins are "periods of intensive practice when you are given the opportunity to devote yourself entirely to practice. A sesshin can last from one to ten days or longer." Many Jews report that they did not appreciate Judaism until they experienced these Zen practices.

A study of Buddhist teachings reveals many gems. Shoshanna quotes a Zen master who offered this cure for suffering, "Do not separate what you like from what you dislike." This means, "Do not accept what you love or reject what you hate...By dividing the world into good and bad, you are creating schism, duality and discord..."

Over the centuries, Buddhist orders have arisen in many countries, but Buddhism has no central authority. There is no

---

[17] Shoshanna, Brenda, *A guide to the practice of Judaism and Zen: Jewish Dharma*, (Philadelphia: Perseus Books Group, 2008), pp. 234–5.

designated successor to the Buddha, no pope or patriarch, and originally, there were no priests. Anyone may join. Anyone can leave. For those who are not monks, there are no required rituals, no prescribed prayers, no initiation ceremony, no need for formal renunciation in case one wishes to leave the community. There only are suggested meditations for those who are interested. Buddhists allow both painted and graven images of Buddha, yet reverence to these images or adherence to their rituals is not required of anyone who wants to go no further than simply meditating.

There are no specific dietary laws, though the prohibition against killing causes most Buddhists to become vegetarians. A monk obtains food by soliciting it as a gift in his little bowl, which surely cannot lead to overeating.

Buddhists have a distinctive tradition that sounds familiar. Highly respected teachers pass their knowledge down to successive generations of students, creating direct philosophical lineages. Some of these teachers, like the Dalai Lama, are believed to have reappeared from a past life in a new reincarnation, and they are revered almost to the point of deification. We should mention that certain communities of religious Jews have prestigious rabbinic genealogies, or lineages. Why are both communities similar?

We have discussed some of the connections between east and west. The Persian conquest of the Indus Valley under Darius I took place at much the same time as the life of Gautama Buddha, and his troops would have brought Zoroastrianism. This may have influenced Buddhism, and the Jain religion, since both began at about the same time.

The Mauryan Empire of India began in 323 BCE. It built Buddhist stupas across northern India, commissioned Buddhist inscriptions, and dispatched Buddhist missions as far as Greece.[18] By the close of the Maurya dynasty, the Parthian Empire had conquered eastern Iran and northwestern India, and it too would leave a Persian imprint on India, especially on Buddhist art.

---

[18] Foltz, Richard, *Religions of Iran – from prehistory to the present* (London: Oneworld Publications, 2013).

Buddhism experienced its greatest growth from the third century BCE to the fourth century CE, becoming the most popular religion in India, but in the fifth century CE when it suffered setbacks in India, it began moving toward China.

Buddhism spread to Afghanistan, Bactria, Tajikistan, Tibet and along the Silk Road to China. Many of the traders who carried it were Persian tribesmen, Parthians, Iranians and Sogdians. The Sogdians were 'traders by nature' according to the Tang Dynasty, and they traveled these routes, buying and selling their wares, disseminating Buddhism, Manichaeism, even Christianity. And along this route, in 75 CE Persian Jews also implanted a Jewish community in Kaifeng, the capitol of the Song Dynasty, in central China. In 1161 CE, a fine synagogue even was built in Kaifeng.

Many of these rich traveling merchants used to make donations to Buddhist monasteries and shrines, and, until the Arab conquests, Buddhism was the major religion along this route. Buddhist Caves, such as the Dunhuang Caves or the Mogao Caves, collected manuscripts of many religions, in many different scripts, among which were Jewish scroll portions dating from the fourth to the eleventh centuries.

Iranian Buddhist flags still fly over Sufi shrines in Central Asia. Two monumental statues of Buddha looked out calmly from a shear mountainside for centuries at Bamiyan, Afghanistan until the Taliban destroyed them in 2001.

Both Iranians and Buddhists left their mark in Central Asia, sometimes together. An image of the Buddha in Qara-teppe, Uzbekistan is inscribed with the name 'Buddha Mazda,' a mashup of Buddhist and Iranian figures. Mithra and even Zurvan appear in a Sogdian tale of the Buddha. The Tibetan Book of the Dead uses Iranian light symbolism, describing the soul as moving toward the light if a person is good, toward ghastly demons if he is evil.

Mahayana Buddhism was a product of Indian, Persian, Greek and Chinese influences, and it flourished among the Kushans of northern India and central Asia in the days of the Emperor Ashoka of India, in the beginning of the Silk Road. In this branch of Buddhism, *Maitreya* is a savior who will come at the end of time. Here we see the Persian Saoshyant, their Messiah figure, but in India. Statues of the *Maitreya* can be seen from Pakistan to Iranian villages close to Tehran, carved in the style of Gandhara, a Kushan area stretching across the Afghanistan and Pakistan of today. This Greco-Buddhist art form fused the artistry of the Hindus and the Greeks, often with Persian imagery. One type of bodhisattva found in that style resembles the Persian *Zurvan*, and another resembles the Persian god *Mithra*.

Today there are many Buddhist practitioners in Asia, especially in Tibet, Bhutan, Sri Lanka, Myanmar, Thailand, and Japan. Various forms of Buddhism have also seized the imagination of the western world. Practices vary from country to country, and so does the imagery. Unfortunately, the Chinese have destroyed much of the unique statuary and many of the monasteries of Tibet, but we were able to see Tibetan style monasteries both in Bhutan and in Dharamshala, India. In Dharamshala, we toured a school, Norbulinka, that was established to teach traditional Tibetan arts of painting, textiles and carving to the younger generation, to keep these skills from being lost in their adopted country.

In Iran, Islam supplanted Buddhism. It was starting to disappear in the ninth century, and by the twelfth century it had vanished. In India too, Buddhism has almost disappeared, except for its works of art. But in India, the Hinduism of today is greatly influenced by Buddhism, to such an extent that observers have characterized it as a joint product of the two.[19]

Now that we have surveyed Zoroastrianism, Hinduism and Buddhism, we are ready to look seriously at Judaism. We have considered some of the many cultural practices that Judaism shares with these religions, but we have not yet considered the many mystical ideas that it shares with them, nor have we discovered the other almost uncanny similarities between them.

We are ready to learn about the beliefs they all have shared, where they shared them, and when. The starting point of course, is in the Hebrew Bible, followed by the Talmud, and the commentaries. After all, the Jews have been known throughout the Middle East and throughout the ages as the People of the Book.

---

[19] Bettany, p. 57.

CHAPTER ELEVEN.
JUDAISM

When did Judaism begin? That is a difficult question to answer. Did it start with the Patriarchs Abraham, Isaac and Jacob? Did it start when Moses led the Children of Israel out of Egypt? Or was the seminal event the giving of the Ten Commandments on Mount Sinai? Perhaps it was when the twelve tribes staked out their land in Canaan. Do we know these dates?

To understand world history, we try to fill gaps in our knowledge with archeology. In some cases, linguists can deduce how one language came from another and how a given language evolved. Scientists have tried to date biblical stories, such as the ten plagues in Egypt and the Exodus, by relating them to known astronomical occurrences. Biblical scholars have calculated the time spans from event to event, using sequences that are spelled out in the bible. And the results of all these calculations have been wildly disparate.

Guessing the dates of the Patriarchal Age is the most challenging of all, even though the staid Encyclopedia Britannica[1] confidently puts Abraham in the early second millennium BCE, based on evidence from archeologic digs in the ancient Sumerian city of Ur, his biblical birthplace. The problem is that highly authoritative works written by religious Jews, secular Jews, and non-Jews all calculate the putative dates in different ways.

---

[1] 'Abraham,' Britannica, Abraham | Facts & Significance | Britannica

In his book,[2] Abba Eban, a scholar and diplomat, writes that the Exodus probably was not one event. It more likely took place in the form of waves of migration during the reign of Ramesses II (1290–1225 BCE). According to a recently published publication, "the Main Exodus occurred during a new moon following the Autumn Equinox. It is after this Autumn Event in which a pharaoh can be proven to have died and whose only son and heir to the throne died just before him."[3] According to this writer, the Exodus would have been in 1206 BCE.

Prominent experts on the Zoroastrian religion write that some of the most important Jewish beliefs come from Zoroastrianism. We also know that the origins of that religion are close to the origins of Hinduism. We might want to ask how these dates compare. We know that the oldest Vedas in India may date back to 1500 to 1200 BCE, and the Avesta, the oldest literature of Zoroastrianism, may date to between 1500 and 1000 BCE. That does put them both potentially within a few hundred years of each other and of the time when the Jewish law was handed down. But that depends on when and where the Jewish law was handed down. Was it at Mount Sinai? Or later? Maybe much later.

Grayzel divides Jewish history into seven periods.[4] The *Patriarchal Age* defies any attempt to date it scientifically. The *First Commonwealth* was between 1200 and 586 BCE, the time of judges, prophets and kings. The *Second Commonwealth* was from 586 BCE to 70 CE, the period between the Babylonian Exile and the destruction of the Second Temple. The fourth period was that of the *Jews of the East*, when the Jews lived in Babylon, wrote the Talmud, and came under the rule of Islam. In the *Middle Ages in Europe*, the Jews experienced the Crusades, the Renaissance, and the first ghettos. Last came the eras of the *Jews of Eastern Europe* and the *Modern Age*.

---

[2] Eban, Abba, *My People: The story of the Jews*, (New York: Random House and Behrman House, 1968), p. 15.
[3] Jacquet-Acea, Russelll, 'Re-calculating the Historical Age of the Israelites in Egypt and the Date of the Exodus Part Two.
[4] Grayzel, Solomon, *A History of the Jews*, (Markham Ontario: New American Library, 1968), p. 25.

The most sacred writings of the Jews are in the Torah. This is the fundamental work that tells the Jewish story of creation, that recounts stories of the founding patriarchs and matriarchs, and that explains the Jewish holidays. It outlines Jewish law and ethics, gives instructions for building the ark of the covenant, – which held the Ten Commandments – and it describes the required rituals that the priests of the temple were to observe. It has been studied, analyzed, interpreted and commented upon for thousands of years.

Of all possible descriptions of the Jews, probably the best is that they are the People of the Book. This book is the Torah, and in it, God makes a compact with the Jews that requires them to follow its laws. Therefore, in order to understand anything about Judaism, we must look at this fundamental book, and later at the Talmud, which is built upon the Torah.

There is both an oral Torah and a written Torah. Traditionalists believe that the oral Torah was handed down at Mount Sinai along with the written Torah. In this oral Torah are rules, interpretations and explanations of the fundamental laws. These were passed from sage to sage for over a thousand years before they ever were written down. Ultimately, most of this material was incorporated into the Talmud.

The written Torah is the first part of the Hebrew Bible. As usually understood, the Torah comprises the first five books of the bible, called the Five Books of Moses. The Hebrew Bible also has 8 books of prophets (Nevi'im), and 11 more writings (Ketuvim), which contain the lyrical literature of Psalms and the Song of Songs. This comes to 24, but some are divided further, which brings the total to 39. Together these are collected in what is called the Tanakh. Yet, just as the Vedas later came to include more than the original four Vedas, in Judaism the word Torah is often used in a broader sense to mean the entire Tanakh.

When were these books written? Strict traditionalists say that God not only gave Moses the Ten Commandments, but He also dictated the entire first five books of the bible to him, or He inspired Moses to write them while He was leading the Jews through the desert for forty years.[5] But some believe that some stories in the book of Genesis come from ancient Mesopotamian myths and legends.

While the first five books may date back to the people of Israel who were wandering in the desert, they have been assigned many different dates, some as early as the tenth to the seventh centuries BCE, some much later. According to the Jewish Encyclopedia, the first five books "received scriptural status in the 5th century BCE."[6] Yet qualified scholars write that final editing of the last books may not have been completed until the second century CE. That would mean that these books have multiple authors.

One reason for the multiple authorship theory is that the books exhibit different writing styles, and some books record historical facts that could only have been known to authors who wrote after the reported events occurred. According to Wellhausen, a German scholar, the Jewish bible had four writers – J, E, D and P.[7] According to him, J (for Jehovah) wrote between 1000 and 900 BCE, the time of Kings David and Solomon. The next, E (for Elohim), wrote about the Northern Kingdom of Israel in the eighth or ninth centuries BCE. D wrote Deuteronomy, and he wrote about the seventh century BCE prophets. Finally, Wellhausen believed that P – the priestly source – wrote much of Genesis and early Leviticus during the Persian period, (539–330 BCE). All this is hotly disputed.

According to another scholar,[8] "However, the 'documentary theory' sequence is only based on an evolutionary theory popularized by German archaeologists during the World War II to struggle against Jewish and Christian fundamentalism." This scholar, Gerard Gertoux, asserts that there is no manuscript evidence of any of these documents. Some skeptics claim that the

---

[5] Bazak, Amnon, *To This Very Day: Fundamental Questions in Bible Study*, (Jerusalem: Koren Publishers, 2020).
[6] Werblowsky, Zwi R.J. and Wigoder, Geoffrey, Eds. *The Encyclopedia of the Jewish Religion*, (New York: Holt, Rinehart and Winston, Inc., 196) p. 66.
[7] King, Justin, 'Torah', *Ancient History Museum*, May 9, 2012, https://www.ancient.eu/Torah/
[8] Gertoux, Gerard, *Dating the Five Books of Moses*.

story of the Exodus is an unprovable legend, and Hebrew writing did not even exist in the time of Moses. To this he responds, "the oldest epigraphs in paleo-Hebrew are dated 1515 +/- 35 BCE".

To those who say there is no historical evidence of Moses, he responds, "Strabo, a Greek geographer and historian, wrote (c. 20 CE): An Egyptian priest named Moses, who managed a portion of the country called the Lower [Egypt], being dissatisfied with the established institutions there, left it and came to Judea with a large body of people who worshipped the Divinity (Geography XVI:2:35)." Some skeptics say that early biblical references to camels are anachronistic because camels had not been domesticated yet. He responds "Several studies mention relics, texts and animal remains that support domestication of the camel in Arabia starting prior [sic] 2000 BCE. Many petroglyphs occurring on rocks in Saudi confirm this." And so forth. He refutes objection after objection.

One important dividing point in biblical scholarship is the distinction between books written before and books written after the Babylonian Exile of 586 BCE. This would have a direct bearing on what could have been influenced by Persian theology. Yet[9] that too is complicated. It now is believed that there were as many as seven exiles between 733 and 586 BCE. In each one, populations were relocated, deported, and dispersed. Certainly, the work of scholars would have been disrupted and subjected to foreign influences through this entire turbulent period.

Practically speaking, only books written during and after the exile to Mesopotamia could have been influenced by Persian theology, but the Persian influence would have continued when Cyrus the Great allowed the Jews to return to Israel. Some claim

---

[9] Knoppers, Gary, 'Exile, Return and Diaspora', ed. Louis C. Jonker; *Forschungen zum Alten Testament II*, 53; Tübingen: Mohr-Siebeck, 2011) 29–61,
https://www.academia.edu/13104332/Exile_Return_and_Diaspora_Expatriates_and_Repatriates_in_Late_Biblical_Literature?email_work_card=view-paper

that the entire Hebrew bible was written during the Persian period, which would have been the 5th to the 4th centuries BCE.[10]

Some material in the later prophets obviously came from Persia. The Book of Esther was set entirely in Persia, with the story of a Jewish queen of Persia who saved her people from destruction at the hands of an invidious vizier. This probably was written in the fourth century BCE. The last book of the Hebrew canon was the Book of Daniel, with stories of the Persian court, in which the courtiers spoke Aramaic. That book was written in about 164 BCE, in Persian-controlled Babylon, largely in Aramaic.

One other language is worthy of mention here – Greek. The word Judaism comes to European languages from the Greek. Judah (*Yehudah*) was one of the sons of the patriarch Jacob, and one of the original 12 tribes of Israel was named for him. The later books of the bible used the name *yehudim* to refer to the entire nation. Based on the Hebrew, the Greeks used the word *Ioudaism*, and this was translated into Latin as *Iudaismus*.

Jewish history is displayed particularly well in two Israeli museums. One, the Rockefeller Museum, is in East Jerusalem. Formerly called the Palestine Archaeological Museum, it was built as a repository for the British excavations that were carried out during the 1920s and 1930s in Mandatory Palestine. The cornerstone was laid down in 1930, but the start of building was delayed, as often happens in the holy land, by the discovery of fifth century BCE tombs on the site. The display starts with artifacts from 2,000 years ago, and it illustrates all the most important eras with stunning local archeologic findings.

The other is the Ralli Museum in Caesarea, built by the Recanati banking family. In the basement of building 1 is an amazingly detailed timeline of Israel, starting from Hellenistic times. The artifacts, and especially the chronology, are so well

---

[10] Petrovich, Douglas, (2019) Interacting with the Patterns of Evidence: The Moses Controversy Film. This article has a scholarly discussion and review of a film on this subject.
https://www.academia.edu/38560919/_2019_Interacting_with_the_Patterns_of_Evidence_The_Moses_Controversy_Film?email_work_card = view-paper

organized that the visitor sees it all fit together in one large graphic display.

Now we return to our texts, moving on to the Talmud. After the Babylonian Exile, the Jews established a self-contained civil-religious community in Babylon. This was organized under the leadership of a powerful Exilarch,[11] who was believed to be a descendent of the biblical King David. This meant that the House of David continued to rule for another 1,844 years from the fall of Jerusalem in 586 BCE to the Mongol invasion in 1258 CE. The Exilarch was considered equivalent to a patriarch, almost a pope, treated with great respect by the Parthians, Sassanids and even the Muslim Abbasids.

Under the authority of the Exilarch, the Jews built world-famous Jewish academies in which they debated the laws that were promulgated in the Torah. The records of these debates were ultimately collected, along with disquisitions on general legal theory, religious instruction, allegories and parables, to become the Babylonian Talmud, the most important set of books in the history of the Jewish religion, after the Torah.

THE TALMUD

The Talmud is composed of two parts, the accumulated result of rabbinic study and debates that spanned more than eight centuries. One part is called the Mishnah. That is a textbook that committed much of the oral law to writing before or after 220 CE. The driving forces behind it were the great sages Yochanan ben Zakkai and Yehuda HaNasi, and their work has been studied for centuries. Additional oral law found its way into other books, but the other main component of the Talmud was the Gemara. This is a compilation that summarizes debates on the Mishnah and that records the *Aggadah,* which consists of homilies, ethics, history, legends and philosophy. Combined with references to four other great documents (including the Tosefta), these form the Talmud, which contains commentary on the Mishnah, tries to harmonize discordant rules, and gives interpretations of complex legal questions.

---

[11] Ben-Sasson, The Exilarch is discussed in multiple chapters of his book.

One combination of the Mishnah and the Gemara was compiled in the Galilee. This is misleadingly called the Talmud Yerushalmi, and it was completed around 400 CE, during the Sassanian Empire. A longer version, the Babylonian Talmud (the Talmud Bavli), was put together in the Mesopotamian academies of Nehardea, Sura and Pumbeditha. This was finalized between 500 and 600 CE, but parts of it were reedited periodically for years, perhaps centuries. Of the two, the *Bavli* is the more highly regarded, and it shows obvious Persian influences. Scholars have disagreed about how much.

Let us stop for a moment and look at this question. One authority, Jacob Neusner, has taken a rather dim view of reported interchanges between Jews and Persians, yet he wrote an interesting book[12] that shows many commonalities between the Babylonian Talmud and the major Zoroastrian Pahlavi literature. Secunda[13] even writes that "there is some evidence that Jews studied orally with Zoroastrian priests."

The Jews compiled the Talmud just as Islam was appearing on the scene. Neusner explains that the Zoroastrians too assembled their major compendia of literature while they felt under threat, just after Islam had invaded Iranian Babylonia and was actively converting Zoroastrians rapidly to Islam. The sages of both religions were under pressure, fearing that if they did not write down their entire tradition of knowledge, it would vanish forever. Both might well have shared these fears. They had lived together for a thousand years. The Zoroastrians had governed the state, and, under them, the Jews ran their own affairs – undisturbed for most of that time – under the Achaemenid, Parthian and Sassanian Persian Empires.

Perhaps not surprisingly, both sets of literature use the question-and-answer technique, but there is a big difference. Neusner explains that the Zoroastrian literature presents elegantly stated questions that are answered by carefully phrased

---

[12] Neusner, Jacob, *Judaism and Zoroastrianism at the Dusk of Late Antiquity: How Two Ancient Faiths Wrote Down their Great Traditions,* (Atlanta: Scholars Press, 1993).

[13] Secunda, Shai, *The Iranian Talmud – Reading the Bavli in its Sassanian Context* (Philadelphia: University of Pennsylvania Press, 2014) pp. 41, 47.

rules, and these are often cast as conversations between God and Zoroaster. In contrast, Talmudic discussions begin with a question based on a citation from a major text, bring in other relevant references and report an analysis of the ensuing dialogue for the reader to evaluate on his or her own. The citations may be from the bible, the Tosefta, or from other respected sources, and there may be quotes from highly respected religious authorities, all of which are presented as the bases for the discussants' reasoning. In some cases, points made by scholars of one generation are disputed or refuted by scholars who lived centuries later. At the end of each topic, the reader has the arguments, and he is free to draw his own conclusion. There is no mandated conclusion, no pronouncement by God. Scholars of both religions promulgate secular as well as religious laws, but it is understood that there is an underpinning of heavenly norms.

Despite differences in approach, Neusner writes that "no two religions have more in common than the Zoroastrianism of the Avesta and the Pahlavi books and the Judaism of the Pentateuch and the Talmud." As he describes it, they have many topics in common, accomplish many of the same purposes, share a devotion to principles of justice and share a conviction that God intervenes in human affairs.[14]

Yaakov Elman has found both Sassanian stories and legal texts in the Talmud.[15] One example[16] is a story found in the Jewish-Christian *Ascension of Isaiah*, in which a Samaritan false prophet slew the prophet Isaiah by sawing him in half. This book probably was written in late first or early second century Palestine. The *Bavli* retells the story with the difference that Isaiah was swallowed by a cedar tree, and when they sawed the tree down to the prophet's lips, he died. Scholars have found this same

---

[14] Neusner, p. 5.

[15] Secunda, Shai, *The Iranian Talmud*, p. 50. Elman and Macuch cite Jacob Neusner, writing in *History of the Jews in Babylonia,* denying that there were outside influences on the Talmud.

[16] Kalmin, Richard, *Migrating Tales – The Talmud's Narratives and Their Historical Context* (Oakland: University of California Press, 2014), pp. 30–45.

motif in the *Avesta Yast* 19.49, which dates from the Achaemenid period.

Geoffrey Herman[17] tells of two Talmudic passages that show real or reputed relationships between Persians and Jews. The mother of Shapur II, Ifra Hormiz, admonishes her son when he tries to chastise Rabbi Rava for corporal punishment, warning him that he should not become involved with the Jews because "Their God gives them whatever they ask of Him." Herman repeats another Talmudic tale in which King Shapur koshers his knife by plunging it into the earth before cutting a slice of fruit for his Jewish guest, Mar Yehudah.

The *Avesta* tells an Iranian legend of the death of their god Yima. Here it is Yima's brother who kills him by cutting him in half. Kalmin agrees that the story in the Avesta differs from the story in the *Bavli*, but he still finds striking similarities between versions of the death of Yima and versions of the Isaiah story. He even suggests that this and other legends may have originated with the Romans, traveled east to Babylonia and from there to Persia, reaching the Babylonian Talmud in the middle of the fourth century. He says that "Mesopotamia and the eastern Roman provinces, and the territory in between, increasingly formed a cultural unity during the period under discussion." This would be the period in which the *Bavli* was written.

Kalmin[18] writes that Babylonian rabbis turned non-rabbinic literature into stories of Jewish sages. He found Babylonian literary texts that had been modified and incorporated into the Talmud, and he also cites numerous stories in the Babylonian Talmud that parallel stories told by Josephus, a first century Jew who became a Roman historian. Cleverly, the rabbis who repeated the original stories would transform the king or priest who had delivered the zinger in the original story into a rabbi.

One such story is of a conversation between a Babylonian rabbi and King Shapur II, in which Shapur supposedly asks what verse in the Torah mandates burial of a body after birth. Another

---

[17] Koller, Aaron and Tsadik, Daniel, Iran, *Israel and the Jews: Symbiosis and Conflict from the Achaemenids to the Islamic Republic*, (Eugene: Wipf and Stock publishers, 2019), chap. 3.

[18] Kalmin, pp. 97, 139.

story is of an encounter between a man named Shmuel and King Shapur I in which Shapur is supposed to have said, "May evil befall me if I have ever killed Jews." Both are parables, written to illustrate particular Talmudic teachings, but, remarkably, in both stories the Jew supposedly spoke directly to the king.

One master of cultural sharing was Sa'adiah ben Yosef (Saadia Gaon), who was born in 882, in Egypt, moved to Israel, and became the Gaon (Eminence) of the Babylonian academy of Sura in 928. He wrote many works in both Arabic and Judeo-Arabic, but his grand achievement was the *Tafsir,* completed in 902 CE. This was a monumental translation of the Pentateuch into Judeo-Arabic. Sa'adiah was familiar with elements of Indian science, and he had access to some Indian texts, which he obtained from traders. Prof. Goldstein explains[19] that, since he was fluent in Arabic, he was familiar with a wide range of intellectual activities that were taking place in the world around him, and these included modern philosophy and science. With much current theology incorporated into his work, his rich translation was the gold standard for hundreds of years, considered to be just as important as the Septuagint. Sa'adiah translation thus introduced foreign ideas into the Pentateuch itself.

Two centuries later, Rabbi Abraham ibn Ezra credited Hindus with originating the system of numerals that was adopted by the western world, and he clearly credits Indians with inventing the idea of zero. Under the Fatimid caliphate in Egypt, ibn Ezra translated Arabic texts into Hebrew, and many of these Arabic texts had originally been translated from Sanskrit. He was particularly taken by the expertise of the Hindu civilization in astrology, and his translations served as a bridge from Sanskrit to Hebrew. From there it was a shorter step to the European languages, which helped spread the science and culture of India to the western world in the early twelfth century CE.[20]

---

[19] Prof. Miriam Goldstein of Hebrew University, webinar.

[20] Weinstein, Brian, 'Traders and Ideas,' Chap. 2, in Katz et al, pp. 50–51. These are two among many examples. Weinstein also cites work by David Shulman, Tzvi Langerman, and older writers, who discuss the influence of Indian yoga texts on the Jews of Yemen.

Weinstein cites more examples, but these were among the best-known illustrations of intellectual links between the Jews of the Middle East and the Indians of the subcontinent, from the time of the First Temple on into medieval times.

BELIEFS

Following a discussion of the basic books of the Jewish faith, a proper treatment of Judaism would have to talk about the many brilliant books and compilations of commentary that have been written over the last 2,000 years, but that would be another book – many books. Even more daunting, in all this time, because of all this history of scholarly disquisition, argument and explication, the beliefs of the Jews broadened, deepened and reached out to reevaluate every law, concept, and – in many cases – every word of Jewish law. For this reason, it is not possible to state confidently *What the Jews Believe,* the title of more than one book, by more than one fine scholar.

What we can do is to give some basic beliefs. Then we will give some examples of the foundational legends of the Jewish people, and we will show how these have counterparts in the mythology of other peoples. After that, we will choose a few historical instances that might help us understand why Jews would feel a kinship with religions of India. This should help us when we analyze the historical pathway that Jews have taken from the Mediterranean through Persia to India, and vice-versa.

This does not mean that we will neglect mystical comparisons between the religions. We will come back to them in later chapters.

Now we come to the most basic question. In what unshakable truths do Jews believe? They believe in one God. They believe that they have an obligation to observe the Ten Commandments. They know that, in order to maintain their covenant with God, they must faithfully follow the laws of the Torah. And in some deeply understood way, not always fully expressed, they believe that they are part of a Jewish people that started with Abraham, continued through the Exodus and that still exists today. Then again, it all may be simpler. A man once sneeringly told the great Rabbi Hillel that he would convert to Judaism if he could teach him the Torah while standing on one foot. Hillel gently answered "What is hateful to you, do not do to your neighbor. That is the whole Torah; the rest is the explanation of this – go and study it!"

Another way to present Jewish beliefs would be to summarize their views, path and goals, in the same way that a Buddhist would summarize his world view. Looking at it in these terms, Katz[21] would say that the view of Judaism is "belief in a Creator God who endows creation with an inherent sanctity." The Jewish path, he would say, would include the study of Torah, the performance of rituals that connect to the transcendent, and acts of loving kindness. The Jewish goal is wholeness, a partnership with the Divine to repair the world. As we will see later, this description makes it sound similar to Buddhism.

Many of the early stories of Judaism resemble those of neighboring lands. The first chapter of the bible, Genesis, sets forth the Jewish legend of creation. It also tells the story of a great flood. The Babylonians told another version of the flood in their Epic of Atrahasis in the 18th to 17th century BCE. The other famous legend of the flood is found in the Epic of Gilgamesh, written in Akkadian during the third millennium BCE, also in the Babylonian period. And there were other versions of a flood story in the Middle East, such as the story of Manu and the great fish that we already have discussed. Can we explain any of them by saying that torrential rains once flooded major rivers so dramatically that people remembered this event forever? That is one theory of how the Indus Valley civilization was destroyed in India. Did people find marine fossils on dry land and wonder why they were there? We do not know how the myth started or why it lived on, among so many civilizations.

In the Book of Genesis – the first book of the Hebrew Bible – one of the most dramatic moments comes when God commands Abraham to sacrifice his only son Isaac. Together they climb Mount Moriah, carrying wood for the fire, but with no animal to sacrifice. Miraculously, just as Abraham raises his knife to kill his son, God stops him, and Abraham sees a ram caught in the

---

[21] Katz, Nathan, *Spiritual Journey Home: Eastern Mysticism to the Western Wall*, (Jersey City: KTAV Publishing House, 2009) p. 104.

brambles nearby, ready to be sacrificed. In this story, Abraham proves his faithfulness to God, and God demonstrates that He rejects human sacrifice. Interesting, all the way over in India the Vedas relate that the gods wanted to kill a man for a sacrifice, but parts of him entered several animals, lingering the longest in a goat. They too believed that a human sacrifice could be replaced by an animal sacrifice. Why such a similar story, so far away?

There are more similarities to India. Both Hindus and Jews anoint with oil. Both light lamps in their temples. Both blow trumpet-like instruments. The Jews blow a specially prepared ram's horn, called a *shofar*, in the mornings leading up to Rosh Hashanah, during the day of Rosh Hashanah, and at the end of Yom Kippur. It also may be blown at times of victory or celebration. Hindus blow a conch shell both before and after worship, and they may also blow it in connection with ritual purification.

The next story is one of ritual practice, and it is a story of loss. The Jews too had priests. After King Solomon completed his great Temple on Mount Moriah, that was where the hereditary priests of Judaism, the Kohanim, fulfilled their priestly duties. This Temple was the center of religious life in Jerusalem and in the whole land of Israel until the Babylonians destroyed it. After it was rebuilt, again the Kohanim were able to perform the rituals and sacrifices that God had commanded, until the Romans destroyed the Second Temple.

Since that date, almost the only duty left to the Kohanim is to give the priestly blessing on specified occasions. The one exception to their relative anonymity is on the holiday of Yom Kippur, when Jews in the synagogue hear a dramatic recitation of the ancient Service of the Kohen Gadol. This recounts the rituals that were required of the high priest on that day, his spiritual preparations, his numerous changes of immaculate clothing, and the special sacrifices that he performed on Yom Kippur while the Temple still was standing. In the finale, the Kohen Gadol entered the Holy of Holies, where he pronounced the ineffable name of the Divine Presence as only he knew how to say it. Is it nostalgia for this pageantry, a wistfulness for what was lost, that kindles the imagination of a Jew when he watches a Hindu priest perform his traditional rites?

One Jewish expert on Hinduism writes that "Temples and sacrifices are one of the elements of Hindu religion that strike Israelis the most." He even says that his own son, who had just completed reading the entire Talmud, was fascinated with them, saying "It was really the first time he could witness the kind of activity that he had spent so much time studying, but could never witness, as Judaism no longer practices animal sacrifices."[22]

After the destruction of the Temple, Jewish practice had to be completely restructured. Of necessity it became decentralized, and Jews learned to worship at local synagogues. Now it was synagogue rabbis who shaped Judaism, guided their flocks, transmitted religious knowledge and led the services. In addition to local leaders, certain rabbis developed exceptional reputations for scholarship, and questions would be sent to them from all over the Jewish world, requesting answers to problems of ritual and belief, the questioners anxious for reassurance that their practices conformed to approved norms.

For centuries, rabbinical scholars, first in Baghdad, later in academic centers in Europe, patiently crafted legalistic answers to these multiple abstruse religious questions. Over two millennia, these responsa and the voluminous writings that were published during that time have created a body of rules designed to preserve the oral and written law of Moses. Colloquially, this is known as Rabbinic Judaism.

Over the centuries, and continuing into the modern era, towering spiritual figures appeared from the Hasidic rabbinic lineages of eastern Europe, and some of them acquired transnational followings. The word used to describe the holiest of them is *tzaddikim*, a word coming from the Hebrew word *tzedek*, or justice. This also connotes righteous, or righteous one, and there is a belief that such a righteous man – and it always is a man – is able to channel divine energy down to the lower realms to sustain the world. The implication is that a tzaddik has a direct, intense, immediate experience of the divine, and this qualifies

---

[22] Goshen-Gottstein, Alon, p. 1331 in the Kindle edition.

him to be an intermediary between the Hasid and God. Of interest, the tzaddik often was believed to have ascended to heaven but then to have chosen to stay on earth for the sake of his followers. This is exactly the defining characteristic of the bodhisattva in Buddhism.

One famous tzaddik was the Baal Shem Tov, the Besht, an eighteenth-century mystic who lived in Poland. The founder of Hasidic Judaism, he taught his followers that every action of theirs is infused with the Divine. He also told them that he was able to ascend to heaven and speak with the sages who debated among themselves in perpetual celestial study. When he died, he bequeathed his leadership to Rabbi Nachman, who also became a famous tzaddik.

A recent example was the Chabad-Lubavitcher Rebbe Menachem Mendel Schneerson, born in Russia, a descendent of rabbis. Until his death in 1994, R. Schneerson was one of the most influential Jewish leaders of the twentieth century. The son-in-law of the leader of the Chabad movement and a Talmudic scholar himself, he came to the U.S. in 1941, and he eventually became the leader of the movement. His followers regarded him with awe as a paragon of spirituality, and he was the epitome of the spiritual, charismatic rabbi that previous generations had so revered. Despite his objections, his followers believed him to be the Messiah.

The guru in Hinduism plays a similar role. The guru is foremost a teacher, but he too is understood to be one who has had a direct experience of the Divine. Often, he too is part of a spiritual lineage. He also may be regarded as the embodied Divine, as distinguished from other humans, one who is next to God, even equal to God.

A tzaddik and a guru have even more in common. Typically, the guru teaches primarily from personal experience. The tzaddik too may teach his students how to live a pious life by setting an example, although many of the most famous rabbis also produced mountains of responsa, interpretations, and written theses.

The enormous body of literature, laws and traditions that have emerged from centuries of rabbinic Judaism gives strict rules for every activity of the religious Jew, but this makes it difficult for the secular Jew to find one simple answer to many of the questions that arise in a modern world.

You cannot light a fire on Shabbat, but can you go online on Shabbat? OK, you cannot turn on the computer, but what if you turn it on before Shabbat and just leave it on? If synagogue services are prohibited during an epidemic; can you watch them on Zoom? If you cannot turn on the Zoom program on Shabbat, can you sign on to Zoom before Shabbat starts? This all is particularly frustrating for modern Jews who want to do the right thing, or at least do the best they can, without all the complicated baggage. Here is where Buddhism beckons. It may be appealing exactly because it looks – for one who does not delve too deeply into it – simplified, refreshingly devoid of complex rules and restrictions. Serious adherents tell us that it is not free of rules, but the average Israeli is quite content simply to meditate, without worrying about lists of prescribed, and proscribed, practices.

Another solution to the problem posed by the plethora of rabbinic rules has been for Jews to treat their religion as if it offered a pick and choose menu. To accomplish this purpose, Judaism has branched out. The Reform Movement – in Europe called Progressives; the Reconstructionist Movement, and non-denominational Judaism have developed out of Orthodoxy. Some of the more lenient of these allow members to follow those rules that are meaningful to them and to ignore those that they find oppressive, though they might not admit it. Another branch is the Conservative Movement, which has tried to reinterpret many of the laws in order to help their congregations better fit Judaism into modern life.

Some Jews follow no traditional religious practices at all; they simply show up at the synagogue on the High Holidays. They are the extreme opposite of the religious Jews who flock to charismatic Orthodox rabbis in the mold of American evangelical leaders with congregations of thousands.

One smaller, newer branch of Judaism is the Jewish Renewal Movement such as Metivta in Los Angeles and Chachmat HaLev in Berkeley. Metivta was founded over thirty years ago by Rabbi Jonathan Omer-man, who had lived in Israel for 26 years, where he worked first on the land, then went into publishing. Metivta is devoted to the renewal of Jewish meditation traditions and to strengthening the personal Jewish quest for spirituality. The center emphasizes the contemplative path within Judaism, and it keeps kosher.

Chochmat HaLev in Berkeley California describes itself as a trans-denominational synagogue that brings spirituality, mysticism and the joy of Hasidism into Jewish life. It is a member of ALEPH, an international community that has multiple centers around the world. They, and organizations like them, hope to bring additional cross-cultural institutions into the mainstream in order to revitalize Judaism, and they are trying to bring back Jews whose spiritual needs were unmet in the past.

Meanwhile, most Jews today settle into an intermediate level of observance that works for them. There even is a small sect called Jewish Humanism, that rejects any belief in God but focusses on Jewish history and secular culture. One of the early leaders was Rabbi Sherwin Wine, of Michigan, and in his synagogue the young person who sought to be Bar Mitzvah would essentially read a book report, never a portion of the Torah. To be clear, none of these variances in belief and practice have been devoid of controversy. Buddhists meditate, but Jews – like Hindus – argue among themselves about everything, with the energy of fans at a soccer match.

Now back to our original question: why are Jews so attracted to Hinduism and Buddhism? We will continue our search for answers by travelling east, seeking connections between Judaism and Zoroastrianism. After that, since Zoroastrianism and Hinduism have much in common, we will continue further east, to examine these commonalities. Finally, we hope to be able to connect all the dots between the Mediterranean and India.

CHAPTER TWELVE.
JUDAISM AND ZOROASTRIANISM

Up to now we have dealt primarily with historical and cultural links between the people of Israel, Mesopotamia and Persia. But do their concepts of creation, death, final judgement, resurrection, the afterlife, heaven and hell, angels and demons, the Messiah, or a final apocalyptic battle between good and evil resemble each other? Did they borrow any of these beliefs from each other? Does that matter to us today?

Other questions we might ask would be whether, when and how these peoples could have come into contact. We know that the Babylonian Talmud was written during the Persian Sassanian Empire, and it does seem likely that the wise men of both religions would have had scholarly exchanges.[1] Did many of the most profound ideas of Judaism came from Zoroastrianism? Did the early Israelites have a clear concept of the afterlife before their contact with Persia? Or even of God? What about the travels, and travails, of the soul after death? Or did Jewish ideas influence the Zoroastrians? Perhaps each had an influence on the other.[2]

Foltz claims that, prior to the Assyrian Exile and the subsequent contacts with Iran, Judaism was 'a sacrificial Yahweh

---

[1] Darmestat Ibid.
[2] Kohler, Kaufmann and Jackon, A.V.W., 'Zoroastrianism', *Jewish Encyclopedia.com*,
http://www.jewishencyclopedia.com/articles/15283-zoroastrianism

cult.'[3] By this he means that Jews only were distinguished from other Semites by their worship of a God named Yahweh, and by the belief that they had made a covenant with this God. He says that the first of the Ten Commandments implies that Jews once believed in multiple gods, since it says in Exodus 2:3 "Thou shall have no other gods before me." Based on that verse, he argues that even the monotheism that is so central to Judaism did not reach its current importance until after the Exile, when the bible was written, or edited, in Persia. Remember, in Persia Zoroaster had artfully shifted the focus of his religion away from the older pagan gods, teaching that Ahura Mazda ultimately will win out over all the gods, with a result that Zoroastrians would call monotheism.

This would mean that monotheism came to Judaism from Zoroastrianism. There is some support for this, as "Thou shalt have no other Gods before me" at the very least acknowledges that there could be other gods. Yet the concept of one God is one of the most fundamental precepts of the whole Jewish religion. The central prayer of Judaism comes from Deut. 6:4, "Hear O Israel, the Lord our God, the Lord is One."

Mary Boyce[4] is a known expert on Zoroastrianism, and she believes that many Zoroastrian ideas influenced Jewish writings after the Babylonian Exile. Among these she would include the idea of one supreme God who created this world for a purpose. She also would include the concepts of heaven and hell. Boyce further claims that Zoroastrianism was the first religion to teach of a Last Judgment, a future resurrection of the body, a final cosmic battle, and an everlasting life for a reunited soul and body.

As Kohler and Jackson saw it: "Ahuramazda, the supreme lord of Iran, omniscient, omnipresent, and eternal, endowed with creative power, which he exercises especially through the medium of his Spenta Mainyu ("Holy Spirit"), and governing the

---

[3] Foltz, Richard, *Religions of Iran – from prehistory to the present* (London: Oneworld Publications, 2013), p. 2112.

[4] Boyce, Mary, *Zoroastrians – Their Religious Beliefs and Practices* (London: Routledge, 1979).

universe through the instrumentality of angels and archangels, presents the nearest parallel to Yhwh that is found in antiquity."[5]

Let us look at these claims in some detail. A good place to start is with the story of creation. As told in Genesis, the first book of the Hebrew Bible, God is the creator. On the first day of creation, He created light, and on the second day he separated the waters of the sky from the waters of the earth. On the third day He created vegetation, on the fourth the sun and the moon, on the fifth birds and fish, and on the sixth animals and man. Another description in the Bible differs in significant details. In that one, after plants came animals, then the primeval ox, and finally, man. Either way, He created the world in seven days. At the close of the sixth day, God looked at His work and "saw that it was very good." Then the seventh day was His day of rest. The culmination of His creation was man.

The great creation story of Mesopotamia is thought to date from the second millennium BCE. This was the *Enuma Elish*,[6] also called the Seven Tablets of Creation. Possibly the oldest creation story in the world, the creator was named Enk or Enlil or Ea in the Sumerian version and Assur in the Assyrian version. The Babylonian version used the name of their main god, Marduk. The story starts out with undifferentiated water swirling in chaos. Then these waters separate, differentiate, give birth to the gods, and a long, complicated saga rolls out.

The Persian *Avesta* describes how Ahura Mazda is the sole creator and how he created the world in seven steps.[7] Zoroastrians describe seven creations, and these are identified with seven divinities of creation. First Ahura Mazda created the sky in the form of a shell of stone, then he poured water into it. Next, he created land, which rested on top of the water. Then he created a single plant, a single animal and a single man. The seventh stage was the creation of fire and the sun. Then hostile gods intervened,

---

[5] Kohler, Kaufmann and Jackson, AVW, 'Zoroastrianism,' *Jewish Encyclopedia*
http://www.jewishencyclopedia.com/articles/15283-zoroastrianism
[6] Enuma Elish – 'The Babylonian Epic of Creation – Full Text,' *Ancient History Encyclopedia.*
[7] 'Ancient Persian Mythology,' *Ancient History Encyclopedia.*

crushed the plant, slew the bull and the man, and sullied the fire. Through the intervention of more beneficent gods, ultimately all of this was purified, and from the ashes came all living things. From the bones of the first man grew a plant. Forty years later, a man and a woman came from the plant, and their children populated the world. Thus, all these descendants came from a single couple, named Mashya (man) and Mashyana (woman), the Iranian Adam and Eve. In the culmination of this story, man is acknowledged as the chief of all creations, and he is responsible for taking care of all the others.

Note that all three stories have one creator; they separate the waters in the first or second step, and they have seven steps.

The Persian version describes the work of Ahura Mazda as perfect. This resembles the Jewish story, in which at the end of the day, on the second through the sixth days, God would look at His work and say it was good. Persians also believed that their king too was obligated to make the world 'excellent,' evidently in the spirit of their god, Ahura Mazda. Can any of these religions credibly claim that their version was first? Elements of any of these stories would have sounded quite familiar to the neighbors.

Cosmology is the study of the origins of the world, and, consistent with what Boyce and other experts believe, much Jewish cosmology was developed during the Babylonian captivity. This certainly could have put a Zoroastrian imprint on Judaism. Chapters 40–55 of the biblical Book of Isaiah (now called Deutero-Isaiah) probably were written after the sixth century BCE by a Jewish exile in Babylon. One reason for postulating that is that some of the verses speak of the fall of Babylon and the intervention of Cyrus.

Deutero-Isaiah lays out the cosmology of the universe. Chapter 45:12 says, "I have made the earth, and created man upon it: I, even my hands, have stretched out the heavens, and all their host have I commanded." This is perfectly consistent with basic Zoroastrian cosmology.

Also, Isaiah 44:24 says, "Thus says the LORD, your Redeemer, who formed you from the womb: "I am the LORD, who made all things, who alone stretched out the heavens, who spread out the earth by myself.""

Yet the books of Proverbs date back as far as 700 BCE before the Exile, and Proverbs 3:19 says "The Lord by wisdom founded the earth; by understanding he established the heavens." We also read in Proverbs 8:22 "The LORD brought me forth as the first of his works, before his deeds of old." Thus, even this pre-exilic book unambiguously declaims God's role in creation.

Rabbis emphasize that the role of the Almighty is told in the Torah, and that the Torah is the foundation of the world. Rabbi Akiva described the Torah as the "instrument by means of which the world was created". In his cosmology, the Torah is among the first of God's works. It is God's architect, the blueprint of Creation, the divine language through which God created everything. It existed before the revelation at Mount Sinai, and it was given to Moses on Mount Sinai.

By the way, it is worthy of note that Zoroaster too received the revealed word from Ahura Mazda on a mountain, "the Mountain of the Two Holy Communing Ones."[8]

The *Sefer Yetzirah,* or Book of Creation, according to some, is one of the oldest existing wisdom books in the history of Jewish mysticism. It could go back to the 18th century BCE, predating the Vedas. Other legends attribute it to the patriarch Abraham. Or it may date back only to the early Talmudic texts, perhaps to Rabbi Akiva in the second century CE. Then again, maybe it was written as late as medieval times. Obviously we do not know. At least the essence of it must have been known to the elders who finished the Mishnah, because the Mishnah appears to reflect its teachings.

In it, we read a quintessentially Jewish explanation of creation – that each of the 22 consonants of the Hebrew alphabet played a role in the act of creation. In exquisite detail, it analyzes the importance of each letter's shape and sound, its permutations and its combinations with other letters. Building on this, the Babylonian Talmud elaborates on how these letters created heaven and earth.

---

[8] Kaufmann Kohler, A. V. W. Jackson, 'Zoroastrianism,' *Jewish Encyclopedia.com 2002–2011,*
http://www.jewishencyclopedia.com/articles/15283-zoroastrianism

There actually may be an Indian connection here. Weinstein writes[9] that the *Sefer Yetzirah* shows the influence of Hindu mysticism, and Saadiya Gaon agreed. Rabbi Brill too writes[10] that the Sefer Yetzirah probably has Indo-Hindu roots, quoting David Schulman of Hebrew University, who remarks on its "highly developed phonology, etymology, morphology, syntax, metrics and grammar." According to one proposal, this exchange of ideas might have taken place by way of northern Mesopotamia. Just to wrap up the discussion of these possible Indo-Judaic roots, a Swiss physicist found that Sanskrit and Hebrew are the two languages in the world in which "the visual characters of their alphabet correspond very precisely to their individual audible sounds." Apparently, he did not know about Korean, but I digress.

The subject of evil is an important part of our discussion of Judaism and Zoroastrianism. Both religions believe in free will. However, in order to exert free will, evil must exist as an alternative. And where does evil come from? The Zoroastrians postulate a god of good and a god of evil. *The Bahir* is a powerful Jewish wisdom book written between the first century CE and medieval times. This teaches that evil fell on earth because the heavenly vessels that once held the divine light had broken, unable to hold the powerful light any longer. This is an important concept in the Kabbalah. The *Bahir* says that 'Evil is a result of the secondary elements of creation, since its purpose is only to allow free choice to exist, and thus bring about the primary purpose, which is man's attachment to God.'

Moving on from the subject of creation, we should look at other beliefs that the Jews share with the Zoroastrians. Jewish literature addresses the problems of heaven, a last judgement and resurrection of the dead, but it shows little interest in hell. All these topics fall under the complex topic of eschatology, which is a whole category of questions about death, judgment, the final destiny of the soul, the transmigration of souls and the end of

---

[9] Weinstein, Brian, in Katz et al, p. 49.
[10] Brill, Alan, p. 34.

time. Miryam Brand[11] explains that there is little about heaven, hell, judgment or resurrection in the biblical literature until after the Babylonian Exile, but Persian ideas can be seen in the manuscripts found at Qumran.

Brand discusses one text found in two caves at Qumran, the *Treatise of the Two Spirits*. In it, the prince of light leads the children of righteousness, and the angel of darkness leads the children of deceit. And neither of the sides seems to have free choice about where they will be led. Brand acknowledges that this dualism is a very Persian idea, though she says that at least the Zoroastrians believed that the two groups would have a choice.

She then cites other texts from Qumran, one of which is the *Visions of Ammon*, which describes a figure of darkness and one of light, both seen in a dream, but in this dream, Ammon has a choice, as in Zoroastrianism. There also is the *War Scroll*, which describes an apocalyptic battle between the children of darkness led by Belial and the children of light, led by Archangel Michael. She contrasts these with the *Damascus Document*, in which the choice is between God's commandments and the desires of self. What were these Persian documents doing deep in the Judean Desert among the Essenes?

Not only were these documents in those caves, but the writings of the Essenes also used Persian loan words, some of which may have entered Aramaic during the Persian period. Persian words and concepts too were used, such as the word *Ruah* for spirit, instead of older Hebrew words.

Reward and punishment after death are other topics that were important in Persian eschatology. The Book of Deuteronomy probably was written in the seventh century BCE, just after the beginning of the Babylonian Exile, and it spoke forcefully about both. Deut. 11:13–21 says that the Lord will reward the righteous thus: "I will grant the rain for your land in season, the early rain

---

[11] Koller, Aaron and Tsadik, Daniel, Iran, *Israel and the Jews: Symbiosis and Conflict from the Achaemenids to the Islamic Republic*, (Eugene: Wipf and Stock publishers, 2019), chap. 2.

and the late. You shall gather in your new grain and wine and oil." And that is just the beginning.

Deut. 28 details what the Lord will do to one who does not obey all of His commandments: "Cursed shall you be in the city and cursed shall you be in the country. Cursed shall be your basket and your kneading bowl. Cursed shall be the issue of your womb and the produce of your soil, the calving of your herd and the lambing of your flock. Cursed shall you be in your comings and cursed shall you be in your goings." And from there it gets much, much worse.

There are many more descriptions of rewards for the righteous after death in Jewish post-exilic apocalyptic literature, but we should remember that this literature was written a millennium before the Zoroastrians ever wrote down their oral tradition. It also comes from the very beginning of Jewish life in exile. Was this too early for Persian influences to have permeated such an important book? We do not know. For all we know, the Zoroastrians could have been influenced by Jewish thought.[12]

In more than one Middle Eastern religion, evil comes from the north. Certainly, that is true in Jewish belief. Ever since the time of the Assyrian invasions, Jerusalem's weakest line of defense has always been against attacks that come from the north. That could have been one of the main reasons why they feared the north.

Since north is on the left when one faces the rising sun in the east, in Latin, the word 'sinister' means left. In the languages derived from Latin, the implication of the word sinister is shady, or worse.

The *Bahir* emphasizes that 'North is associated with evil in many places.' According to Jeremiah 1:14, "Out of the north disaster shall be let loose upon all the inhabitants of the land." Ezekiel prophesies stormy wind, great clouds and burning fire in the north. In Kabbalah, all the manifestations that are associated with the north are evil. And evil is represented by the left hand in the Kabbalistic diagram of the body.

---

[12] Secunda, Shai, p. 116.

Is there any reference to the north in other faiths of the region? In Persia, it is Ahura Mazda, and in India, it is Mitra who will judge the souls of the dead. As these souls arrive for judgement after death, they are met either by a sweet breeze from the south or by a stinking wind from the north, depending on the soul. In either case, the soul must cross a dangerous place, sometimes described as a glowing river. After that, its fate depends on whether or not it receives a favorable verdict at the Last Judgement. A soul that is consigned to Hell is met by a horrid hag and carried off to misery. A more fortunate soul is escorted to Paradise by a beautiful maiden, and there it will be resurrected and reunited with its body "when the earth will give up the bones of the dead."[13]

The idea of a final battle at the end of time was held by many Indo-European cultures before it was adopted by the Persians. It is not an idea that particularly caught on with the Jews. However, Ezekiel 38–39 references a war involving "Gog, of the land of Magog," in which God says to Gog, "You will come from your place in the far north." Note, the north again. Then comes verse 20, "The fish of the sea, the birds of the air, the beasts of the field, every creature that moves along the ground, and all the people on the face of the earth will tremble at my presence. The mountains will be overturned, the cliffs will crumble, and every wall will fall to the ground."

And that may be a description of the final battle, though after these momentous verses we hear little or nothing about any of this again in the Hebrew bible. The concept was adopted by Christianity, and in the early days of that religion there was a strong belief that the End of Days was about to come, culminating in an imminent final battle and the coming of the Messiah. This is the Christian tradition of an Apocalypse, an idea that we know even today in the west since Christianity is so pervasive.

Resurrection of the dead and posthumous punishment of sinners are Persian ideas, and Hindus share these same beliefs. However, the *Bahir* attributes the idea of *Gilgul*, or rebirth, to the

---

[13]Boyce, Mary, Zoroastrians – *Their Religious Beliefs and Practices* (London: Routledge, 1979), p. 27.

second century CE Rabbi Akiva. Yet in the sixth century BCE the post-exilic prophet Ezekiel had already foreseen a field of dry bones ready to rise again. And in America, we sing about 'them bones, them bones, them dry bones.'

The idea of Resurrection could have entered Jewish thinking after contact with Zoroastrianism. Resurrection is first mentioned explicitly in the post-exilic Book of Daniel and in the portions of Isaiah that were added later. We read in Isaiah 26:19, "But your dead will live, LORD; their bodies will rise – let those who dwell in the dust wake up and shout for joy – your dew is like the dew of the morning; the earth will give birth to her dead."

Isaiah 66:24 speaks of posthumous punishment of sinners: "And they shall go out and look on the dead bodies of the men who have rebelled against me. For their worm shall not die, their fire shall not be quenched, and they shall be an abhorrence to all flesh."

Resurrection of the dead is explicit in Daniel 12:2: "And many of those who sleep in the dust of the earth shall awake, some to everlasting life, and some to shame and everlasting contempt." Using a phrase that also is found in the *Book of Enoch*, Daniel 7:13 says: "I saw in the night visions, and behold, *one like the Son of man* came with the clouds of heaven, and came to the Ancient of days, and they brought him near before him." This sounds like a description of the *saoshyant*, the Persian Messiah, and it also uses the language – son of man – that Christians use to describe Christ. Significantly, the *saoshyant* is supposed to have been born of a virgin, in this case a virgin who conceived a child after she waded into a lake that contained the seed of Zoroaster.

What about Jewish books in which the dead are brought back to life? In 2 Kings 13:21, "Once while some Israelites were burying a man, suddenly they saw a band of raiders; so they threw the man's body into Elisha's tomb. When the body touched Elisha's bones, the man came to life and stood up on his feet." In 2 Kings 4:32–37, Elisha, a man of God, brings a dead boy back to life, and in 1 Kings 17:17–24, Elijah also brings a little boy back to life. While some of these miracles may have been successful resuscitations rather than actual resurrections, they at least exemplify a Jewish belief in the possibility of the dead coming back to life.

There was great controversy about resurrection of the dead in the Second Temple period, with strong disagreements between the Sadducees and the Pharisees, but in the Talmud, it says that Jews had better believe in resurrection! Sanhedrin 10.1 says, "And these are the ones who have no portion in the world to come: He who maintains that resurrection is not a biblical doctrine, that the Torah was not divinely revealed". Then again, the Talmud was written under Persian influence.

Brill quotes the seventeenth century Rabbi Menashe ben Israel, who states clearly, "The belief in reincarnation is a firm belief for our entire congregation, and none are to be found disputing it...it is a true belief and one of the fundamental principles of the Torah..."[14] Ironically, Brill says that the Hindu belief in reincarnation "is generally quite vague and consists mainly of being rewarded for one's deeds..." This is true even though most westerners think all Hindus believe in reincarnation. It turns out that it depends on which sect of Hinduism we are talking about, because Hindu beliefs vary considerably. Any comparison is complicated, depending on which group of Jews we cite and which sect of Hindus, to say nothing of the difficulty of making additional comparisons with the various Persian religions that were practiced at different times through the ages.

Belief in an afterlife remains strong among Orthodox Jews today. The Chabad website[15] instructs "Belief in an afterlife is core to Judaism. It's a foundation stone without which the entire structure would collapse." The same Chabad reminds us that belief in an afterlife is the reason why Jews recite the prayer called the Kaddish for their parents after their death. It is to help their souls ascend to the greatest heights, "to assist them on their journey to that lofty peak."

Angels played a far more prominent role in Persian thinking than in early Jewish lore. Admittedly, angels made important

---

[14] Brill, p. 121.
[15] Freeman, Tzvi, 'Do Jews Believe in Heaven?' *Chabad.org*, https://www.chabad.org/library/article_cdo/aid/4848230/jewish/Heaven-and-the-Afterlife.htm

appearances in the first book of the Hebrew bible, Genesis, but most of them appeared in the form of a man, a herald of events to come or a carrier of a message from God. They rarely manifested as flocks of spirits, nor did the bible give explicit descriptions of angels with wings. In one story, Abraham was visited by three mysterious men, who he graciously served a meal, and they turned out to be angels bringing important messages for him. One message was a warning about the imminent destruction of Sodom and Gomorrah, and another was a reveal that Sarah miraculously would have a baby.

After she fled into the wilderness, Abraham's Egyptian wife Hagar was visited by the Angel of the Lord, and in the wicked city of Sodom, Lot was visited by two angels. The standout episode though was in Genesis 28:10–17, when Jacob dreamed of a ladder to heaven, with "the angels of God ascending and descending on it." In that scene there did seem to be flocks of angels, not just anthropomorphic apparitions. Then in Genesis 32:22–32, Jacob strove all night with an angel when "a man wrestled with him until the breaking of the day." Except possibly for the angels on the ladder, all these other angels had a human appearance. We could give other examples, but these should suffice.

On the other hand, demons barely make an appearance in the Hebrew bible, only assuming importance after the Exile and after extensive contact with the Persian civilization. The one exception in the bible would be Azazel, a demon that lurked in the desert, waiting, and to whom, every year on Yom Kippur, the Jews would send a scapegoat bearing all their sins.

This is in contrast with the Zoroastrian literature, in which both angels and demons played elaborate parts from the very beginning. In the early Avestan language of the ancient Gathas (hymns), there was a word for angel, *Fraasht*, or *Fraaesht*, and the concept was of a divinely inspired being, an angel, or a messenger.[16] Also in the Gathas, *daevas*, or demons abounded, and, along with angels, they played an active role in the mortal

---

[16] "Angels and Demons in the Poetic Gathas," September 24, 2012, *Authentic Gatha Zoroastrianism.*

world. They are described in multiple Yasnas (Avestan texts), and they assumed multiple forms.

All kinds of angels floated into Jewish thinking after the Babylonian Exile, and angels, some of light, some of darkness, play prominent roles in the wisdom literature. For example, the Book of Daniel mentions two angels – Gabriel and Michael – who fought a prince of Persia. The books of Daniel, Ezekiel, and Enoch outline a whole hierarchy of angels. As contrasted with the Iranian literature though, these angels are depicted not as independent entities, but as servants of God, spirits.[17] Both religions have angels and demons, but under Persian influence Jewish angelology and demonology became ever more elaborate. For one thing, the Jews picked up the concept of a battle between good and evil, in which righteous angels and men fought evil angels and men.

When the Jews returned from Babylon, the angels returned with them, with names. Now there were seven archangels, and they all had Hebrew names that could be broken down into Hebrew components. We will consider three of them. The 'chief prince' of the angels was Michael (*Mi-cha-el*), whose name means 'like God.' In Daniel 10:13, it says "But the prince of the Persian kingdom resisted me twenty-one days. Then Michael, one of the chief princes, came to help" Another important angel was Gabriel (*Gaber-el*), whose name means 'warrior of God', and a third was Raphael (*Rofe-el*), whose name means 'healer of God'.[18]

Jeremiah (Jer. 9:23) warned against this Persian influence with dire imprecations, finishing with, "Let not the rich glory in his riches." Presumably he meant that Jews should not adopt foreign beliefs from their rich and successful Persian neighbors. Apparently, the Jews did not heed this advice.

The wisdom book called the *Book of Tobit* was written between the second century BCE and the second century CE, about the same time as the Book of Daniel. It is canonical in

---

[17] Carter, George William, *Zoroastrianism and Judaism*, (Boston: Richard G Badger, The Gorham Press 1918), Classic Reprint, available on internet archive.

[18] Puhvel, Jaan, *Comparative Mythology*, (Baltimore and London: Johns Hopkins University Press, 1987), p. 104.

Christianity, but not in Judaism, possibly because the book was of late authorship, but fragments of this book, written in Hebrew and in Aramaic, were found in the Dead Sea Scrolls. It tells the story of Tobit, a righteous man living in Nineveh after the Assyrian Exile, who was blinded by the evil actions of a demon. In the end his sight is restored by the healer Raphael, a good angel sent by God. Raphael goes on to produce a wife for him and to deliver him from Asmodaios (Asmodeus), the demon of lust. The latter name comes directly from the name of an Iranian demon, *Aeshma daeva*. In Persian, *Aeshma* means wrath. The name *Ashmedai* also appears in the Jerusalem Talmud. Curiously, in Hebrew, *ashma* means guilt. Perhaps it is a loan word from Persian.

The biblical Daniel lived in Persian Babylonia, and he was buried in Susa (Shush), Iran, possibly in the second century BCE. Along with the books of Isaiah, Ezra, Nehemiah, Chronicles and Esther, the Book of Daniel refers liberally to Jewish life in Persia, and it shows many Persian influences. For instance, we could look at the metals described in the dream of Nebuchadnezzar. According to one commentator, "Zoroastrians today have divided the last period into four lesser periods, each being symbolized by a metal. Gold for the period when the religion was revealed to Zoroaster, silver for the period when king Gashtasb was converted, steel for the Sassanian period and iron for the present age."[19]

As it happens, Daniel's interpretation of Nebuchadnezzar's dream refers to four metals, associated with four kingdoms. In Daniel 2:31–3, Daniel speaks to King Nebuchadnezzar about a troubling dream, telling him, "before you stood a large statue...The head of the statue was made of pure gold, its chest and arms of silver, its belly and thighs of bronze, its legs of iron..." Strikingly, these verses name three out of the four metals that we just listed. Also reflecting the Babylonian environment, large

---

[19] Price, Massoume, 'Zoroastrian Myth of the End,' *Iran Chamber Society*, http://www.iranchamber.com/religions/articles/zoroastrian_myth_end.php

portions of this text are written in Aramaic, and they contain many Persian loanwords.

The *Book of Enoch* is believed to date from 300 to 200 BCE, perhaps as late as 100 BCE. This tells of a miraculous ascent to heaven, of demons and giants, of angels, of the flood, and of the coming of the Messiah. It is part of the Christian canon, but it is not in the Jewish canon, probably because it describes fallen angels coming to earth to engage in generally naughty activities with humans. In it, through parables and visions, Enoch describes the end of days, the last judgment, and future life. Fragments of this book have been found written in Greek and in Latin. They also have been found among the Dead Sea Scrolls, in Aramaic and generally dating from 300 BCE to the first century CE, though some of the oldest could go back to the 8th to the 11th century CE.

Many of these are the scribal product of the Essenes who were in that desert. In addition to descriptions of a last battle between the Prince of Light and the Spirit of Darkness, these scrolls contain other Zoroastrian ideas.

The Essenes seem to have believed that death is the liberation of the soul, an idea they held in common with Persians and Indians. Did Zoroastrians come traipsing through the Judean desert bringing these ideas to the Essene monastic community? Did the Essenes develop these ideas independently, or did they bring the concepts with them when they entered the desert?

Recent findings provide an alternative version of the story. The September 3–9, 2021 International Jerusalem Post reports that the site at Qumran served, not as a permanent settlement, but as the site of an annual celebration of "the passing of the covenant." For this event, members would assemble from all over the country, the numbers perhaps rising into the thousands. The rules of these proceedings have been found in so-called Community Rule documents, and they are in the Damascus Document, which was copied in 1,000 CE, and was stored in the Cairo Genizah. Thus, the Essenes would not have been isolated desert dwellers, but a widely spread community which brought their precious scrolls to the Qumran caves each year for safe storage.

Thus, our old concept of the Essenes as only living in the dessert, with a celibate lifestyle, vegetarian, foreswearing private property or money, rejecting animal sacrifice, and cultivating the esoteric arts, may be more extreme than the reality. We have found evidence though that they believed in angels, believed that the soul is immortal and thought that it will come back after death. That may be true.

There are several parallels between Essenes and the Zoroastrians. The Essenes are believed to have been conversant in mystic lore, and to have passed these beliefs to sages who continued to pass them on until these ideas came to the writers of the Talmud. They also had many names for angels, and they claimed to foretell the future. Perhaps they had a wider network of contacts than we might have suspected.

My friend Ram had no doubt that a group of Buddhist monks from India came to the land of Israel bringing their philosophical ideas with them and debating with Jewish sages in the time of Jesus. He said that they even instructed Jesus. There are serious advocates for this theory. Judea was on the trade route between the Mediterranean and India; Zoroastrians, Jews, Hindus and Buddhists traveled along this route. Not only was there routine commerce, but we know that as far back as the third century BCE the Indian emperor Ashoka sent Buddhist missionaries along the Silk Road and over the Hindu Kush as far as Alexandria. The respected historian, Will Durant, wrote that Ashoka "sent Buddhist missionaries to all parts of India and Ceylon, even to Syria, Egypt and Greece, where, perhaps, they helped prepare for the ethics of Christ."[20]

One writer[21] says that the primary link between the Buddhists and Jesus appears to have been the Essenes, quoting the scholar Melamed who wrote "Numerous scholars long ago discovered Buddhistic elements in the Gospel of John and also recognized the Buddhistic background of Essenism, by which Jesus was greatly influenced. The conclusion is inescapable that

---

[20] Durant, Will, *Our Oriental Heritage*, p. 449.
[21] Hansen, James, 'Was Jesus a Buddhist?', *researchgate.net*. This article is on several sites.

Palestine, together with many other parts of Asia Minor, was inundated with Buddhistic propaganda for two centuries before Christ."

He further says that the records indicate there was "a steady stream of Buddhist monks and philosophers who, living in that area, which was at the crossroads of commerce and ideas, influenced the philosophical currents of the time. There are strong similarities between Buddhist monastic teachings and Jewish ascetic sects, such as the Essenes, who were part of the spiritual environment of Palestine at the time of Christ's birth."[22]

This same author adduces much more evidence for this thesis, including a possible origin of the Essenes "from Indic origins" about 150 years before Jesus and well after Ashoka's Buddhist emissaries came from India.

John the Baptist is said to have been an Essene, and some believe that he studied in their community near the Dead Sea. This is significant because it is known that John the Baptist was an important influence on Jesus. According to the scriptures, he even baptized Jesus.

It is difficult to know whether we should accept the proposed connections between Buddhist monks and Essenes as authoritative, but it may not be fair to dismiss them out of hand. The story of Ashoka sending monks to the land of Israel seems to have a lot of support. A specific connection to the Essenes or to Jesus could be legend, or it could be folklore. It would be intriguing if true, because it might explain many of the differences between Judaism and Christianity.

Before we leave the Essenes in their caves by the Dead Sea, we should mention two other ascetic sects. At the time of Christ, it was not uncommon for individual Jews to become Nazarites, leaving their hair unshorn, renouncing the comforts of life, living in a state of poverty and dedicating their lives to God, precisely the life of Hindu and Buddhist holy men.

We also know that early Christians lived in monasteries for centuries in the Middle East. But from the fifth through seventh

---

[22] Yvette Rosser, 'On Buddhist Influence on Christianity', rajeev2004.blogspot.com

centuries, the most extreme were the stylites, who would stand on top of a high column for days, exposed to the elements from above and to curious observers below, worshipped as saints. Could Buddhist emissaries have brought the idea of this renunciation to any of them? Could Buddhist emissaries have learned this from the Middle East?

Now, we will continue travelling from west to east to India, carefully inspecting what history, religions, and people lie between. We know that there were important similarities and mutual influences between the Judaism of the land of Israel and the Zoroastrianism of Persia. We also know there were ancient, primal connections between Zoroastrianism and Hinduism, and this is what we will study next. In the end, we should be able to complete the chain of connections between Jews and India, in the light of history.

CHAPTER THIRTEEN.
ZOROASTRIANISM AND HINDUISM

Hinduism and Zoroastrianism both grew out of an Indo-Iranian migration[1] that started in the steppes of Russia and moved into Europe, the Middle East and South Asia between 2000 and 1600 BCE, but at some point, the two religions diverged, developing in different directions. Most Persian religions came to believe in a god of good and a god of evil, but Hinduism[2] evolved a broad pantheon with many gods and baroque symbolism.

Despite those differences in their evolution, many similarities continued between the gods of Zoroastrians and Hindus and between their respective languages. Fortunately for scholars, these provide helpful illustrations of their common origins, and they are of inestimable value for interpretations of both religions. As we will discuss now, knowledgeable linguists often can identify a god or a legend from one religion with an analogous god or a legend from another, which helps educated academics explain and translate verses that would otherwise remain obscure. Many philosophical comparisons between these two religions can be made, but we will save the more arcane for a subsequent chapter dedicated to the world of mysticism.

---

[1] Mallory, J.P., *In Search of the Indo-Europeans*, (London: Thames and Hudson, 1989). This book has many dates, and I have simply chosen some representative ones.

[2] *The Zend Avesta Part I The Vendidad*, translated by James Darmestet, is a republished ancient text. It shows how, in Iran, dualism became Mazdeism, and how Mazdeism anticipates a future war between good and evil.

The oldest part of the Zoroastrian Avesta, the *Yasna*, is written in an Old Avestan language that is not far removed from the Sanskrit of the Vedas, the earliest texts of India. Many words are almost the same in the two languages. Persian priests speak *manthra*; Hindu priests recite *mantras*. Iranians used the word *yasna* for priestly acts of worship; the Indians called their rituals *yajnas*.

The first and second parts of the Avesta are composed of hymns. Bryant writes that lengthy passages in these portions of the Avesta may be translated to Vedic Sanskrit by making minor grammatical alterations.[3]

Comparisons between the Avesta and the Hindu Vedas show strikingly similar gods. For instance, after the most powerful gods of the early Vedas receded in importance over the years, two twin gods, *Varuna* and *Mitra*, moved to center stage. *Mitra*, we remember, was *Mithra* in Persia.

One goddess in the Avesta, *Spenta Armaiti*, is the same as the Vedic goddess *Aramati*. Scholars identify *Ahura Mazda*, the supreme Zoroastrian god in the Avesta, with the Hindu *Varuna*, the most important of the *Asuras* in the Vedas. In the Avesta, the word *Ahura* means 'the Lord.' In the Sanskrit of the Vedas, the *Asuras* were powerful demigods.

In the Rigveda, Indra was the *deva*, the god who creates the sun, heaven and dawn. In India, the word *deva* means a god, or deity. The root *div* means 'to shine.' It is *deus* in Latin, and these two roots gave rise to the English words divine and devil. In the Avestan language (the language of the Avesta), *daevas* are demons of lust or doubt. The Avesta has many demons, and many of them resemble the demons in the Vedas. Other related words are the Avestan word *Sauru* and the Vedic word *Saru* (or *Sarva*). Both mean 'the arrow of death.' Hebrew has a word, *sar*, which means prince. Is there a relationship?

The Hindu god of fire is Agni. Fire is *atas* in Persian, *ignis* in Latin, the root of the word igneous, which is a type of rock that comes from hot lava. The Hindu moon god was Soma. And the *soma* plant was the source of the divine juice that Hindu priests

---

[3] Bryant, pp. 131–3. Bryant discusses this along with the linguistics of river names.

use in their rituals. The Persian counterpart to Soma is Haoma, an intoxicant used by Zoroastrian priests in their ceremonies. Priests of both the Avesta and the Vedas used hallucinogens. We are not sure what plants either the Soma of India or the Haoma of Iran came from originally, but today priests might use ephedra, crushed pomegranate leaves or pomegranate juice. One could speculate about whether this traditional use of drugs in ritual explains why the Indian subcontinent is so open to the recreational use of marijuana.

Experts tell us that the ceremony of drinking Haoma in Persia resembles the Soma sacrifice in the Vedas, and that it also resembles the Lord's Supper.[4] The Lord's Supper is supposed to have been a Jewish Passover Seder, in which the participants drank wine, but they ingested no drugs, as far as we know.

The Zoroastrian Yima (also called Yama), or first man, corresponds to the Hindu Yama, the son of the sun god. Yama was a twin, a common theme in both traditions. In the Rigveda, the twins Yama and Yami were chosen for populating the world, but they refused. In the Iranian tradition a similarly named first couple appears, but the female somehow evaporates from the scene. This same story of Divine Twins entered the Islamic tradition as a story of a young woman who was pursued into heaven by twin angels.

The Zoroastrian Yima and the Hindu Yama both go on to have complex and elaborate histories, many aspects of which are similar. Most important, both play a literally seminal role in populating the world. The excellent discussion by Puhvel provides more details, but their complexity may leave us wading in the weeds.

There are more correlations. Among the gods in the Vedas is Aryaman, who corresponds to Airyaman in the Avestas. In fact, the word Aryanam stands for Aryan, and the word airya referred to Iran. The great god Indra of the Vedas was the most important god in the literature of that era, and in the Avestas, Indara is a god of the warrior class.

---

[4] Paul Carus, *The History of the Devil and the Idea of Evil*, (1900) (Reprinted 2004 by Kessinger Publisher LLC, Whitefish MT).

Priests are called "athaurvan," in the Avesta, clearly related to the word "atharvan" in India."[5] Both societies had priests, and early Indian and Persian societies were organized along similar lines. Even today, Hindu society is divided into castes: Of the four major castes, at the top are the Brahmins, who are teachers and intellectuals. Next are the Kshatriyas, the warriors; followed by Vaishyas, the traders; and last the Shudras, who were assigned menial jobs. Below these were untouchables, though this category officially no longer exists. In Persia before Zoroaster, there were three main categories – priests, warriors, and herders – all of whom had their own gods. These formal distinctions were erased in Iran with the advent of Islam, though sociologists point to stratifications that remain by income, occupation and geographic location. In India, Gandhi faught the caste system, working especially hard to eliminate the untouchable category. This was daunting, but one could say that he had a modicum of success.

By the ninth century CE, a major work of literature appeared in Persia, the *Bundahishn*. This combined generous heapings of Zoroastrian mythology, cosmology and astronomy, and it mixed them with a thick brew of Indian, Greek and Jewish cultures, flavored with Christianity, Gnosticism and Manicheanism. All these contemporary domestic and foreign influences make it almost impossible to disambiguate the Zoroastrian roots from this new material. Only using the *Bundahishn*, it now would be difficult to separate ancient Persian thought from the influences of other religions.

Now we are getting closer to answering our original question: why do Jews keep travelling to India?

Is it the historical network of ancient commercial connections? Is it the surprise of finding familiar customs in a strange land or the attraction of enjoying something completely different? Have Jews come to escape threats to their way of life? Do Jews have a special predisposition for studying Indian philosophy? If so, why?

Or is this the allure of India's pure exoticism?

---

[5] Kohler, Kaufmann and Jackon, A.V.W., 'Zoroastrianism', *Jewish Encyclopedia.com*,
http://www.jewishencyclopedia.com/articles/15283-zoroastrianism

CHAPTER FOURTEEN.
SO MANY TRAVELS AND
COMMONALITIES

Jews are drawn to India for many reasons, but surely part of it is the pure wonderment of travel there.

> *In the 1970s, we visited north India, attempting to schedule our trip late enough in the year for the Himalayas to thaw out from the long winter, but early enough to avoid the onset of the monsoons. One day we went to a park where the visitors ride on an elephant. The elephants were decorated with colored chalk patterns on their foreheads, and tourists were seated on cushions atop the elephants.*
>
> *The elephants marched majestically, the tourists swaying gently from side to side, entranced, as we progressed through the jungle. Greenery caressed us on either side. A party of south Indian girls was riding ahead of us, resplendent in brightly colored silk saris, smiling happily. Suddenly the sky opened. The monsoon had started, a month early, and we were soaked. The decorations on the elephants' foreheads were washed away. The girls ahead of us were drenched, sputtering with mouths full of water, their silk saris stuck to their skins, and giggling uncontrollably. That was my India.*

The Israeli who travels in India will find ancient walls, temples, and picturesque archeologic remnants scattered across the country, many of them dramatically reminiscent of those in Israel, where spectacular Roman ruins are found in many tourist sites, not only in Caesaria, but also in locations such as Bet Shean and

239

Tzipori. As Israelis know, archeologists working at Tel Dan in the Galilee have found a Canaanite stele (carved monumental rock) with an inscription in Aramaic dating back to 802 BCE. On it, the King of Damascus brags of his victories over the king of the House of David and the king of Israel, the first mention of King David in all the archeological findings of Israel.

In the enormity of India, spectacular archeology may be seen in seemingly countless sites. In the southeastern state of Tamil Nadu, in the city of Maduri, sits the vast complex of Meenakshi Temple. It is believed to be at least 2,000 years old, and legend has it founded by Lord Shiva 2,500 years ago. It has 14 gopurams – high carved towers over entrance gates – a hall of a thousand pillars, and an estimated 33,000 sculptures. When we visited, we were stunned by the huge, elaborate structures that surrounded us as we walked through the grounds, and by the incredibly profuse amount of sculpture, all painted with lovely, faded colors. In contrast to many archeological sites we have seen across the world, it was completely intact and in daily use. Since then, as part of their continuing upkeep, they have repainted portions of it with colors that are jarringly bright, but they will fade.

Some of the best conserved archeologic findings are in Delhi. It would be hard to forget the first time I saw Humayan's Tomb. At that time, many years ago, it looked like a run-down preliminary model for the Taj Mahal. Now it has been cleaned, beautified and landscaped. Then, it was sleeping in a state of dusty, picturesque neglect. What I remember best was a rather aggressive snake charmer strategically positioned in a sand lot outside of the tomb.

One of the most beautifully preserved sites is in central Delhi, anchored by the towering Islamic Qutub Minar, which is surrounded by a mosque, tombs, and a magical iron pillar. Walking around the grounds felt like a visit to the old city of Jerusalem, all monuments, old walls and giant stones. And one of the featured artifacts is the iron pillar of Emperor Ashoka, one of many that he had erected all over the country, well over 2,000 years ago. Famed for being made of cast iron but never rusting, it is quite remarkable. I, as every tourist must, put my back to it and tried to touch my hands behind the column. As I already knew, nobody can. What I did not know at the time was that there are many more Ashoka pillars in northern India.

> *In 2006 my husband and I were in India for a legal conference in Bhopal, which is in the middle of a rural region.[1] A British judge with us, Michael Fysh, was an old India hand, and he had read about a nearby village that was supposed to have an Ashoka pillar. Several of us accepted his invitation to visit it with him. We drove there along something that passed for a road but really was just a narrow strip of asphalt slaloming around massive potholes. When we arrived, we found that the village was celebrating a local festival in a rather barren looking park that surrounded the pillar, and their animals were left to rest. As a result, we had to tiptoe to the park between massive black water buffalo, with huge horns, who were taking a bovine midday nap in the streets around it. Not knowing what their attitude toward us would be, we virtually held our collective breath as we made our way around them. Once we reached the park safely, we could see the pillar up close. It was the same as the one in Delhi, black cast iron, no rust, standing proudly in its ancient glory, entrusted to the loving care of rural India.*

Travel from the land of Israel to India is not new. The Bible is clear that there was trade between King Solomon's Israel and India. It is written in 1 Kings 10:22: "...once in three years came the navy of Tharshish, bringing gold, and silver, ivory, and apes, and peacocks." Tharshish may have been Carthage or it may have been in North Africa; at least it was located on the Mediterranean. Apparently, King Solomon wanted gold from India for his temple ornaments. We read in 1 Kings 9:27, "And Hiram sent his men – sailors who knew the sea – to serve in the fleet with Solomon's men. They sailed to Ophir and brought back 420 talents of gold, which they delivered to King Solomon." Ophir was India, according to tradition. The sea trade that these verses describe apparently consisted of joint expeditions of King Solomon and

---

[1] The reader may recall that this was the site of one of the worst industrial accidents in the history of India, the result of a gas leak in a Union Carbide plant in 1984.

King Hiram of Tyre in the ninth century BCE,[2] departing either from a Red Sea port or the Mediterranean and sailing to India.

But there was more than one ancient connection. A recent article[3] reports on research in Tel Megiddo and Tel Erani in which archeologists studied food found in dental remains from as far back as the 16th century BCE, 3,600 years ago. Caught in these teeth, they found traces of soybeans, bananas and the spice turmeric, which must have come from India. According to the researchers, this is the oldest evidence ever found of trade between the land of Israel and Southeast Asia, presumably passing through Mesopotamia or Egypt, with which the Mediterranean communities had a lively trade.

We know that the Persian Achaemenid King Darius I sent an expedition to the Indus Valley, and we know that the Royal Road of Persia connected with branches of the Silk Road that passed through northern India and Kashmir. From there it connected with the capital of the Maurya Empire, a city in India now called Patna. Chakravarti writes that the Hebrew word for India, *hodu*, may have come from the name for this land that was used in the Achaemenid Persian inscriptions of that time.

The Muslim Abbasid capital was Baghdad, and the principal port was on the Persian Gulf. Contemporary authors documented trade between Baghdad and India, describing the merchants as Arabs and multilingual Jews. Their ships traveled west to Spain and east to India; their trade networks transported merchandise to and from China. Also, merchants from the Egyptian Fatimid Caliphate plied their trade through the seas. In time, many Jews and Syrian Christians from these trading communities eventually settled in Cochin and other coastal cities of India during the tenth and eleventh centuries CE.

One incomparable source of information on this Jewish trade, as well as on other religious, cultural and political matters,

---

[2] Ranabir Chakravarti, 'Reaching out to Distant Shores: Indo-Judaic Trade Contacts (Up to CE 1300),' Chap 1 in Katz, Nathan et al ed, *Indo-Judaic Studies in the Twenty-first Century: A view from the Margin*, (New York: Palgrave MacMillan, 2007), p. 22.

[3] Benzion, Yakir, 'Israelis Discover Holy Land was Global Trade Center in Biblical Times,' *United with Israel*, Dec. 22, 2020.

was found in a repository of Jewish documents in a synagogue in Cairo. This is known as the Cairo *genizah*, from the Persian word *ganza*, meaning treasury. Accumulated over 900 years, this contained medieval letters and records of Jewish merchants whose business affairs stretched from North Africa to the Malabar and Konkan Coasts of India. And many of these letters demonstrated cordial relations between Jewish, Muslim and Indian merchants, both on a business and on a personal level.

Richard Marks writes[4] that he has found 19 references to India in the Jewish medieval literature. Many of these are hearsay or speculation, but at least some seem to reflect actual visits to India, in which the travelers did learn something. In other cases, the stories were legends or parables in which an Indian wise man is given brilliant lines to speak. Or, as the sources confabulate, telling exaggerated tales of exotic beasts and people, adding to the mystique of India as a home of forest women with hooves as feet, of a great river that flowed out of the Garden of Eden, of sly conjurers, and of bearded sages.

How did any of these traders travel such distances? The distance from Baghdad to Jerusalem is 646 miles, today a 13-hour drive on a good day. In the American west, the old pony express made 30 miles a day. Using that metric, the trip from Baghdad to Jerusalem would have taken a good 22 days, even with navigable roads and without highway robbers. The trip from Baghdad to India would have been 1,963 miles longer by road, if there was a road. In short, it would have been 88 days of travel by pony express, if there were roads, and no mountains, wars, bandits or monsoons. On top of that, we learned in Petra, Jordan, that the ancient Nabateans supported themselves by levying taxes, or transit fees, on travelers who came through a chokepoint on the King's Highway. We do not know how many other entrepreneurs along that highway utilized the same economic model. We do read that the ancient Romans could sail from a Red Sea Port in

---

[4] Marks R.G. (2007) 'Hindus and Hinduism in Medieval Jewish Literature,' Chap. 3 In: Katz N., Chakravarti R., Sinha B.M., Weil S. (eds) *Indo-Judaic Studies in the Twenty-First Century*. Palgrave Macmillan, New York. https://doi.org/10.1057/9780230603622_4

Egypt to Cranganore in South India in 40 days. Sometimes travel by ship is better.

We know that first century BCE Buddhist traders sailed back to the Middle East from India with Alexandrian merchants, and they are believed to have influenced Gnostic, and possibly Christian thinking. We also know that Jews were exposed to Hindu thought through books written by Greek historians. Thus, Hindu and Buddhist ideas could have invaded the Jewish world through multiple channels. At least one famous philosopher thought so. Aristotle[5] wrote that Jews were descended from Indian philosophers, meaning that they were their intellectual heirs. They have even referred to themselves using the same descriptions. Brahmins have been called a community of priests. The Jews called themselves a Kingdom of Priests. Of course, neither one had a monopoly on priests.

A Greek writer from 300 BCE[6] once served as an ambassador to Tamil Nadu in southern India. In his writings, he mentions "the sea margarita [pearl] as it is called in the Indian tongue." This caught my eye, because *margolit* is the Hebrew word for pearl.

In a dialogue between the Dalai Lama and a group of learned Jews, as chronicled in *The Jew and the Lotus,*[7] the Jewish participants told the Dalai Lama that there had been many past contacts between Jews, Buddhists and Hindus.

Nathan Katz began with the linguistics. In the Hebrew Bible, the words for ginger and for ivory have Sanskrit roots, presumably because of ancient trade relations. The word *pilpul* – the technique by which pairs of Jewish religious students study and debate – also has a Sanskrit root, the word pepper, used in this case to indicate a sharp debate. He said that the Buddhist concept of *shunyata*, or emptiness, passed from India to the Jews, then to the Arabs, and in Arab writing, it became the basis for the concept of zero. We might add that the Hindi word *darshan* means

---

[5] Goodman, Hananiya Ed, *Between Jerusalem and Benares – Comparative Studies in Judiasm and Hinduism* (Albany: State University of New York Press, (1994), pp. 46–7.

[6] Parpola, p. 153.

[7] Kamenetz, Rodger, *The Jew in the Lotus,* (New York: HarperSan Francisco, 1994), pp. 68–9.

a teaching session with a holy person or the viewing of a deity. In Hebrew, a lesson in biblical interpretation is called a *drash* (or *midrash*), and in Arabic *daras* means lesson. The common root is apparent.

Jewish ceremonies during the holiday of Sukkot feature a large citrus fruit called an ethrog. This word can be traced from the Tamil of southern India to Persia, where it became a *turung*. It also became the Mandaic word *trunga*, and it finally appeared in Jewish Babylonian Aramaic as *ethroga*.[8]

Next, we come to the six-pointed star.[9] This originally was a Mesopotamian fertility symbol. Only in medieval times did it become known as the Jewish star. It may have been brought to India by the Aryans, and in India it became a symbol of Shakti, the Mother. This star remains a good luck symbol in India, and it is often depicted on stone monuments. In the Hindu esoteric tradition, the star consists of two triangles, one pointing upward to represent the male, and the other pointing downward to represent the female. In tantric Buddhism, the six-pointed star is the symbol of the cervix.

There is an analogy in Zoroastrian art, which used a Persian mandala with a *Shamseh* motif. This is a circle surrounded by rays and other patterns, representing the sun. Sun is *shemesh* in Hebrew, *Shams* in Arabic. Interestingly, In Persian wood inlay work, the shamseh patterns are six-pointed stars, what we call Jewish stars. Who got the star from whom? Writers have ventured that some Hindu traditions, such as the six-pointed star, could have entered Jewish Kabbalistic thought through Sufism.

All that said, it may be something of a surprise while you are huffing and puffing up steep steps to a Hindu temple in India when you look down and see a six-pointed "Jewish star" carved into a mossy stone along the stairs. Of course, it also is a shock to see a swastika carved into another step, even if it is displayed 'backwards'. Both the star and the swastika are considered auspicious signs in Hinduism.

---

[8] Goodman, p. 30.
[9] Kamenetz, p. 221.

Indian traders may have brought Tamil and Sanskrit words to Israel through their trade with southern Arabia,[10] but they brought more than that. Goodman writes that a rabbinic parable about the patriarch Abraham has its origin in an Indian legend.

> In the Jewish parable, Abraham saw the stars come out, and he thought they were gods, until they disappeared at dawn. When the sun came up, he again thought it was God, until the sun set. Then the moon came up, but it too went down. Abraham now exclaimed that it must be God who set them all in motion.

> In the Indian tale, a sage saved a little mouse from death, and when he brought it home, he changed it into a maiden. When she came of age, he asked the sun to marry her, but the sun said that the clouds are more powerful because they can hide the sun. He went to the clouds, but they said that the wind was more powerful because the wind could blow the clouds away. He went next to the wind, but it said that the mountains are more powerful, because they remain standing no matter how hard the wind blows. Then he went to the mountains, who said that mice are more powerful because they can gnaw holes in mountains. So, he changed the maiden back into a mouse, and he found a fine young mouse to be her husband.

A leader of the Babylonian Jewish community, Saadia Gaon, discussed Hindu theological views in his books. Kalilah wa-Dimnah, a medieval Muslim writer, based many of his stories on Indian fables, and it was a Jew who had translated the fables from Sanskrit to Arabic.[11] Several medieval Jewish writers discussed Indian culture, though mostly they treated it as a semi-mythical source of wisdom.

More recently, a nineteenth century Hindu thinker, Arumuga Navalar, published a booklet of arguments borrowed from the Torah, written in Tamil, to defend the worship of Shiva and to refute Protestant critics of Hinduism.[12] In the booklet, he presents

---

[10] Goodman, p. 10, 34–5.
[11] Brill, p. 19.
[12] Goodman, p. 55–84.

the worship of Shiva as inherently monotheistic, describing all the other Hindu deities as minor gods who were servants of Shiva.

Sarmad Kashani was a sixteenth century Armenian-born Jew who traveled as a merchant to India. A poet and mystic, he was responsible for a translation of the Torah into Persian. He also may have converted to Islam, while remaining a secret Jew. In India, when Aurangzeb rounded up accused infidels, he beheaded him.[13] Because he was involved with Sufism, Islam and his own Jewish faith, it has been speculated that Kashani introduced some Jewish ideas, through Sufism, to India.

IDEAS WE HAVE IN COMMON

Holdrege[14] has taken a serious look at whether Hindu or Buddhist thinking resembles Judaism. She starts from the texts. In the Brahmanical tradition of India, the Vedas are the absolute authority for orthodox practice. In Judaism, the ultimate authority is the Torah. Both religions have important traditions of practice, observance and legal systems, and their legal systems cover sacrifices, purity codes and dietary laws. To this Nathan Katz would add that both "value practice over doctrine."[15]

Both have sacred languages and a sacred land. Both go back so far in time that their origins are impossible to date. From the beginning, both had oral traditions that their priests memorized and transmitted flawlessly from generation to generation. In both, the oral law eventually was written down to form a massive body of sacred texts that synthesize parable, poetry, prayer, legalisms and commentary. Both also have a tradition of revelation that they believe is the direct word of the Divine. Both have rites of passage like the Jewish Bar Mitzvah, and there are similarities between their ceremonies.

Holdrege also writes[16] that the two religions are "concerned with issues of family, ethnic and cultural integrity, blood lineages,

---

[13] Kamenetz, p. 249.
[14] Holdrege, Barbara A., *Veda and Torah – Transcending the Textuality of Scripture* (Albany: State University of New York Press, 1996).
[15] Katz et al, p. 115.
[16] Holdrege, in Katz et al, p. 89.

and the intergenerational transmission of traditions." Both religions historically have been confined to one people, who lived in one land, with a distinctive culture, to which each has been deeply committed for many centuries.

In 2007, a Hindu-Jewish summit took place in Delhi.[17] In part the impetus for this meeting was anxiety felt by Hindu participants because Christian missionaries were pressing to convert them. As they made clear, they wanted to join forces with the Jews, on the theory that both Judaism and Hinduism had been persecuted, were targets of terror attacks and of proselytism, yet remained non-missionary. Discussions between the two groups of representatives focused on what the religions have in common. The ones they cited were the idea of a priesthood, laws of purity and impurity, legal codes, dietary laws, and devotion to a sacred land. The Hindus also wanted to correct the record and to assert clearly that they are not idol-worshippers; they are monotheistic believers in one God. In the joint statement, God was not defined, but was characterized as universal, as the first cause and as comprising all things. The question of whether all Jews and all Hindus would agree on this definition was set aside for the moment.

Among the speakers were distinguished representatives of both religions. Sri Swami Gurusharnanandji said that the four Vedas were not written. They were revealed. And he knew that Jewish traditionalists believe that the first five books of the Jewish bible were revealed. He also mentioned some lesser points. Both religions employ immersion in water for ritual purity. Both have lunar calendars. And much more.

Sri Sadhu Madhava Priyadasji said, "Abraham, in our meaning, is connected to a famous phrase, "Aham brahmasmi." He continued, "This is similar to the word "Abraham." We have mentioned this, but the reader also may see the relationship to the word 'Brahmin'. Another speaker noted that the Hebrew greeting Shalom (peace) can be divided into Shal- and -om.

---

[17] 'Report of the Hindu-Jewish Leadership Summit', Feb. 5–7, 2007, New Delhi, India,
http://www.millenniumpeacesummit.org/1st-Hindu-Jewish_Summit_Report-Final.pdf

Shalom is said constantly in Israel, especially to mean hello and goodbye. In a sense, this word is the mantra of the country. And in India, the syllable *Om* is the best-known of all Hindu mantras.

With much covered and much more left to address, the two parties agreed to set up mutual work groups and to plan their next summit in Israel. Accordingly, the Second Hindu-Jewish Leadership Summit took place in Jerusalem in February 2008 as an initiative of the World Council of Religious Leaders, with the participation of the Chief Rabbinate of Israel, the American Jewish Committee and a Hindu umbrella group called Dharma Acharya Sabha. On the Hindu side, a prime mover was Swami Dayananda Saraswati, and on the Jewish side it was Rabbi David Rosen. After the plenary summit in Jerusalem, follow-up meetings were held in Haifa.

One more summit was held in 2009 in Washington, D.C., but there were no more, because the first two had "sparked violent protests by Muslims in and outside India, [suspicious of] the emergence of an anti-Islamic alliance."[18] Nevertheless, the declarations that emerged from the 2007 and 2008 summits were impressive.

Of all the affirmations released by the 2008 summit, several points are particularly worth quoting verbatim in whole or in part:

1. "the participants reaffirmed their commitment to deepening this bilateral relationship predicated on the recognition of One Supreme Being, Creator and Guide of the Cosmos; shared values; and similar historical experiences."

2. "It is recognized that the One Supreme Being, both in its formless and manifest aspects, has been worshipped by Hindus over the millennia. This does not mean that Hindus worship 'gods' and 'idols.' The Hindu relates to only the One Supreme Being when he/she prays to a particular manifestation."

---

[18] 'Religious Dialogues: Hindus and Jews; Indian Muslims and Jews' | *The Jewish People Policy Institute* (jppi.org.il).

3. "Svastika is an ancient and greatly auspicious symbol of the Hindu tradition. It is inscribed on Hindu temples, ritual altars, entrances, and even account books...The participants recognize that this symbol is, and has been sacred to Hindus for millennia, long before its misappropriation."

The theological points in this statement tell us where the participants believed they were at that time, but would other representatives of the two faiths necessarily agree with this politically correct joint statement? Were some potential points of contention left out? Is this closeness between the two faiths something new?

YES, NO, AND A POTPOURRI OF OBSERVATIONS

Having posed the question of the antiquity of the connections between Judaism and Hinduism, and having given it careful consideration, we will have to admit to the reader that we find it unanswerable. We can illustrate many, many examples of closeness between the two traditions and religions, but, apart from some objective dates in the historical record, it is impossible to date most of the mutual influences or connections. Anyhow, they would have taken place gradually, and, considering the age of these traditions, it would be reasonable to think that the relationships between them could have developed over the course of centuries.

We cannot make a scholarly, definitive argument about who influenced who, or when, but on the other hand we have not set out to prove such a thesis. In the end, all we really want to know is why Jews feel such an attraction to Hinduism and such comfort in a Hindu milieu, nothing more than that. We invite the reader to join now in a survey of similarities, going beyond the ones that we have discussed already. Some of these are striking, some subtle, but all are highly evocative.

While the Temple still was standing on Mt. Moriah in Jerusalem, the Jews held three pilgrimage festivals a year, observed on the holidays of Passover, Shavuot, and Sukkot. On these occasions, they bathed in the Pool of Siloam, then they joined a vast procession of pilgrims who carried or led their animal sacrifices up a broad Roman road to the Temple. Today, with no Temple and no sacrifices, Jews simply hold small processionals around their synagogues, carrying their Torah. In Israel they also have large yearly gatherings in front of the Kotel, a wall of the platform that King Solomon had built for the Temple, but these are not pilgrimages.

Hindus today continue their ancient tradition of a *yatra*, a religious pilgrimage in which large groups trek to a holy site, often a famous temple, the Ganges or a revered mountain. And they hold local processionals in which elaborately decorated chariots transport elegantly attired gods through the streets of their city and back to their temple. We once watched a small local procession in which worshippers paraded their god through the streets and then back, accompanied by joyous music and song.

Every fall, Jews observe Yom Kippur as a Day of Atonement; this is a 24-hour fast day that comes ten days after the Jewish New Year. Hindus observe Navarti, also in the fall, also spanning 10 days, and often distinguished by fasting. On that holiday they celebrate the triumph of good over evil. On Yom Kippur the Jews seek to triumph over their own evil, meaning their own sins, but a direct analogy between the two holidays would be a stretch.

The Hindu festival of spring is called Holi, and that celebrates the triumph of good. And what a triumph it is! They sing, dance in the streets, drink and throw colored powder all over each other and over any hapless bystanders, with reckless abandon. Would-be observers are warned that they must wear their oldest clothes, because they will end up drenched by water pistols and water-filled balloons, ultimately looking like they had been attacked by a very wet rainbow.

In their spring festival, Purim, which falls at almost the same time, Jews celebrate with a huge costume party. Little girls love to dress as Queen Esther and little boys as King Ahasuerus or the wicked Haman. They swing noisemakers, sing, dance and hold street fairs all over Israel. Once in Florentin, an old neighborhood in south Tel Aviv, we elbowed our way through crowds of costumed revelers, dodging street stands sloshing with free beer, and trying not to eat too many of the refreshments that were handed out everywhere.

A major festival of the Hindu year is Diwali, celebrated for five days as the 'Festival of Light.' As both religions have a lunar calendar, with an extra month added every few years, the Jewish holiday of Chanukah regularly falls in the same lunar month as Diwali, and Chanukah is celebrated for eight days as the 'Festival of Light.'

Both religions have traditions of ritual immersion. Hindus travel to bathe in the Ganges on ceremonial occasions, and most large temples have an adjacent temple tank, or pool, that may be as large as a small lake. These can be used for bathing, or they may function as water reservoirs. For their immersion rituals, and for Orthodox women to use monthly, Jews bathe in a *mikveh*, a pool that must have flowing water.

Hindus, Buddhists and members of the closely related Jain religion typically are vegetarian. Jews are not necessarily pure vegetarians, but there are strict dietary rules for the observant. From the sea, they are limited to eating only fish, no shellfish. They cannot eat birds of prey or land animals that do not chew their cud or have split hooves. Rules are strict about who can slaughter an animal and how they can do it (It must be with one stroke of a knife). The blood must be drained, because of the prohibition against consuming blood. Jews also are prohibited from eating milk and meat products at the same meal, and the rabbis have devised a long list of ancillary restrictions to make sure they comply with the basic rules. Of course, many of these rules are short-circuited if one is vegetarian. Jews say that the laws force them to be as close to vegetarian as possible without giving up meat. Lately though, many Jews, especially the young, have become vegetarian. Because of the dietary rules, India does not present a big problem for Jews who limit themselves to its delicious vegetarian food, a big advantage for Jewish travelers.

In a sense, Hindu dietary laws have much in common with Jewish laws. Hindus cannot drink the milk of sheep, camels or any other animal that does not have a split hoof. They cannot eat a variety of five-toed animals, and they have additional restrictions that resemble those of Judaism.[19]

---

[19] Bettany, pg 36. Many or most Hindus are vegetarian, so these detailed laws matter to very few people.

Now we return to the matter of ascetics. Apart from some historic monastic orders, asceticism is not a normal part of Jewish culture or life. Judaism is focused on this world. Rabbis are expected to marry and to have children. Wine is enjoyed at festive meals, and the Sabbath evening meal is supposed to be as tasty and as beautifully presented as possible. During the day on the Sabbath, people enjoy a leisurely walk to and from the synagogue, guests may be invited for lunch; they study a bit, and perhaps they take a midafternoon nap with their spouse.

There is no normative tradition of monks or nuns in Judaism. There are no religious orders in that sense, strictly observant sects yes, but no convents or cloistered religious communities. That is significantly different from Christianity, and from many Buddhist traditions. Yet, numerous Tibetan Buddhist monasteries used to be massive, elaborately decorated near-fortresses, dramatically located on mountain sides and home to thousands of monks, before the Chinese takeover. In Nepal we met a Tibetan nun from a community of Buddhist nuns who had been displaced from Tibet. In Dharamshala we saw whole replicas of Tibetan monasteries. Meanwhile in Tibet, the Chinese destroyed some 6,000 Buddhist monasteries, the cultural and religious riches of an entire civilization.

Again in contrast with Judaism, India has a long tradition of Hindu ascetics, regarded as holy men, *sadhus*. Some Hindus choose, after they have fulfilled their responsibilities to their families, to leave home and become ascetics, *sannyasis*. These are itinerant holy men who have renounced the world, who only own the clothes on their backs and who beg for food. They might live as hermits, or they might belong to a type of monastic order. They may wear saffron robes, or they may wear no robes. Often, they leave their hair long, and they mark their foreheads with the symbol of their god, today usually Shiva or Vishnu.

India has an estimated 4–5 million Hindu holy men. In addition, there may be another 6,000 Jain ascetics, conspicuously dressed in white clothing, or no clothing. The Hindus often are solitary itinerant men who have renounced the trappings of society, although women too – less commonly – may choose a life of renunciation. Usually these are widows who choose to live within religious communities.

Among the few Jews who could be called ascetic, one was Judah ha-Nasi, a second century rabbi noted for his asceticism who was the chief editor of the Mishnah. On a visit to the Cave of Judah ha-Nasi in Bet She'arim in the Galilee, we could see that his has the place of honor among all the burial caves. Another group given to fasting and ascetic practices were the early Karaites of the seventh and eighth century. Some Jewish mystics in the Middle Ages, well into the 13th century, were ascetics too, and they inflicted severe mortifications on themselves in order to merit ascending to heaven and meeting the heavenly sages.

Some Jews knowingly have undergone actual martyrdom, but usually they were martyred because they refused to convert. One of the prayers recited on Rosh Hashanah is *unetaneh tokef*, written in the eleventh century by Rabbi Amnon of Mainz. On that High Holiday he was horribly tortured, by order of the Bishop of Mainz, for refusing to convert to Christianity. From there he was carried to the synagogue where he was able to stay alive just long enough to recite the prayer to the congregation, and then he died. Today this story is part of a martyrology service read on that holiday, one from which many congregants recoil in horror.

Almost two thousand years ago, one community became martyrs because they had no choice. This is the story of Masada. During the 73–74 CE Roman conquest of the land of Israel, a group of 960 besieged Jewish rebels made their last stand at Masada, on a mountaintop overlooking the Dead Sea. Finally, the Romans built a great ramp up to the top of the mountain. Once it was clear that they could not hold out any longer, according to the story, all the Jews on the mountain committed suicide. This is a popular tourist site, and for many years, the Israeli army was sworn in here, until Israelis insisted that they stop it. They objected in part because some aspects of this tale are in question, and in part because critics say that mass suicide is not an Israeli ideal. Israelis admire those who live and fight.

In India holy men are regarded with great respect. In the vast masses of humanity at the Magh Mela every year, they stand out distinctively. And at the Kumbh Mela festival that is held every

12 years, with up to 10 million pilgrims bathing in the Ganges to obtain *moksha* (liberation from the cycle of rebirth), these holy men, stark naked, their bodies smeared with ashes, cadaverously thin, heads shaved, are the first to be granted the honor of ritually dipping into the water, the assembled pilgrims contemplating them in awe.

Let there be no mistake though, there is a parallel India – the world of Bollywood. Here, well-fed actors in gorgeous clothing portray a life of luxury while they sing of broken hearts and heartless mothers-in-law. They portray the same over-the-top aspirations as those of Jewish families that follow their son's Bar Mitzvah with an outrageous party that costs thousands. And that is little different from the Hindu custom of throwing wedding parties that last a full week, each evening more lavish than the last, if they are rich enough. Finally, on the day of the actual wedding, in his big moment the groom may ride a white horse to the festivities, escorted by joyous revelers, who are singing, dancing and playing music. At its most decadent, the entire wedding party may be dripping with gold and diamonds. Though wretched excess is not exclusive to either community, I would give the edge to the Indians from what I have seen.

Continuing the comparisons, Jews always say that if there are two Jews in a room, there are three opinions. This is true of Hindus too, who are nicely captured in the title of a book by Amartya Sen, *The Argumentative Indian*. Indians are endemically chatty, love to argue, and do not hesitate to take their disputes to court. The early Parsi community in Bombay benefitted from all the legal cases that fell in the laps of their lawyers, and when the Sindhis came to Bombay after partition, their lawyers too were awash in lawsuits. A surgeon colleague of mine from India, very political and very much of an activist, loves to give speeches. Colleagues have always said that the most dangerous place to be in a room was to get between Dr. X and a microphone.

Outside of that room, culturally, Israelis and Indians may most resemble each other in a market. In Middle Eastern markets, one can buy ancient Nabatean coins, and not-so ancient ones. The shopper can buy Roman glass or Phoenician glass that is 1,000 to 2,000 years older, made by the people who first invented glass blowing. She can browse shops filled with bronze ritual objects and other artifacts that the owners brought back from Iran, or she can buy questionable antiquities from a dubious store in the flea market. Whatever it is, wherever it is, bargaining is expected.

The Khan Market, or any other market in Delhi feels exactly like the Arab souk of the Old City of Jerusalem or the Flea Market of Jaffa. All these markets delight the traveler with endless shops that are festooned with imported textiles and embroidered clothes that hang over barrels of beads, bins of colored stones, antique buttons, valuable antiquities, tee-shirts with funny sayings, and charming counterfeits, luring them in with a come-hither look. The new is artfully larded with the old, the rusted with the shiny, the ancient with not-so-ancient. Again, bargaining is required.

In India, markets like this are all over Mumbai, Delhi, large cities, small cities, tourist sites, small towns and posh neighborhoods, but for serious antiquing, I enjoy Sundar Nagar, its shops arranged around a quiet corner of Delhi, all filled chockablock with treasures. Then again, the completely unexpected is a specialty of India. Once on a rickshaw in the noisy market of Old Delhi, while navigating precariously around pedestrians and goats on the street, I saw a camel caravan. And this was not even the Middle East!

So far, we have compared Israel and India, Judaism and Hinduism, but we not compared Judaism and Buddhism. There are similarities between Jews and Buddhists, and there are differences too. Now we should get a feel for the Buddhist atmosphere before we go on to the next chapter, where we will explore mystical ideas that inform all these religions.

ON BUDDHISM

In dramatic contrast to the chaos of modern India, Jews may turn to Buddhism for tranquility. Buddhists seek calm, renunciation of worldly attachments, and a way to relieve suffering. For Jews, it is comforting to find that Buddhists do not pray to a god, but they see the divine in everything. Buddhists, like Jews, seek to improve and correct the world, what Jews call *tikkun olam*. Both Jews and Buddhists emphasize ethical action, and both teach that actions have consequences. Neither community shies away from theological dispute; both incorporate debating in their religious instruction. Both cultures have a tradition of devotion to teachers, and they have great respect for scrolls, texts and manuscripts, many of which are thousands of years old. Neither of them discards worn-out books or other writings. Instead, they bury them reverently.

Struggles with anti-Semitism, attacks on Zionism and actual persecution have dogged Jews throughout their history. The so-called wandering Jew moved ceaselessly to escape attempts to convert or kill him, and even when he settled in his own country, the surrounding nations forced him to fight for survival. Buddhists, apart from the Chinese take-over of contemporary Tibet, historically have lived in quiet environments that allowed them to meditate and to work toward inner peace.

The differences between a Jewish, or Hindu environment and a Buddhist one may be profound. The quintessential Jewish city is Tel Aviv, the city that never sleeps, throbbing with activity, the people in a hurry, beset by intractable traffic, but blessed with limitless opportunity for the ambitious. Oddly, one could say all the same things about the largely Hindu city of Mumbai. In contrast, one classic model of a Buddhist site is Sanchi.

Located in central India, Sanchi admittedly is an archeologic site, not a bustling city, and it is impressive to feel how it envelops the visitor in serenity. The center of the complex is the Great Stupa of Sanchi. This massive domed structure is one of the oldest stone buildings in India, commissioned by Ashoka in the third century BCE. Later, four ornamental gateways were built around it. These are called *toranas*, and they are the prototypes of the tori gates of Japan. These, as contrasted with their counterparts in Japan, are covered with intricate carvings of mythological scenes. Next to one of the gates is the broken base of another Ashoka pillar. Surrounding this complex are fifty other Buddhist temples and stupas, which, along with the main stupa, have been meticulously restored by the Archeological Survey of India. The effect is of absolute calm.

Some ten years ago in Dharamshala, we had the good fortune to meet the 17th Gyalwang Karmapa, Ogyen Trinley Dorje, the most important Tibetan Buddhist leader after the

Dalai Lama. He was chosen by the traditional method, in which a designated group of senior Buddhist monks identify a young child who can pass tests that prove he is a reincarnation of the previous Karmapa. At age seven he was taken from his parents to his monastery to be given the necessary training. Unfortunately, the Chinese intervened, picking a different child to replace the choice of the monks. At age fourteen, the Karmapa who the Buddhists had selected, Ogyen Trinley Dorje, felt he needed to leave Tibet, and he escaped over the Himalayas to India to resettle in Dharamshala, India, near the Dalai Lama.

When we met him, he was about 24 years old. He had a wide, open face, perfectly serene, with a gentle smile. Despite a waiting room full of people bringing gifts for him, he was friendly and unhurried. Since we were introduced as friends of Ram, and Shobha was introduced as Ram's daughter, he was interested in talking with us. "Ram?" he smiled, "He is very old." Simple, direct, unpretentious, that was the impression he made. He acted like he had not a care in the world, as if he had all day to spend with us, even though the Chinese were watching him on the other side of the Himalayas, and his monks were waiting in the wings downstairs, ready for us to move on.

Buddhism evokes tranquility. Is this what Jews seek in India? If so, why study Hinduism? The raucous jousting of Mumbai intellectuals is like the loud debates of Jewish scholars in their busy study halls.

But now we are coming to the mystical, or spiritual connections that so many Jews have looked for in India, and that some have found by chance. And we have been asking whether these connections have grown out of our shared history or from the shared wisdom of our holy men. Surely, many Jewish travelers to India only know that they have found much that was familiar in what they thought would be a strange land, but they do not know why. To just take one example, why do we all hold the same number to be sacred?

CHAPTER FIFTEEN.
MYSTIC CONNECTIONS AND THE
PERSISTENCE OF MEMORY

Do Jews and Indians share memories of an ancient past, a time when our cherished sagas, allegories and legends were born? Are these the primordial memories that Carl Jung describes? He has written[1] that "as far as the collective unconscious are concerned, we are dealing with archaic – or I would say – primordial types, that is, with universal images that have existed since the remotest times." By this he means myths, esoteric teachings, and fairytales.

Yet Jung writes that much of this intuitive belief has become rote, stiff, devoid of 'wings' in the west, so that "the philosophical speculations of the educated European are attracted by the symbols of the East – those grandiose conceptions of divinity in India and the abysms of Taoist philosophy in China." That may be why Jews who grew up in a Reform Judaism that has been modernized, and stripped of its rich tradition, may look elsewhere for majesty.

In *Religion as a Chain of Memory*, Daniele Hervieu-Leger[2] goes back further, writing of *anamnesis,* a memory of things from a supposed previous existence. This occurs "when a group demonstrates...that they belong to a distinctive religion by

---

[1] Jung, C.G. *The Archetypes and the Collective Unconscious* (Princeton: Princeton University Press, 1990), pp. 5–8.
[2] Sigalow, Emily, *American JuBu,* (Princeton: Princeton University Press, 2019), p. 156. While group memories are not the same as Jungian individual memories, the concepts have something in common.

recalling the past to memory through rites." In other words, "Thus, like cultural tradition, religion may be understood as a shared understanding with a collective memory that enables it to draw upon the deep well of its past for nourishment in the increasingly secular present."

Jewish values and traditions certainly are rooted in the past. And elements of these traditions come from Jewish peregrinations through Europe, the new world, the Middle East, Africa, India, Persia and even Turkey. And before this was that ancient Aryan migration from Central Asia, whose culture still underlies theirs.

HOW DO IDEAS PASS FROM ONE RELIGION TO ANOTHER?

How much did Jews, Zoroastrians, Hindus, and Buddhists borrow from each other? Look at their stories about the creation of the world, the flood, and the end of times. They echo each other. Look at the early legal codes of the Sumerians, the Code of Hammurabi and the legal codes in the Torah. Even if wise men in times of old did not meet in academic conferences, we know that ideas have a way of floating up into the atmosphere, like spores, later to land, germinate and grow.

This phenomenon occurs in the world of science. An inventor who files a patent application may learn that similar work is being done in a laboratory of another country, or even in his own country. The idea must have been one whose time had come. Even when an idea does seem to be borrowed, it may be difficult to know who borrowed from whom. It simply may have been in the *zeitgeist*.

The Semitic alphabets are a good example. Between the seventh and eleventh centuries, both Jews and Christians created systems of dots to denote vowels in their alphabets. In Babylon between the 6th and 7th centuries, vowels were added to the Hebrew alphabet, but these were small notations on top of the consonants. In Tiberias, up to the end of the tenth century, Jewish scribes of the Ben Asher school,[3] possibly refining an older

---

[3] Werblowsky, R.J., and Wigoder, Geoffrey, *The Encyclopedia of the Jewish Religion*, (New York: Holt, Rinehart and Winston, 1965).

system,[4] added dots and other diacritical marks below the consonants of the Hebrew alphabet, and this became known as the Masoretic system, a word that came from the Hebrew word *masoret*, meaning tradition. Between the fourth and the tenth centuries, Christian scribes in Nisibis and Edessa (both now in Turkey),[5] and in Ctesiphon (close to Baghdad) instituted a similar system of dots for vowels in Aramaic (Syriac).

In Basra in the seventh century, scribes such as Al-Khalil ibn Ahmed al-Farabidi added dots and other notations to Arabic, and in the eighth century much of this work moved to Baghdad, while continuing in other locations in present day Iraq and in Damascus. By the tenth and eleventh centuries, elements of the Aramaic (Syriac) and Hebrew notation systems had merged with elements of the Arabic system.[6] It should not be a surprise that linguists see considerable overlap between these systems. If you look at a map, you will see that none of these cities are far from each other. Remember the travel times in the days of the pony express.

Did they copy each other? Well, they worked in adjacent geographic areas and during roughly the same period of history. Some think they even collaborated. Consider the evidence. My husband is a law professor and an expert on intellectual property. He says that, according to copyright law, in order to demonstrate that copying took place, the lawyer must show at the very least that the two sides had access to each other's work, and he must show similarity. Finally, he must show that one side copied. In this case, there is at least circumstantial evidence that these vowel systems were transmitted from one group of scholars to another. And just as scribes and scholars must have exchanged ideas about scripts, they must have exchanged other ideas.

We know that the scholars who compiled the Babylonian Talmud lived in Babylon under the Sassanian Persian Empire, and

---

[4] Rollston, Christopher, personal communication.

[5] Goldenberg, Gideon, *Semitic Languages*, (Oxford: Oxford University Press, 2013), p. 37.

[6] Posegay, Nick, *Connecting the Dots: The Shared Phonological Tradition in Syriac, Arabic and Hebrew Vocalization*, in *Studies in Semitic Vocalization and Reading Traditions*, ed. Aaron Hornkohl and Geoffrey Khan, (Cambridge: Open Book Publishers, 2020).

we know for instance that the Jewish concept of resurrection of the dead resembles that of the Zoroastrians. Did they ever talk while they were doing business? Did one scholar's sister ever marry the brother of a scholar from another community? Did people of either religion convert, bringing new ideas with them to their new congregations? Did a Jewish scholar occasionally argue about ideas with his Persian counterpart, or with another foreign intellectual? Or do all these ideas go back to even more ancient traditions?

The archeological record[7] shows that the people of Sassanian Mesopotamia were a mixture of Zoroastrians, Mandaeans, Manichaeans, Christians and Jews. This would have been a veritable cauldron of ideas. Talmudic anecdotes do describe meetings between Jews and Persians. Some of these interactions were in the sphere of magic and in the use of incantation bowls. These were metal bowls that had prayers engraved around their circumference, which people from all communities used in their supplications for health, babies and success.

Other interactions would have been in the field of law, because under the Sassanian legal system, the various communities were permitted to rule themselves, according to their own laws. The Ottoman Empire used this same system centuries later, dividing their subjects up according to a *millet* system. In it, each religious group would form its own self-governing political entity, called a *millet*, and each had its own court of law. Thus, adjacent communities would have been able to compare their legal systems with those of their neighbors.

Were they able to talk to one another? Jewish Babylonian Aramaic was closely related to Mandaic and to the Aramaic dialect of Eastern Christians. Middle Persian was a different language, but some Aramaic speakers could read and speak it. There are numerous stories of rabbis conversing with Persians, and there are many Persian loan words in the Bavli (the Babylonian Talmud). One rabbinical warning[8] implies that Jews studied with magi even though it was considered anathema: "And

---

[7] Secunda, Shai, pp. 16ff.
[8] Secunda, Shai, pp. 43–50.

he who learns something from a magus is worthy of death." The Persians were just as intense about preventing Zoroastrians from studying with Jews. Obviously, they must have studied with each other, or these efforts to stop them would not have been necessary.

Rabbi Gamliel is quoted[9] as saying: "For three things I like the Persians. They are modest in their eating, in the bathroom, and in sex." If he knew all that, he must have talked with them too, a lot.

THE NUMBER SEVEN

Now we come to the strange matter of the number seven[10]. No other number appears as often, with so much importance, or in so many religions of the Middle East and India as the number seven. This phenomenon is so impressive that it is worth exploring in depth. It may be one of the best illustrations of how these religions must have come from a common substrate of ideas and myths that predate all of us - ancient material that we subconsciously recognize when we travel to a new country.

In Judaism

At the beginning of the Hebrew Bible, in the Book of Genesis, God creates the world in seven days. Well, six days, because He rests on the seventh day, but the seventh day was critical. This was the one that completed and perfected creation. Moreover, in this biblical account of creation, the phrase 'it was good' occurs seven times. Note that we already have seen the number seven in other Mesopotamian creation myths, and in the Avesta.

Jewish tradition describes seven levels of creation: form, matter, combination, mineral, vegetable, animal and man. In fact, prior to the creation story in Genesis, according to mystical

---

[9] Secunda, Shai, p. 67.
[10] This section is presented with little footnoting. To do justice to the research involved would require extensive, pedantic footnotes that would try the patience of the nonacademic reader. Many of the sources are in the appended bibliography, and many others are available in standard references on Judaism, Zoroastrianism, Hinduism and Buddhism. Additional specific points may be searched by topic by asking Mr. Google.

tradition there were seven preexistent entities. Among the mysteries of the Kabbalah is the concept of seven chambers in the universe of the world of creation, *Beriyah*. Also, Kabbalah describes seven universes, and seven firmaments.

The Jewish day of rest is on the seventh day of the week, and the name of that day is *Shabbat*, שבת. The word comes from the Hebrew word for seven, *sheva*, שבע. In the Exodus story, the Israelites who entered the promised land took seven years to divide the land, and they are said to have required seven years to conquer it. For that reason, in Israel, every seventh year is consecrated as a Sabbath for the land. Called the *Shmita*, in that year the farmer cannot plow, plant or harvest. This is part of the Sabbatical cycle, which has seven cycles of *Shmita*, followed by a Jubilee (Yoval) on the fiftieth year. In that year, as we read in Leviticus 25, "each of you shall return to his own property, and each of you shall return to his family... In it you shall not sow, neither reap." In that year too, prisoners are to be freed, and debts are to be forgiven. And there will be seven Jubilee periods. Thus, in ancient Israel all slaves and prisoners were to be set free after seven years. Today, the Jubilee is problematic because all twelve tribes do not live in the land.

The saga of the number seven continues. At an Orthodox Jewish wedding, the bridal couple says seven blessings. Seven days of celebration follow the wedding, and before each meal there are seven blessings. When a baby boy is born, a ritual circumcision is performed on the eighth day, after allowing the child to remain perfect for seven days. The religious Jewish woman counts seven days for her period, then adds seven more days, after which she can resume marital relations. After a death in a Jewish family, the relatives sit home in mourning receiving well-wishers for seven days. This is called sitting shiva, again from the Hebrew word for seven. In some traditions, a ritual bath (mikveh) requires seven immersions.

On the days of the week when the Torah is read, the reading is divided into seven portions, each one with its own blessing, seven blessings in all.

The seventh month of the year, Tishrei, is sacred, and this month has been accorded the honor of four major holidays and festivals. According to the sages, Tishrei was allotted these holidays in honor of being the seventh month after the Exodus from Egypt. On the ancient Jewish calendar, there were seven major days of celebration. On Yom Kippur, the day of Atonement, the priests in the Temple sprinkled blood on the altar seven times. Two of the major Jewish holidays, Passover and Sukkot, are seven-day festivals.

The holiday that follows Passover on the Jewish calendar is Shavuot, commemorating the giving of the Ten Commandments, and the Commandments were handed down on Mount Sinai after the Jews had spent 49 days (seven times seven) in the desert. Still today, Jews carefully count out seven weeks between Passover and Shavuot, a spiritual preparation for receiving the law. On Sukkot, seventy bullocks were sacrificed as burnt offerings at the altar of the Temple in Jerusalem.

While it is not commemorated by a specific holiday, we read in Joshua 6:8 that Joshua brought down the walls of Jericho after "seven priests carrying the seven trumpets before the Lord went forward, blowing their trumpets." In all, they marched around the city each day for six days, until, on the seventh day, they marched around the city seven times, and the walls came down.

In Genesis 7:2, God commands Noah to bring seven pairs of every kind of clean animal into the ark. After the flood was over, God sealed a covenant with Noah, promising to send no more floods to the earth and giving him the Seven Laws of Noah, which – according to legend – had been given first to Adam. These are the basic moral laws for all humanity, and they are listed in the Babylonian Talmud: not to worship idols, not to curse God; not to commit murder; not to commit adultery, bestiality or sexual immorality; not to steal; not to eat flesh torn from a living animal; and to establish courts of justice. These laws are believed to be incumbent on all people. If non-Jews follow them, they are known as righteous Gentiles.

There were seven biblical matriarchs and patriarchs. Ancient Israel had seven holy cities: Beersheba, Hebron, Bethlehem, Bethel, Shechem, Safed and Jerusalem. The biblical King David was the seventh son of Yishai, and he married Bat Sheva, a name meaning 'daughter of seven'.

In the Jewish tradition, the Hebrew word for seven is the root of the word used for an oath. In the Bible, the patriarch Abraham offers a sacrifice of seven (*sheva*) lambs to satisfy an oath (*sh'vu'ah*) that he took at Be'er Sheva. This city's name consists of be'er, the word for well, and sheva, for oath. Thus the city of Beersheba is 'the well of the oath.' Alternatively, it could mean 'seven wells.'

In Egypt, Joseph is called out of prison by pharaoh to interpret two frightening dreams. The first dream is of seven lean cows and seven fat cows, and the seven lean cows devour the seven fat cows. The second dream is of seven heads of full, ripe grain growing on one stalk and seven heads of dried out grain. As in the first dream, the seven heads of dried out grain swallow the seven heads of ripe grain. Joseph explains that this meant that there would be seven years of plenty followed by seven years of famine. Joseph recommends that pharaoh choose a wise man to collect the grain from the good years and to save it for the seven years of famine. And pharaoh appoints Joseph.

Four hundred years later, the Jews escaped from Egypt and trudged through the Sinai desert, where Exodus 15:27 tells us they came across 12 wells and 70 palms in a desert oasis. These palms have been interpreted[11] as standing for 70 elders, or the 70 faces of Torah.

The great biblical commentator Ibn Ezra wrote that there were 70 aspects of the Torah, and in the 12th century CE, the eminent scholar Nahmanides, known as the Ramban, agreed with him.

The number seven plays an outsized role in Jewish wisdom books. These books teach proper behavior based on good thoughts, good words and good deeds, and they are still read today. And, these same three principles of good behavior are basic to Zoroastrianism as taught in the Avesta.

Seven wisdom books are in the Septuagint: Job, Psalms, Proverbs, Ecclesiastes, the Song of Songs (Song of Solomon), the Book of Wisdom (Wisdom of Solomon) and the Wisdom of Sirach

---

[11] Trugman, Avraham Arieh, 'The Healing Power of Trees,' *Kabbalah Online*, Chabad.org.

(Ben Sira). There also is another, the Book of Baruch, which Jews consider apocryphal, i.e., of doubtful authenticity. Among the many other wisdom books are Tobit, Judith, Maccabees I-II, Enoch and addenda to Esther and Daniel.

The wisdom book *The Bahir* lists seven voices of God heard at Mt. Sinai: 'the God of glory thunders;' 'the voice of God comes in strength;' 'the voice of God is with majesty;' 'God's voice breaks the cedars;' 'God's voice draws out flames of fire;' 'God's voice shakes the desert;' and 'God's voice makes hinds to calf, strips the forests bare and in [the] Temple, all say Glory.' The Torah was given with seven voices. As it is written, 'And all the people *saw* the voices.'

The Hebrew apocalyptic *Book of Enoch* describes seven archangels and a miraculous ascent up through multiple heavens, with a vision of the Almighty sitting above them all on a throne of glory. The highly esoteric literature called Hekhalot mysticism describes ascents through seven heavens and seven throne rooms. This material is so secret that is not even available for us to summarize it, but again it has the theme of seven heavens. We will see this theme over and over.

The Book of Ezra, written between the fifth century BCE and the second century CE, describes how God sent Ezra seven angels to lead him to heaven and how Ezra subsequently saw seven visions. In the end of his life, Ezra is given the Torah, the entire bible and 70 books of secret apocalyptic lore. Then he finally ascends to heaven.

In some works of Jewish mysticism, he who strives to reach the highest level of the heavens must pass through seven palaces. We also read about seven heavens in the Hindu Puranas, and in the Tibetan Book of the Dead. In the Tibetan book, we find descriptions of sequential stages, called *bardos*, that a soul must pass through following death. The whole process takes 49 days – seven days a week for seven weeks[12] – and there are "seven

---

[12] Bromage, Bernard, *Tibetan Yoga*, (London: The Aquarian Press, 1952), p. 54.

successive [critical or] dangerous pathways."[13] During this time, in the middle stage, the soul is met by seven Peaceful Deities, one for each day of the week. In the next part of the same middle stage, the soul is met by seven legions of Wrathful Deities[14]. At this point, the soul is subjected to frightful tests and tortures, not dissimilar from the tests that the Jewish sages faced in their ascents.

Proverbs 9:1 writes: 'Wisdom has built its house; it has carved its seven pillars.' These seven pillars have been described variously as the seven days of the week, seven pillars that support the world, or the seven sciences: grammar, rhetoric, logic, arithmetic, music, geometry and astronomy.

In biblical times there were believed to be seven planets: Mercury, Venus, Mars, Jupiter, Saturn, Sun and Moon. According to Kabbalah, there are seven gates in the Soul and seven openings in the head. There also are seven primary traits: wisdom, wealth, seed, life, dominance, peace and grace. There are seven earths, seven seas, seven rivers, seven continents, and seven deserts through which the Israelites had to pass. As the children of Israel wandered through the wilderness to the promised land, they were surrounded by seven clouds.

The ancient Sumerians[15] were the first we know of to use the term Seven Seas, and they linked them to seven planets as well as to seven heavens. The Talmudists described Israel as the land of seven seas. These were the Dead Sea, Mediterranean, Sea of Galilee, Red Sea and the Sea of Aspamia (once in northwest Syria) that surrounded Israel; the Hula Lake within it and the Birkat Ram in the Golan Heights.

---

[13] Padmasambhava, *The Tibetan Book of the Dead*, (New York: Penguin Books, 2006), p. 255. This book is long, and this was not the only source used in the above discussion. Unfortunately, summaries of this material differ from one another, so we have tried to give a general sense of it, without being pedantic.

[14] 'The Tibetan Book of the Dead: Summary, Translation and Quotes', 2003, *Study.com*, https://study.com/academy/lesson/the-tibetan-book-of-the-dead-summary-translation-quotes.html

[15] Zimmerman, Kin Ann, 'What are the Seven Seas?', Mar 6, 2013, *LiveScience*.

Persia too had seven seas, by which they meant seven tributaries of the Oxus River. Medieval Arabs spoke of navigating seven seas in their maritime trade, and the Phoenicians understood the seven seas to be parts of the Mediterranean. The ancient Greeks referred to seven seas, but these were the Aegean, Adriatic, Mediterranean, Red Sea, Persian Gulf, Black Sea, and the Caspian Sea. Medieval Europeans too named their own versions of seven seas. And today again we speak of seven seas.

The Arch of Titus was erected in Rome in honor of the Roman destruction of the Temple of Jerusalem. A dominant symbol on this arch, featured more prominently than any other plunder the Romans carried away, was a seven-branched menorah. The branches have been interpreted as representing the five planets plus the sun and the moon, seven branches of human knowledge, or the seven days of Creation.

The prophet Jeremiah (29:10) said, "For thus says the LORD: After seventy years are completed at Babylon, I will visit you and perform My good word toward you." He predicted that the Jews would remain in the Babylonian Exile for seventy years. In fact, the exile started in 586 BCE and Cyrus began liberating the Jews in 539 BCE, so it was closer to 47 years, but who is counting?

The number seven signifies completeness, repenting and returning. On the Sabbath before the New Year, the Torah reading that day uses the word for return, or to return, seven times, in order to make the return to Torah complete.

In Zoroastrianism

The prehistoric Indo-Iranian supreme deity was conceived of as sevenfold, and in Zoroastrian Persia the chief god, Ahura Mazda, was the Ruler of the Seven Worlds. The ancient Persians believed that the universe was created in seven stages, starting with the sky, and ending with primeval man. And they also believed that the earth has seven *Karshvars*, meaning divisions or climates.

According to Zoroastrians, the "world endures fourteen thousand years from the Creation to the Resurrection, "seven thousand spent in the act of creation and seven thousand in maintaining it." The world will be renovated, or rejuvenated, by seven lords.[16]

Zoroastrians describe seven heavens, seven earths and seven creations, guarded by seven gods, called *Amesa Spentas*. These are the divine entities that emanate from *Ahura Mazda*: the holy or creative spirit, good purpose, righteousness, desirable dominion, holy devotion, wholeness and immortality. The first seven days of the month are dedicated to them. Ahura Mazda and the *Amesa Spentas* were worshipped through a seven-part liturgy known as the *yasna haptanghaiti*, also known as the "worship of the seven chapters." This entailed a seven-part sacrifice.[17] Avestan texts were divided into seven chapters, like the Koran and several other major books of Persia.

The constellation Ursa Major was referred to as *Haptoiringa*, meaning seven thrones, and it was known in the Christian world as the constellation of the seven souls.

Traditionally Zoroastrians celebrate seven holy days, or feasts of obligation. The first is the Persian New Year, Nowruz; the others are called the Gahambars, six seasonal festivals that honor earth, water, plants, animals and humans. On festivals and other joyous occasions, Persians serve seven cups of wine and in some regions, they burn seven bundles of wood. In many regions, they celebrate holidays with trays that may hold seven kinds of grains, seven sweets, seven kinds of fruits, and seven varieties of dried roasted seeds.

In the Mithraism that the Romans adopted from the Persians, the soul journeys upward through seven spheres, and it passes through seven stages of secret initiation. Mithraism has seven gods, believes in seven planets and describes seven levels of heaven. The Yezidis too, although they believe in one God,

---

[16] Shahbazi, Shapur A., 'Haft (Seven) The "Heptad" and its Cultural Significance in Iranian History,' *CAIS The Circle of Ancient Iranian Studies*, 1998–2020, HAFT (seven), the "heptad" & its cultural significance in Iranian history, © cais-soas.com

[17] Boyce, pp. 21–37. Portions of this discussion have come from Mary Boyce's book, but the exact references are found in multiple places throughout the text.

believe in seven angels that all are emanations of God. They also believe in seven mysteries.

We read that there were seven wise men in Persia. In the Book of Esther, King Ahasuerus chose Esther in the third year of his reign, but he took her into his bed in the seventh year of his reign. At a great banquet, as told in Esther 1:14, "Then the king consulted the wise men who knew the times, for it was customary for him to confer with the experts in law and justice." His closest advisors were Carshena, Shethar, Admatha, Tarshish, Meres, Marsena and Memucan, the seven princes of Persia and Medea, also called the seven counselors of the king. The king employed seven eunuchs to tend the harem, and their names were variations on the names of the wise men.

The Persians had seven field commanders in their army, and Xerxes set out for war against the Greeks in the seventh year of his reign. When a Mede overthrew the Persian throne, seven nobles overthrew the Mede. This event was foreshadowed by an omen of seven eagles. These nobles then established Seven Great Houses that essentially ruled the empire under Darius.[18] This number was a constant theme in Persia. The feudal lords of Parthian and Sassanian times were called the Seven Magnates, and the lords of seven provinces continued to play a role during Safavid times and beyond. Several rebellions in that time were said to have been led by seven rebels.

Prof. Shahbasi writes that the Mazdakites had seven viziers and seven gods. And, in a continuation of ancient Mesopotamian tradition, early Persians would build seven palaces, fortified by seven walls and painted in seven colors, in the belief that these colors corresponded with seven planets, which in turn were guardians of the seven climes.

A traditional bride wears seven items, is presented with an armband woven of threads in seven colors and may enjoy a banquet in seven colors. A newborn baby is named after seven days.

---

[18] Shahbazi, Shapur, 'Haft (Seven) The heptad and its cultural significance in Iranian History', https://www.cais-soas.com/CAIS/Culture/haft.htm. This article also is the source of several other points in this discussion, which I will not cite separately. For more details, the reader should consult this article by Prof. Shapur.

In Hinduism

In the Vedic tradition, there are seven different groups of *rishis* – seers of truth, sages, even saints. R*ishis* are said to have existed prior to creation in the form of seven primordial *pranas* (life forces or breaths). Among these rishis are seven divine *Brahmarishis* – sons of the god Brahma, enlightened ones, the highest class of rishis – and they include the poets who composed the Vedas. They are also called the Saptarishi, meaning Seven Sages, who are believed to have transmitted Vedic knowledge to humans.[19]

The Seven Sages appear in the Vedic version of the Flood story, and they are regarded as the ancestors of the Brahman clans.[20] In Vedic ritual, seven priests officiate at a row of seven fireplaces, offering soma sacrifices, and they represent the Seven Sages. The Jains believe in what they call Saptrishi. In India, Hindus call the Ursa Major constellation the Saptarishi, or 'Seven Sages,' the same name that the Sumerians used.

Seven great personalities live eternally, the *Chiranjeevis*. These seven immortals will remain alive until the end of the current stage of the world. Among them are two incarnations of the god Vishnu and one incarnation of the monkey god, Hanuman. In the Puranas there are said to be fourteen worlds, seven below the earth and seven above, just as in Zoroastrianism.

In the Bhagavata Purana 6.16.37, "Every universe is covered by seven layers – earth, water, fire, air, sky, the total energy and false ego." The same Purana says there are innumerable universes besides this one.

The Vedas speak of seven sense organs, the 'seven vital airs of the head'. There are seven major collections of Sanskrit sacred writings (Puranas), most of them dating from 300–1000 CE.[21] There are seven planes of consciousness, corresponding to seven musical notes. The *Mandaka Upanishad*, the Upanishad most often

---

[19] 'Significance of 7 in Hinduism', *WordZZ*,
https://www.wordzz.com/significance-7-
hinduism/#:~:text=In%20Hindu%20calendar%20number%20seven,is%
20known%20as%20Bhadra%20thithi
[20] Parpola, p. 197.
[21] Holdrege, pp. 30, 193, 244.

translated, describes seven tongues and seven forms of the fire god *Agni.*

The Hindu goddess of destruction, *Durga,* manifested herself in seven forms when she fought the demon *Raktabija.* The sun god *Surya* rides on a chariot drawn by seven horses, which represent the seven days of the week and the seven colors in the rainbow. Surya is the lord of the seventh lunar day. Lakshmi, the goddess of wealth, is represented by the seven-faced Saptamukhi. There are seven metals. There are seven addictions. There are seven planets in the solar system in Vedic astronomy.

Astrology is very important in Hinduism. Marriages and other important contracts are only made on auspicious days. Kings would not declare or initiate a war on an inauspicious day, and virtually all persons of influence have their astrologer, who they consult frequently. In Hindu astrology, Saptama Bhaava, the seventh house, is particularly important.

We read about seven *chakras,* or *shaktis* (forces, energies or powers), the points at which energy is concentrated from the crown of the head to the base of the spine. These are supposed to be the foci that regulate the flow of energy throughout the body.

Ancient India was called the Land of Seven Rivers, the *sapta sindhu.* India also was supposed to have had seven holy cities, seven great islands, seven battlefields, seven holy seas and seven sacred hills.[22] The *sapta puri,* or seven cities, were sacred pilgrimage sites: Ayodhya, Haridwar, Mathura, Varanasi, Kanchipuram, Ujjain, and Dwarka.[23]

The seven holy rivers were particularly precious in this land of many deserts: the Ganges, Yamuna, Saraswathi, Godavari,

---

[22] 'Significance of 7 in Hinduism', *WordZZ.* While this material came from multiple sources, the reader is referred to this site as a valuable summary of much information.
https://www.wordzz.com/significance-7-hinduism/#:~:text=In%20Hindu%20calendar%20number%20seven,is%20known%20as%20Bhadra%20thithi.

[23] The reader might recognize Ayodhya, because it was in the news in 1992 when Hindus destroyed the Babri Masjid, protesting that it had been built on top of a former Hindu temple that was dedicated to the important god Rama. Ayodhya is revered as the birthplace of Rama.

Narmada, Sindhu and Kaaveri. Of these, the Saraswathi has disappeared as an actual flowing river, though some remains may be seen from the air.

Buddhism has many of these concepts in common with Hinduism, but Buddhists also believe that when Buddha was born, he arose, took seven steps and lotus flowers sprang up in his footsteps. These seven steps symbolized his ascent of seven cosmic stages. Buddha's pedestal is a lotus flower with seven petals. Buddhists describe Seven Factors of Awakening: mindfulness, investigation, energy, joy, tranquility, concentration, and equanimity. And they have Seven Factors of Enlightenment. In the earliest Pali texts, there were Seven Buddhas of Antiquity.

The number seven also is important to other related religions and cultures. We will name a few.

In other religions and cultures

It is not easy to separate out all the traditions. The Hindu bride and groom walk seven steps together, recite seven vows and circle a sacred fire seven times. At her wedding, the Muslim bride circles the groom seven times. We already know that the Orthodox Jewish bride circles the groom seven times, and seven blessings are recited in the wedding ceremony.

Before the Jews arrived, there were seven Canaanite nations: Canaanites, Amorites, Hittites, Girgashites, Hivites, Jebusites and Perizzites.

In classic times, the Seven Wonders of the World were The Great Pyramid of Giza, the Hanging Gardens of Babylon, the Temple of Artemis at Ephesus, the Statue of Zeus at Olympia, the Mausoleum at Halicarnassus, the Colossus of Rhodes, and the Lighthouse of Alexandria. Speaking of this classical world, Rome has seven hills.

The number seven continues to be important in Islam. All the Abrahamic religions have seven-day weeks. Koran 67:3–4 says *"[Allah] is the one who created seven superimposed Heavens."* Muslims believe that the heavens are superimposed, one upon the other, with man on the lowest level and the angels who sit on our shoulders on the seventh level. Above these heavens is paradise, or the garden, *Jannah.* This word is a cognate of the Hebrew word

Gan, as in Gan Eden, Garden of Eden. There are seven levels of Jannah.

"The early Isma'ilis believed in "seven higher letters" ... "seven prophets," "seven imams," and seven cyclical eras... The ideology of the Isma'ilis, or the Sevener Shi'ites, is still dominated by various heptads."[24] The Ismailis also believe in seven incarnations of the godhead. All Muslims must proclaim Seven Pillars of Faith, and the Druze have Seven Precepts, which they believe are the essence of the Pillars of Islam[25].

At the Hajj, pilgrims walk around the Kaaba in Mecca seven times and they throw seven small stones. The Kurds believe in seven divine forces and seven evils. Sufis believe that there are seven valleys or seven cities of love leading to God. They also describe seven spiritual points of the body and seven mystical degrees.

We see the number seven throughout Christianity too. They warn against seven deadly sins, and they count seven virtues, seven sacraments, seven heavens. In the Christian Book of Revelations, Revelation 1–8, John of Patmos describes the following vision. "Then I saw a Lamb, looking as if it had been slain, standing at the center of the throne, encircled by the four living creatures and the elders. The Lamb had seven horns and seven eyes, which are the seven spirits of God sent out into all the earth." John also describes a vision of God holding a scroll with seven seals.

The Book of Revelation refers to Seven Churches of Asia, to which seven messages were sent, addressed to each of seven angels. Further, it speaks of seven trumpets and seven stars. Matthew 15:34–37 says that Jesus fed the multitudes from seven loaves of bread and "a few small fish" and after they had eaten, they picked up seven baskets of broken leftovers. Mathew 1:17 writes: "So all the generations from Abraham to David are fourteen generations; and from David until the carrying away into Babylon are fourteen generations; and from the carrying away

---

[24] Shahbazi.
[25] 'Druze,' *International Fellowship of Christians and Jews*, Druze | The Druze Religion - The Muwahideen | IFCJ |

into Babylon unto Christ are fourteen generations." These times and dates may not satisfy historians, but they show the importance of the number seven, and its multiples, in our common religious heritage.

Christianity has many more examples in which seven is a holy number. We have just scratched the surface, but these points illustrate how much we all have in common. They also show why what seem to be foreign religions may have an uncanny resemblance to each other.

We have discussed quite a bit of mysticism already, but several special esoteric subjects are worth consideration.

CHAKRAS AND KABBALAH

At first blush, one might think that the god that the Jews worship could not be more different from the gods that the Hindus worship. Consider the sculptures of Hindu gods with multiple arms and hands, each hand holding a representation of the god's attributes. Yet, sophisticated Hindus do not take these multiarmed images literally. Some describe them as "only sensory representations needed for humans to focus during rituals and devotional practices."[26]

That abstract, philosophical way of thinking is far different from that of agriculturalists in rural mud brick villages, who follow a 'village Hinduism' of local cults and guardian deities.[27] This is the Hinduism of their fathers and of their great grandfathers, a tradition that dates back thousands of years.

Hinduism continues to evolve. And, over centuries, in a land that has a several-thousand-year history, over twenty languages and almost thirty states, it is no wonder that it has formed sects. If we want to understand this at all, we must know a bit about Tantra, Shaktism and Kundalini.

Some Tantra is a bit risqué, but it may be considered just "another name for the... literature that contains the basic temple ritual and daily worship rituals that most Hindu denominations

---

[26] Brill, p. 137.
[27] Parapola. Several parts of this discussion come from his book, which should be consulted for details.

use." It has rules for temple building, ritual worship, the use of mantras, mandalas, visualization exercises and philosophies of worship. As far as worship, Brill writes that "Tantra converts ritual into acts that change the cosmos and require an intention to enact the unity." To Jewish ears, this sounds like the goal of Kabbalah, in which mitzvot are acts of great cosmic import.[28]

In Buddhism, Tantra is one of the 'secret teachings.' Probably this is because sexual practices may be associated with it. In comparison, Kabbalah too uses sexual imagery in interpreting texts, but there is no associated physical activity. Even so, there are restrictions on who could learn Kabbalah. During the eighth to the twelfth centuries, Tantra played an important role in the Buddhism of Tibet, Kashmir, and Cambodia, as Buddhism spread across Asia.

Shaktism is one form of Hindu Tantra. In it, spiritual energy is described as a feminine spiritual force. This too has an analogy in Judaism, the concept of the *Shekhinah,* the feminine aspect of the Divine.

Last, Kundalini yoga adherents seek to visualize – ideally to feel – an energy that is described as like an electrical current, that begins at the base of the spine and courses up to the chakra at the top of the head.

The chakras that are arrayed along the axis of the body are believed to concentrate energy. Hindus describe six or seven chakras. Buddhists describe several numbers, but one diagram has five: foundation, abdomen, heart, throat and crown. Chakra diagrams depict side channels branching off into the limbs, and this also is true in the humanoid diagram of Kabbalah. Each chakra is associated with a color, just as each of the Kabbalistic spheres (*sephirot*) has its own color.

Continuing to compare the Kabbalah to the Hindu chakras, the Kabbalistic idea of spheres existed in the *Sefer Yetzirah,* but the names of the spheres did not become fixed until medieval times. The ten spheres on the Kabbalistic diagram of a human body are: crown, wisdom/understanding, mercy/power, beauty, eternity/splendor, foundation and kingship. Reminiscent of the

---

[28] Brill, pp. 183–8.

chakras, these are located at the crown of the head, on the four extremities, on the torso, and on the foundation, which means the organs of procreation. In kundalini yoga too, the chakra for spiritual energy starts just behind these same organs, a location described primly as the base of the spine.

Each Kabbalistic sphere represents one attribute of the Almighty. The three highest represent, respectively, the intellect, the superconscious and the conscious. Below are seven spheres that resemble the seven chakras. While the names vary, there clearly is a correspondence between Hindu symbolism and this Kabbalistic symbolism. How did that happen?

One image frequently depicted in Kabbalah is that of a man, *Adam Kadmon*, on whom the ten sephirot are superimposed. This is the Primal Man, the Divine Man, or the Holy Ancient One. Another image is the 'Tree of Life' or the 'Tree of the World,' which grows upside down, is rooted in the heavens, branches out below, and is watered by juices that flow down to it from above.

The Hindu Bhagavad Gita describes a Primal Man, *Purusa*, who resembles the Kabbalistic Primal Man. The Rigveda describes a cosmic tree, called *Aswattha*, that grows upside down. Is this just a coincidence? In a very learned and opaque fashion, Prof. Braj M. Sinha[29] explains the mystical significance of all these images. The reference is below. Good luck.

Moshe Idel is a leading modern exponent of Kabbalah. He describes a Kabbalistic image with the ten Sephirot arranged in concentric circles, each with its own color, in a form that resembles a Hindu or Buddhist mandala.[30] The word mandala means universe, and a mandala normally consists of a painted picture with an intricate pattern of multi-colored geometric shapes, often using the meme of a circle that encloses a square, symbolizing the universe.

---

[29] Sinha, Braj M., 'Divine Anthropos and Cosmic Tree: Hindu and Jewish Mysticism in Comparative Perspective,' Chap. 5 in Katz et al.

[30] Idel, Moshe, *Kabbalah, New Perspectives*, (New Haven: Yale University Press, 1988), p. 107.

ALTERED CONSCIOUSNESS AND REACHING FOR THE DIVINE

Hindus, Buddhists and Jews have long tried to attain an altered state of consciousness in order to reach a spiritual experience. One of the principal ways in which Hindus and Buddhists seek to achieve enlightenment is by meditation. Jewish mysticism, while probably older, goes back at least to the Book of Ezekiel and its dramatic description of a heavenly chariot adorned with esoteric symbols. This chariot was the *Merkabah,* and explanations of its symbolism are so secret that they can only be taught to qualified students. Only in the 12th and 13th centuries did Kabbalah come into its own.

In the eighteenth century, eastern European rabbis created the Hasidic (Chasidic) movement, a spiritual revivalist movement whose members follow the teachings of a famous rabbinic dynasty. Besides their piousness, they also are known for their joyous celebrations, feasting, singing and dancing. They are the very prototype of Orthodox Jews in Israel today, with their long coats and large showy fur hats, even in the heat of summer.

Recently, the modern Israelis created a massive military tank. They named it the Merkabah.

But what are the goals of these mystics who work so hard to achieve a higher state of consciousness? Hindus and Buddhists seek enlightenment. Sufis try to achieve a state of ecstasy. Medieval rabbis wanted to make perilous nocturnal ascents through the seven heavens to study with the ancient sages and to see the throne of the Almighty. And some of their students tried to emulate them.

A Talmudic legend named Pardes (orchard) tells of four first century CE rabbis who reached Heaven:

> "Four men went up into the heavenly garden, and they were: Ben Azzai and Ben Zoma, Asher and R. Akiva. Ben Azzai gazed and died; to him the scriptural passage may be applied..."
> Grievous in the eyes of the Lord is the death of his pious ones."
> Ben Zoma gazed and went mad; to him the scriptural passage

may be applied [...]." Asher cut the plants. R. Akiva departed in peace."" [31]

In other words, Ben Azzai died because he looked at God. Ben Zoma went mad, and Asher became a heretic. The three who tried to ascend to heaven without the necessary preparation came to a bad end. Only Rabbi Akiva was ready, and only he survived.

No doubt the average young Jewish backpacker in India knows nothing about any of this. Nor does the hip New Yorker who attends Buddhist meditation sessions suspect that anything of spiritual value could be found within his own religion. They have yet to learn about Jewish mysticism.

We might make some direct comparisons of great figures from the Jewish and the Hindu traditions. Margaret Chatterjee[32] compares Rabbi Abraham Isaac Kook (1865–1935), the former Chief Rabbi of Jerusalem and the leading Jewish mystic of his time, with the Indian philosopher-mystic Sri Aurobindo (1872–1950). Aurobindo was born in Calcutta, and he studied the classics in Cambridge before he returned to India. There he became a political figure, and a legendary philosopher.

Both these mystics had "an apocalyptic vision which may or may not have had as one of its main inspirations the powerful darkness/light archetypes of ancient Persia." Rabbi Kook derived much of his thinking from a leading Jewish scholar, Rabbi Isaac Luria, who described how he ascended to the heavens, braving many dangers, to study with the sages.

Rabbi Luria also taught that the Divine Light had caused its enveloping vessel to shatter, sending divine sparks of light down into the souls of humans. Remarkably, Aurobindo spoke of a "concealed soul-spark," writing, "There dwells the little spark of the divine which supports this obscure mass of our nature and around it grows the psychic being, the formed soul of the real

---

[31] Tosefta Hagigah 2.2.
[32] Goodman, Hananiya Ed, *Between Jerusalem and Benares – Comparative Studies in Judaism and Hinduism* (Albany: State University of New York Press, 1994), pp. 243–66.

man around us." They both taught almost exactly the same idea. How could that be?

One of Aurobindo's major works, *Savitri,* appears simply to be a paean to the conquest of death through love. But the deeper philosophical message is about a mystic ascent toward a life filled with the love of God. Rabbi Kook described the same ascent, and so did the medieval Jewish followers of *merkavah* mysticism, who sought to travel through multiple heavenly palaces (*heikhalot*) up to the Divine Throne. Paradoxically, they expressed it as descending into the Divine. Did they mean descending deep into oneself? This sounds like a Hindu or Buddhist idea.

Thus, masters of Kabbalah sought to 'descend' into heaven, and Aurobindo described "bringing down of the Divine consciousness into the heart, mind and body to remove the veil which our present consciousness sets up between us and the divine." Rabbi Kook sees the individual expanding to become part of that which is universal, and so do Hindus and Buddhists. Kook dreamed that when man's spiritual powers fully mature, all will come together. Aurobindo dreamed the same dream.

MASCULINE AND FEMININE PRINCIPLES

Unification with the supreme has erotic connotations, both in Judaism and in Hinduism. It also may involve both a feminine and a masculine divinity, even in Judaism, which may surprise many readers.

Many Hindu temples are lavishly adorned with sculptures of male Hindu gods in sexual congress with their female consorts. Not only are these sculptures found at Khajuraho, but they also appear on many other temples. Surprisingly perhaps, the Kabbalah teaches of a mystic union between a male and a female divine principle. This is not usually shown as graphically as the union of the god Shiva and his consort Shakti depicted on Hindu temples, but the idea is the same. Some Jews might look askance at the erotic sculptures in India, but a female divine entity is not as foreign to Jewish tradition as they think.

The Kabbalah does employ sexual imagery, which is why neither a woman nor an unmarried man is permitted to study it. In one explanation of the four-letter name of God, Kabbalists say that two of the letters represent the masculine entity, two the feminine, and all four are joined in an esoteric union.

In wisdom books, wisdom is female.[33] The *Wisdom of Solomon* portrays her as a partner in Creation. She is called the "breath of the power of God," and she is "a pure emanation of the glory of the Almighty." She reaches across the entire earth, and she is "continually ordering and renewing the entire creation."

Idel describes how, according to the Kabbalah, the Creator and the feminine form of the Divine presence (the *Shekhinah*) are joined in unity, the true unity of God. The root of the word *shekhinah* comes from the Hebrew word for a dwelling. The implication is that she is the dwelling of God. The word first appeared in the liturgy after the destruction of the Second Temple, and it could have been introduced under the influence of Persian and Babylonian cosmology.

Even in non-Orthodox synagogues today, the *shekhinah* is honored as the Sabbath Bride, who is invited into the home and honored on the Sabbath.

In Judaism, relations between husband and wife are sanctified. Genesis says, "And Adam knew Eve his wife; and she conceived." Not only Kabbalah, but also traditional Judaism, attributes a cosmic importance to the marital relationship, yet that does not preclude Judaism from conceptualizing a separate Shekhinah, or any other feminine wisdom entity.

According to one writer, three Jewish inscriptions found in the Sinai Desert[34] suggest the existence of a female goddess. Two inscriptions refer to "Yahweh of Samaria and his Asherah," the third to 'Yahweh of Teman', and 'his Asherah.' Yahweh is one spelling of the Hebrew name for God. Asherah is an alternate name for the Babylonian goddess Astarte. The writer believes that these references imply the existence of an ancient Jewish belief that God had a wife. He concludes that the Israelites and Judeans were polytheistic until the Babylonian Exile of 586 BCE, and they only became monotheistic after that. Startling as that idea might

---

[33] Holdrege, Barbara, *Veda and Torah*, p. 138.
[34] Jacquet-Acea, Russell, 'In Search of the Sacred Tetragrammaton Name of God – Part 3', (*Jacquet Publishing*, 2019), Academia.edu

be to Jewish traditionalists, if true it would lend support to Zoroastrian claims that the Jews adopted monotheism from them. It also would support the view that Jews once believed in a female goddess just as Mesopotamians, Iranians and Indians did. At least we cannot reject the idea out of hand.

UNITY, REALITY AND ILLUSION

Hindu and Jewish mystics always have searched for unity.[35] Rav Kook identified the inner self with God, and he sought "to light a true self that is identified with God [that] is also the supreme wish of the Upanishads." Correspondingly, in the Upanishads, "The purpose of humanity is to realize that Atman, the inner self, and Brahman, the infinite, are one and the same."

The Paramahamsa Upanishad contains the following passage, "I know the Unity; my soul is no longer separate but united to the cosmic soul; this is indeed the supreme union...no more 'me' nor 'you' for [the liberated], the very universe has disappeared."[36]

Buddhists understand the entire world to be one perfect, changeless unity. Ellis Potter calls this belief monism[37]. In Buddhism, suffering results when we forget this unity.

We should discuss one more important set of concepts – illusion vs reality. This is where we encounter the Sanskrit word *maya*. According to one author[38], "in the spiritual parlance, maya means unreality, distinct from the reality represented by God or Brahman." Maya is illusion, but it is not the same as magic or witchcraft. The Encyclopedia Britannica pulls these two ideas together, saying that "Maya originally denoted the magic power with which a god can make human beings believe in what turns out to be an illusion." Judaism, in contrast, sees humanity burdened with the responsibility of fixing the world and

---

[35] Nagen, Yakov, *Be, Become, Bless: Jewish Spirituality between East and West*, (Jerusalem: Maggid Books, 2019), p. 20.

[36] Chalier-Visuvalingam in Goodman, pp. 195–6.

[37] 'Buddhism for Beginners' | *Union Resources* (uniontheology.org). The author is a lecturer and a former Buddhist monk.

[38] Jayarm, V., 'The Definition and Concept of Maya in Hinduism," *Hinduwebsite.com.*

improving reality. Here there is a clear difference. Hindus and Buddhists see this world as an illusion. Jews see it as reality.

Needless to say, there are major differences between Jews and Buddhists, but in some respects, there are fewer differences than we think. For example, Hindus and Buddhists do not have a monopoly on mantras. When we think of eastern religion, we typically visualize an acolyte sitting cross-legged, chanting a mantra, but the wisdom book *Sefer Yetzirah* tells us that mantras exist in Judaism. The Hebrew word for "to hum," is spelled using the letter 'm' twice, and even the word for hum, *zimzum*, has a humming sound. Kabbalists used this sound repeatedly in order to achieve a higher level of consciousness. Hindus will no doubt recognize that it sounds like their mantra: *Ommmm*. Perhaps this is more than coincidence.

One book, *Letters to a Buddhist Jew*,[39] demonstrates the doubts that David Gottlieb, an articulate and sensitive Jewish man, has about the faith of his fathers. At the beginning of the book, Gottlieb is practicing Buddhism, but he appears to be looking for a way back to Judaism. The book contains letters that Gottlieb writes to Rabbi Akiva Tatz, asking 15 specific questions, and we have answers from Rabbi Tatz, which raise more questions, leading to further exchanges. The Gottlieb letters represent such sharp challenges to Judaism that they are worthy of consideration here:

As contrasted with Judaism, Gottlieb argues that Zen Buddhism "does not deny the existence of a divine force at work in the Universe, it does not focus on a God who must be obeyed or, more importantly, believed in." Gottlieb cannot fathom how Jews can worship a Supreme Being who may or may not care about them. Gottlieb next complains that Judaism is encumbered by laws, texts and incomprehensible language, while, in his view, Buddhism just requires mindfulness. The reader will know by now that this is an oversimplification.

Gottlieb thinks that the idea of being chosen people unnecessarily sets Jews apart from the rest of humanity, and that

---

[39] Tatz, Akiva and Gottlieb, David, *Letters to a Buddhist Jew*, (Israel: Targum Press, Inc., 2004).

it compares poorly with the universality taught by Buddhism. Likewise, he does not believe in the revelation from Mt. Sinai, which he takes to mean that he cannot ever be a Jew. He is repulsed by the gratuitous savagery of sacrifices, wars, plagues and punishments in a bible that was written thousands of years ago. One of his last points was that he had never heard of Jewish meditation. Apropos, a rabbinical student with whom I discussed these matters believed that meditation requires visualization of the Buddha, which would not be kosher for a Jew.

We will not give Rabbi Tatz's lengthy answers here, in part because that would preempt his fine book. Suffice it to say that his responses were excellent, and when we last hear from Gottlieb, he is studying Torah.

The reason for dwelling on this dialogue is to show what Judaism is up against in the modern world, what Jews are trying to escape, what they find lacking in Judaism, and what they have not looked for at all in Judaism.

In the next chapter we will ask what so many Jews are running from, where they are running to, and what they hope to find when they get there. We have proposed a number of answers in the course of this book, but more questions remain. Finally, we will consider one more question: must Jews look to Hinduism and Buddhism to find the answers that they are seeking?

Chapter Sixteen.
What Are Jews Running From and What Are They Looking For?

Now that we know the history and a bit about the religions, do we understand yet why so many Jews are attracted to India? Is it a matter of shared history or philosophy? Or is it mundane – cheap travel and drugs? Is it the exotic, or is it a way to fill a hole in the heart?

For Israelis, if the trip to India comes between the army (IDF) and college, or a job, is it this the soldier's last fling before settling down? In the IDF, soldiers may be under constant tension, anxiously protecting the homeland from threats on all sides, or they may be bored to death, stuck in desk jobs during their entire term of service. Whatever they did in their army service though, when it is over, this is their opportunity to go away to a destination of their choice. The question when they have almost finished their service is not "What are you going to do now?" It is "Where will you be traveling now?" Wonder of wonders, everyone considers this trip legitimate, well-deserved. Even their family expects it.

So, without pressure, without the need to think about the future, without having to listen to what anybody else tells them to do, they can, for once, do what they want. Some Israelis say that this was the best time of their lives. But it also is a time to learn about the world. Many Israelis have never traveled beyond the obligatory trip to relatives in New York or London. Now they have a chance to see the orient, to think, to take a gap year during which they make decisions that will determine the rest of their lives. Alon Goshen-Gottstein calls it a rite of passage, a trip taken between one's youth and the next stage in life.[1] The trip must be important too, because they work, plan, borrow and save for it with great fervor.

When they arrive, some discover Hinduism for the first time. Goshen-Gottstein writes that the Jewish encounter with Hinduism in India is completely different from encounters that Jews have had with other religions. Jews have lived for centuries in countries whose rulers and population practiced religions that were hostile to Jews. In contrast, for these travelers, this encounter normally is for a limited time, is nonpolitical, and does not involve living side-by-side next to Hindu or Muslim neighbors. In a way, it is not real life. It is a voyage into someone else's reality.

The trip is not just a visit to another religion, culture and country. It is a time-out. It provides "a lost home for Israeliness... where the latter can be repaired." And for those seeking spiritual guidance, the trip "allows exploration of, but not commitment to, the rules of the mystical path."[2]

Not every trip to India comes after the IDF. Some American and European Jews just go, willy-nilly, as they would go anywhere. Others appear to be running away to India. There are many theories about what they are running *from*. Some young Jews feel disconnected from their own tradition if they were not exposed to it as children in a meaningful way. Matzos on Passover and candles on Chanukah may not be enough to teach the child that that his people have a deep spiritual heritage. Many Jewish holidays seem only to look back, commemorating past attacks on the Jewish people or on a Temple that stood in Jerusalem 2,000 years ago. As cynics say about these holidays, "They tried to kill us; they failed; let's eat."

---

[1] Goshen-Gottstein, Alon, *The Jewish Encounter with Hinduism: History, Spirituality, Identity,* (London: Palgrave Macmillan, 2016).
[2] Goshen-Gottstein, p. 2680 in the Kindle edition.

WHAT ARE THE JEWS RUNNING FROM?

Many Jews who become alienated from their own tradition will seek an alternative that will be more congenial, more fulfilling. My father never had his Bar Mitzvah as scheduled because his Orthodox grandparents objected to his mindlessly reciting the Hebrew words that he had memorized uncomprehendingly. And he was loath to attend services for the rest of his life. As a result, I picked up his early aversion to attending a synagogue.

My husband and I never joined a synagogue until my in-laws decamped for California, leaving us alone with no immediate family to be with on the holidays. So, we called some second cousins, who immediately began inviting us over for the holidays. We joined a synagogue too, and there we soon met Israeli friends.

The most important lessons in being a Jew came from my surgical practice in the Lebanese community of Dearborn, Michigan. In that environment I practically lived in the Middle East. I studied Arabic in order to talk with my patients, and I became friends both with my patients and my Arab colleagues in the hospital. There I learned, to my surprise, that they seemed to believe that Jews are superior, smarter, and better doctors. I saw that patients did not want to go to Arab doctors; they wanted Jewish doctors, and lawyers. Some of my Arab doctor friends even complained to me, saying, "They don't trust us."

Even before I started working in Dearborn, I once ate a ham sandwich in a laboratory at the university, and an Arab student looked at me with disapproval, chiding me that I should follow my rules. The Arabs respected my rules. For them, being Jewish was something special. It is like the old joke in which a Jewish man is reading an Arab paper, and his friend asks why he does not read a Jewish paper. He answers that Jewish papers always write about how bad the Jews are, and Arab papers write about how clever the Jews are.

Later on, my husband and I begin travelling frequently to Israel, and much later I began studying Hebrew, while still enjoying chatting with the Arab staff in our hotels. Meanwhile, we began traveling to India, made close friends there, and returned to India, over and over. But I felt like that Indian part of my life was not the usual story, until I learned what I know now. It is one of the commonest Jewish stories of all.

Other Jews have had their own obstacles and disincentives to full participation in their Jewish heritage. The young pioneers who first came to Israel were highly secular and socialist. Many of those who came from Communist Russia knew only that the word 'Jewish' was what they were supposed to write down on the blank for nationality on their passports. They knew they had come to the land of Israel because they were Jewish, but this meant little to them. Even a large number of the most recent immigrants from Russia are half Jewish, or a quarter Jewish, and they may have received little information to confirm any of this from their grandparents, if their grandparents were even alive.

As a result, in Israel, Russian Jews find themselves unable to have a Jewish wedding if they cannot furnish written proof that they really are Jewish to the rabbinic authorities or if they cannot obtain testimony from an approved rabbi. How are they supposed to do that if they came as refugees who fled with whatever shards of their life they were able to collect before leaving? What about the reality that when they and their parents lived in the USSR, Jewish practice was actively discouraged, and their family never had a real Jewish wedding, much less a rabbi who could vouch for them? What about Holocaust survivors who were lucky enough to escape with the clothes on their backs, hardly in a position to pack and bring their parents' Jewish ketubah, (wedding certificate)?

In Israeli, if Jews marry without the approval of the rabbinate, or do not marry at all but cohabit, then their children cannot marry legitimately according to the rabbinate. Do you think they might become even more alienated than I was?

What about Ethiopian Jews, who the Israeli rabbinate initially looked at skeptically, "But they do not look Jewish!" What about Indian Jews from rural villages in which they observed some of the rituals and traditions of the Jewish people, but not others? Is the testimony of their rabbis accepted in Israel? Did they have rabbis? What about the Jews of Europe, Armenia or Turkey who changed their names and identities generations ago to escape anti-Semitic persecution? Their parents had no

Jewish wedding papers, nor did they have any rabbi who could verify that they were Jewish.

What about sophisticated, college-educated American Jews who moved to the Big City, shortened their names, cut themselves off from their Jewish connections, worked 24-7 through the Sabbath and the Jewish holidays, and essentially became part of the surrounding Christian community? When they suddenly feel the need for a spiritual life, will they turn to Judaism, or will they seek another tradition that permits them simply to meditate once a week in a room with no statues of gods?

Ever since WW II, the Holocaust has affected the Jewish community profoundly. For many, their parents' or grandparents' memories of the Holocaust essentially define what it means to be Jewish. Being Jewish means suffering and persecution. This is not an appealing message for Jewish youths who need help with their own problems, now. If they are taught that the essence of Jewishness is the memory of a catastrophe that killed one third of the Jewish people and 80% of their rabbis and teachers, that just may make them mad at God. How could a beneficent God do such a thing?

What about the children of Orthodox Hasidic households in which television or the internet are forbidden, where the men wear long silk coats and extravagant fur hats, and where the women wear wigs and long dresses to maintain their modesty? Many secular Jews find it embarrassing to read about, or to see, Hasidim out on the street dressed like 14th century Polish counts. Many Israelis today cringe when they see an energetic group of men in black hats and prayer shawls jump out of a car at an intersection, loudly sing "Na, Na, Nachman Meuman," and dance wildly in circles.

What if the children of these families want to join the modern world, but they feel guilty about leaving the world of their father and mother, the world in which they grew up? Maybe all they want is a modernized practice that is less restrictive. Or maybe they want to completely transform themselves, go to Hollywood and become rock singers.

What about Jews who grew up in towns where there were almost no other Jews? What did they learn about Judaism, or about the Jewish community? What about Jewish children who were saved when their parents quickly handed them to Christian families before they went off to their deaths during the Holocaust? These children were loved and well taken care of, but do they feel Jewish? Did they even know they were Jewish while they were growing up?

What about the Jews who marry non-Jews who are loathe to relinquish their Christmas tree or midnight mass? Many synagogues refuse to give mixed couples full membership, though increasing numbers do go out of their way to welcome both members of such families. The problem is that, according to Jewish law, if a non-Jewish wife does not convert, the children are not Jews. In Israel when they want to marry, they face the dilemma of the Russian Jews. Even in America, these children run into resistance if they want to marry someone from an observant family.

Many of these alienated Jews never had a real desire to be part of the Jewish community, yet they may sense that something is missing in their lives. Then they begin to look for it, or a substitute for it. Some of them have become Christian clergy. That is the story of Cardinal Aaron Jean-Marie Lustiger, the former Archbishop of Paris, sometimes called the Jewish Cardinal of France.

WHAT MAKES THE JEWS KEEP RUNNING?

Many American, European and Israeli Jews have roots that go back to Lithuania, where the prewar tradition was distinctly rationalist. One of the greatest teachers was Elijah ben Solomon Zalman, known as the Gaon of Vilnius. Born in 1720 in the Brest Litovsk area, he fought tirelessly against the Hasidim, a sect that he disdainfully equated with ecstatic singing and dancing. He even excommunicated them, twice, clearly setting the tone for the Jews of Lithuania and adjacent parts of Poland. We saw his statue in Vilnius, a larger-than-life black bust still glaring out defiantly at any who dared to venture into the Hasidic side of the Jewish tradition.

In the United States, the older generation watched Israel miraculously transform itself from a patch of sand into a start-up nation, but many younger Jews today are more interested in politically correct politics than in their religion, or Israel. That is especially true of college students who are being taught a globalist world view in which allegiance to one country or religion is viewed with disfavor. Universities also are seeing a resurgence of anti-Semitism, with visible signs of Jewish observance potentially problematic on campus. And the student who is actively harassed in college will learn to conceal his Judaism, internalizing the message that being Jewish is embarrassing, or dangerous.

A proper description of the hostile environment on today's college campuses would require another book, but we should at least mention some of the reasons why young university students may be intimidated into feeling uncomfortable about their Jewishness. Every year in the U.S., college campuses have Israel Apartheid Week, in which vile lies about Israel are written on placards and loudly proclaimed. Anti-Israel organizations regularly pressure college administrations to divest their investments in Israel or in any entity that makes products for Israel. Not only does the BDS movement – Boycott, Divestment, and Sanctions – engage in this effort, so does the JVP – the Jewish Voice for Peace – along with other elements.

On many campuses, JVP and other anti-Semitic organizations loudly oppose pro-Israel speakers, programs and groups. Many beleaguered young Jewish students, just teenagers, are completely unprepared to fight back. They often have had minimal Jewish education, and they just withdraw in silence. It is little wonder that they might be happy to find a welcoming room with Buddhist decorations where they can simply sit beside like-minded others, with no need for a public profession of faith, take a deep breath, relax, and meditate.

Linzer[3] observed that in one course that she attended, the dominant themes in her reading list were self-hate, self-denial, and an attempt to hide one's Jewishness – what she calls internalized anti-Semitism. It is no wonder that some might feel

---

[3] Linzer, Judith, *Torah and Dharma – Jewish Seekers in Eastern Religions* (North Bergen: Jason Aronson Inc., 1996).

the need for, as Monty Python would say, 'something completely different'.

TOO ORTHODOX OR TOO REFORM

In Israel, the Reform and Conservative movements of Judaism play a relatively minor role; most people are either Orthodox or secular. For that reason, in Israel, and even in the multidimensional milieu of America, most serious students of Judaism study in Orthodox institutions. This is a problem, because, according to traditional Orthodoxy, Kabbalah can only be taught to students who have studied Torah. Oh, and they must be married men. With very few exceptions, even today this teaching is only available to men, though this is changing. We recently walked by a large study hall filled with observant women in the middle of a very Orthodox neighborhood of Jerusalem. Still, studying Kabbalah properly requires years of poring over abstruse texts and navigating a maze of intellectual complications. This is assuming that the student finds a teacher, which may be a problem. Much of the rabbinic establishment is uncomfortable with Kabbalah, and the lasting influence of the European establishment, especially the Gaon of Vilna, persists.

As we have seen, Orthodox youths in Israel study for hours a day in a yeshiva, intensely debating fine points of Talmud. If they later gravitate toward Buddhism or Hinduism, they take their finely honed skill in analysis and their intellectual curiosity with them, to the great benefit of their new field of study. We have seen some examples in earlier chapters.

Do American Jews actively look for a Jewish esoteric tradition? Do Orthodox teachers explore abstract metaphysical concepts? Or do they simply teach legalistic thinking and how to read the voluminous Jewish literature?

Many American Jews are descended from European Jews who brought liberal Judaism with them; in America this is Reform Judaism. In my own childhood, as a Reform Jew, I had no idea that there was an esoteric tradition in Judaism, and I doubt that my parents knew either. Even in Conservative Judaism, Jewish mysticism only is taught in synagogues where the clergy have an interest in the subject. So, would-be students may look for courses in Jewish esoterica, but they may not find them without putting in more effort than they are moved to make.

As we have seen, in America, Reform Judaism – and to a lesser extent Conservative Judaism – has eliminated much of the tradition, ritual, mysticism, Hebrew language prayers, and anything else that is inconsistent with European rationalism. This leaves a Judaism of holiday dinners, Bar Mitzvahs and social justice. The *raison d'etre* becomes *tikkun olam,* making the world better. As a teenager, I returned home from Reform Jewish summer camp convinced that the primary meaning of Judaism was *tikkun olam,* forgetting about the actual 613 commandments of Judaism. This only provided 613 reasons for the nonobservant Jew who finds out about these commandments to feel guilty. This is not the kind of Judaism that retains its young. Observers have remarked that many American practitioners of Buddhism come from Ashkenazi, often Reform Jewish, homes.

Goshen-Gottstein writes that modern Judaism is in crisis. Standard teachings emphasize ritual, not enlightenment or inner spiritual development. The student is given Jewish literature to read, with little or no guidance in reaching spiritual insights. Few teachers are willing to ask the big questions about God. Where is He? How do I find Him? Is He everything in the universe, or did He create everything, but remain apart from it all? Young Jews today are seeking a direct experience. They are engaged in "a quest for those parts of the self that cannot be made manifest within one's home space." As a result, they go elsewhere looking for what they need.[4]

Rabbi Alan Lew and his friend Norman Fischer decided to offer a meditation workshop at a Zen Center called the Green Gulch Farm. Lew hoped to help Jews deepen their Jewish practice through Buddhist meditation, and Fischer too wanted to reach out to Jewish Buddhists to help enrich their Judaism. To their shock, the Jewish service that they designed for the workshop caused a furor. The Jews rebelled, complaining bitterly that they did not understand Hebrew; they felt shut out by the service, and "the language was archaic and sexist." They questioned the biblical

---

[4] Goshen-Gottstein, p. 2680.

idea of reward and punishment. They questioned everything about God, and they complained that "The God of the prayerbook seemed like an abusive father."[5]

In another workshop they held at another location, the responses were the same. "...the language was archaic and not what we felt in our hearts...the service excludes us...we feel repelled by the religion and the people we're supposed to belong to." Thinking about it, he realized that these Jews felt a deep frustration with Judaism, but had they been indifferent, they would not have signed up for the workshop. The next observation was particularly poignant.

"The truth is," Rabbi Lew writes, "I had already begun to suspect that there was a connection between these people's anger at Judaism and their anger at their fathers and mothers." One student told him, "Judaism is my family, and I just don't know if I want to be part of my family anymore." Yet at the conclusion of the workshop, one of the angriest students approached him to ask if he would say Kaddish for her father, something she had never been able to do.

Lew feels that Orthodoxy has frozen the religion and left it unable to deal with new challenges, such as sexual identity or modern views of the status of women. Yet rejecting Orthodoxy leaves Jews from that background without observance or commitment, the very factors that have kept Judaism alive for thousands of years.

WHAT ARE WE RUNNING TO?

Israelis love adventure travel. They go to Thailand, to South America, and to Turkey as well as to India, but how many of them stay for long periods of time in these other countries? How many feel a personal connection to them, beyond the pleasure of just seeing something new? The trip to India is different.

India is enormous and full of pageantry. The British were enchanted when they saw elaborately caparisoned elephants parading down broad avenues in eye-popping ceremonies, so much so that they brought some of this spectacle back home to

---

[5] Lew, Alan, pp. 288, 294.

London. Even today in India the visitor can see temple elephants, chockablock bazaars, and cremation rituals at the ghats of Varanasi. India has magnificent temples, amazing art, and rich textiles, not to mention the food. The scenery varies from the Rajasthan Desert to the breezy hill stations, from white beaches on the Arabian Ocean to green tea plantations on the hills of Assam.

The Jewish traveler feels that there is something familiar in India, though it may be hard to put a finger on it. The people are friendly and hospitable, curious and chatty, gracious and nonjudgmental. Many of them remind you of people you know at home, the argumentative uncle, the sweet auntie, the wise old man, the twenty-something striving to get ahead, the sharp merchant trying to outbargain you, the smart little kids typing away on their computers.

Once almost fifty years ago in Madras, we started talking with some kids at a tourist attraction, and we were surrounded immediately by a whole group of eager schoolboys, all talking at once, peppering us with questions about what they needed to do to get into an American medical school.

Just as King Solomon sent his traders shopping in India, bargain-hunters today flock to India from New York or Tel Aviv. Jews fled to India after the destruction of the Temple in Jerusalem, and they came when Islam made their lives untenable. Their Hindu counterparts made them feel welcome then, and they do now.

The welcome may come as a surprise. In northern India, an Israeli or an American Jew may be taken for a Punjabi. I used to be, all the time. And communication is easy; after years of British rule, educated people speak English over much of the country. One gets to know people far faster In India than one does in Thailand, China, or anywhere else in Asia.

In India, picturesque ancient temples and ruins are interspersed with modern neighborhoods, just as they are in Israel. Indian history goes back seemingly forever, just as the history of Israel does. Yet in Pune, Bangalore and many other cities, software designers are everywhere. In the ancient city of Hyderabad sits a huge Microsoft campus.

In India, the traveler feels free, unconstrained by the expectations of those around her. For those who want them, drugs are plentiful and cheap; and the traveler is free to do what he or she wants, hopefully within the limits of common sense. As the song goes, 'the livin' is easy'. Or the traveler may have a different plan. Looking for an ashram? There is one across from the city airport in Mumbai. You will be in Pune next week? Is there one there? Indeed yes, a huge one. Almost anyone can refer you to one that her auntie likes, or her uncle, or the one her family visits regularly.

Some of the Jews who go to India are hungry for spiritual guidance or for a special kind of religious experience. In some cases, once they have learned more about the religions of India, they discover analogous teachings in their own religion. More than one guru has suggested to a prospective student of Hinduism that he learn about his own religion first. Trungpa Rinpoche told Nathan Katz several times that he must observe his own Sabbath.

Katz tells of a respected Chairman of the Benares Hindu University Department of Philosophy who was approached by a young Christian student who enthused that he was so impressed by his courses that he was going to convert to Hinduism. To the amazement of the other students, the professor became angry and said "If you think you should convert to Hinduism, then you have utterly misunderstood everything I have been trying to teach. You insult both Hinduism and your own Christianity." To the student's shock, the professor summarily dismissed him. Katz explains that the professor considered his teachings to be a means of understanding religion, not to be a religion.[6]

A seeker of spiritual guidance will find gurus, ashrams, holy men and highly educated Brahmins throughout India. It is not even necessary to seek out a full-time holy man. One could find all this in a lawyer.

One year we were in India on a trip with lawyers, law professors and judges from around the world, attending a series of conferences. At one of them, we met an eminent Indian lawyer, a partner in a huge law firm, who had a

---

[6] Katz, Nathan, p. 44.

striking yellow vertical line on his forehead, a symbol of Vishnu, the god to whom he prayed. When we asked him about it, he told us that every morning he got up, bathed, brushed his teeth and, alone in his room, chanted from memory lengthy verses of Hindu holy scripture. After that, he donned clean clothes, drew this tilak on his forehead with a mixture of sandalwood and turmeric, and went to work. On special days of the calendar, he chanted certain extremely long passages, from memory.

Not only that, he and his family were very generous contributors to a temple that was special to them in Kanchipuram. And it turned out that their temple was the same one that I once had remembered with such clarity, before I ever visited it with my husband. This lawyer would never have spoken of his spiritual practice, had we not asked him about it. It was just who he is. Only the thin yellow line on his forehead gave us a clue.

COMING BACK HOME

Not everyone explores Hinduism or Buddhism in India. Earlier in this book we talked about many Jews, both prominent and not, who meditate or who have adopted selected Hindu or Buddhist practices in the U.S. or in Israel. These choices have worked well for them, and they are at peace. Those who have settled on a regular meditation practice are not required to travel for religious purposes or to believe in God. Their meditation does not conflict with other religious beliefs that they may hold, and it does not require them to visualize any foreign god. It may be done in short sessions that suit a modern lifestyle, and it can fit into weekend retreats. The teachers do not need to be ordained priests; they can be friends and contemporaries.

In the west, many Buddhist meditation centers avoid displaying any statues of Buddha, and they have very relaxed rules about who can attend. Attendees are free to see themselves as Jews first, Buddhists first, or simply recognize that they are practitioners of both. In one study of Jews who were involved to a greater or lesser extent in Buddhist practices,[7] all the interviewees identified as Jewish, fewer than half as Buddhist.

Many of the leaders and meditators are women, and feminism was an element in the appeal of these groups. In the meditation sessions I attended, women clearly were in the majority, and women told me that they were attracted by the nonpatriarchal nature of these sessions. There is a certain irony in this, because both Hinduism and Buddhism have always been patriarchal, just as Judaism has, but in the western environment, the Indian religions have been exceptionally nimble about adapting to a changing world.

In both America and Israel, Buddhism has transformed the lives of many Jews, but Jews have transformed Buddhism. They have shed some of the orientalism, softened the rules, and positioned it neatly in the main stream of the self-help culture of the western world.

Why have Hinduism and Buddhism become religious homes for so many Jews? Sigalow[8] writes about Buddhism, but her observations could be applied to Hinduism too. In her view, Buddhism does not annoy or upset the would-be practitioner, and it does not carry the burden of the Holocaust. It also does not come with fractious relatives or Jewish guilt over being 'bad' Jews if they do not keep the Sabbath or the dietary laws. Both Judaism and Buddhism are concerned with the problem of suffering, but Buddhism teaches a uniquely gentle way to handle suffering – just let it go. Practicing this version of Buddhism, with no deity or savior pushed on them, secular, atheistic Jews can feel comfortable. Their practice feels permissive, non-threatening.

We could add more positive reasons. In a world full of wars and threatened terrorism, of hostile neighbors and dangers within our own communities, many of us simply seek peace. Some are also seeking silence, freedom from computers and cell phones, perhaps freedom from constant reminders of our own sins or inadequacies. Meditation offers a way to quietly pursue these

---

[7] Linzer, Judith, *Torah and Dharma*, p. 187.
[8] Sigalow, Emily, *American JuBu*, (Princeton: Princeton University Press, 2019), p. 5.

goals, or, if we are more ambitious, to work calmly toward our own personal fulfillment. And those of us who seek that fulfillment do not want to see this wish as selfish, or unattainable.

> Better than a thousand useless words is one single word that gives peace. Better than a thousand useless verses is one single verse that gives peace. Better than a hundred useless poems is one single poem that gives peace. (Dhammapada 100–103)

WHAT DO THE JEWS HOPE TO FIND?

Do they find peace?

Some Jews look toward Buddhism and Hinduism for other reasons. Some put it simply, "to be happy." Some may even become involved in the beginning because they are curious. One student signed up for a course in college on a whim, and the course just spoke to him.

When Charles T. Strauss converted to Buddhism in 1893,[9] he might have been attracted to its romantic, rational or intellectual aspects. The American counterculture figures of the 60s and 70s were attracted to all this, and they were smart enough to build on it, adding social activism to the mix. As these enthusiasts matured, they crafted the concept of mindfulness.

Several of the most successful U.S. programs teach meditation under the rubric of mindfulness. This makes it a psychotherapeutic treatment, a professionally acceptable adjunct to conventional medical therapy. Some teachers[10] suggest that Buddhist techniques can help one to achieve the coveted Jewish ideal of correcting social and political injustice – *tikkun olam*. This is marketing at its most effective.

Goshen-Gottstein writes of *ba'alei tshuva*, Jews who have left and then rejoined the Jewish community, often with redoubled faith. He says that this phenomenon happens less frequently in Israel, in part because Jewish identity is so central to Israeli existence. Still, the Jewish establishment in any country would be wise not to simply sit back and wait for homesick Jews to return.

---

[9] Sigalow, Emily, p. 180.
[10] Sigalow, Emily, p. 76.

In the U.S. today, unless Judaism is willing to meet the needs and interests of its young, these youths will look for more satisfying alternatives, and they will find them. Reform and Conservative synagogues understand this. Apropos, they are learning to diversify their services, and they are adding contemporary music. Female rabbis and cantors are becoming common too in these branches of Judaism, though they are not yet accepted in Orthodox synagogues. Many synagogues offer yoga, classes in meditation, and studies in religious syncretism. My own synagogue schedules a yoga session immediately after Saturday morning services. Some have formed groups, called *hevruta*, in which a few members study and debate texts together, following the pattern of the Orthodox yeshiva. To make up for early gaps in Jewish education, Jewish community institutions and local federations offer courses in Jewish history, theology, Torah and Hebrew, some of them in the familiar format of a college class.

Yet, outside the supportive environment of an Orthodox yeshiva, how many young people today have a rabbi, grandparent or other role model who can act as their Jewish teacher? Do they have anything like a Jewish guru to help them in their own search for peace? This is not the focus of most contemporary Jewish studies. Only those Jews who have been lucky enough to find the right program of instruction and the right role model will have the privilege of steeping themselves in this knowledge.

There actually are options for the serious student, but most Jews have never heard of them. The Spertus Institute was founded in 1924 in Chicago to educate new immigrants about Jewish studies. It now provides fully accredited graduate degree programs and individual workshops. The student may earn an MA or a doctorate in Jewish studies or may obtain a certificate in Jewish leadership.

Another program is the Florence Melton School of Jewish Learning, known as the Melton Program, founded in 1986 as a project of the Hebrew University in Israel. This offers programs in 50 communities across the U.S., and these programs range from individual seminars to two-year programs. Several universities across the country also offer Jewish, or Judaic, studies, but students are required to enroll in the university. Are there informal programs? Yes, often at a local Jewish federation building, in a classroom, in the evening, after work.

Is there such a thing as Jewish meditation? Yes. Informal sessions, analogous to Buddhist or Hindu meditation sessions, are held in some cities, but not all. But it depends on how one defines meditation. Even prayers may be a form of meditation.

An observant Orthodox Jew repeats two special prayers – the Amidah and the Shema – three times a day. The Amidah is a series of up to 19 blessings that are recited while standing. The Shema is the central prayer of Judaism, declaring "Hear O Israel: The Lord our God, the Lord is one". The Kaddish is another important prayer, said in the Aramaic language, praising God's name. It is recited twice daily for eleven months after the death of a parent, every year in memory of this parent, and in short form at other services during the week and on holidays.

Rabbis tell us that the daily prayers are forms of meditation, perhaps even mantras, even though that would surprise most Jews. In repeating these prayers over and over, many pious Jews find solace and peace, the same peace that comes from meditation, but nobody ever tells them that when they pray, they are meditating.

Sylvia Boorstein reads Psalm 121 as a set of instructions for meditation, but one would need her years of experience in Buddhist meditation to recognize it. She also compares another Jewish prayer, the v'ahavta, as comparable to Buddhist instruction. In this prayer, the Jew is enjoined to love God while "sitting in your house, walking on the road, lying down and standing up". She says that Buddhists too have four positions for their practice: "sitting, standing up, lying down, and walking."[11]

Alon Goshen-Gottstein quotes Moshe Idel, who takes the comparison with Indian religions even further. He says that yogic breathing exercises "made their way into the works of Abraham Abulafia."[12] Abulafia, an important 13th century Kabbalist who

---

[11] Boorstein, Sylvia, *That's Funny*, pp. 78, 162.
[12] Goshen-Gottstein, Alon, *The Jewish Encounter*, p. 1096.

has been much studied and much quoted, apparently even incorporated mantras and mandalas in his works. Who knew?

What the Jew seeks in Hinduism or Buddhism may be the way to a quiet place deep inside. With luck, a young Jew may discover this in India, or through an Indian religion. In Delhi, a Hindu lawyer prays quietly, devoutly, each morning in the privacy of his own home, after which he makes his personal *puja* – a devotional offering to his god. His Sikh neighbor reads a portion of her holy book, the Granth, that morning, and the Buddhist in a nearby village meditates early in this same morning. At the same time, the observant Jain family in the next city finishes their morning prayers. In Israel, a religious Jew stops at the synagogue before going to work, and there he says his morning prayers together with at least nine other men. In New York, a secular Jew does ten minutes of meditation before going off to work. And they are all doing the same thing.

The Dalai Lama told Nathan Katz, "If you want to keep your people in your religion, then you must open your doors to spirituality. If you have an esoteric tradition to offer them, then they will not want to leave."[13] The Dalai Lama went on to say,

> Many of your people have keen intelligence and very creative minds, and if they are not personally satisfied with what you offer them, then nobody could stop them from leaving and taking a new religion. Provide them with all the materials, all spiritual teachings. If you have these spiritual values, then there is no reason to fear; if you have no such values, then there is no reason to hold on. If you cannot provide spiritual satisfaction to others and at the same time insist on holding on to them, then that is foolishness. This is reality.

In Judaism we have many wise rabbinic tales, and sometimes one of them will say it all, with great economy of words.

Here is a story from Rabbi Nachman of Bratslav:

> Once a Jewish man from Austria dreamed that a valuable treasure was buried under a bridge in Vienna. He quickly

---

[13] Katz, Nathan, "A Meeting of Ancient Peoples: Western Jews and the Dalai Lama of Tibet", *Jerusalem Letters of Lasting Interest VP*:113, Mar 1991.

traveled there, anxious to find it, but when he arrived at the bridge, he just stood there. He did not know what to do. If he were to try searching during the day, people would wonder what he was looking for, and if it might be valuable.

Eventually a soldier passed by and saw him. The soldier stopped and asked the Jewish man what he was doing there; what he was looking for. After thinking about it for a while, the Jew told his secret to the soldier, offering to share the treasure with him if he helped him find it.

But the soldier just laughed, saying he felt sorry for such a crazy dreamer, and he told him he also had such a dream. His dream was that a valuable treasure was buried in the cellar of a certain Jew in a particular town. Still, he said, "Am I going to set off on a journey there?"

The name of the Jew was this man's name, and the town was his town. The Jew quickly excused himself, immediately hired a wagon and two horses, rushed back home, hurried down into the cellar, and dug up the treasure.

The Jew then understood the mystery that had been revealed to him. The treasure had always been buried there, but he had to leave town and travel far away to Vienna in order to discover it in his house

Chapter Seventeen.
Epilogue

One day I wandered along the wooded paths that crisscrossed the University of Washington campus in Seattle, and a massive log beckoned me into the forest. It lay in a small clearing, and young trees crowded around it, jostling to replace the old grandmother. I sat down on the log, and, to my amazement, I noticed tiny branches sprouting here and there directly out of the log itself, right where small branches had been cut away. I stood up to inspect, to see how that could be.

At least two feet across and five feet long, the log was all that remained of one of the great, primeval giants that dominate the forests of the Pacific Northwest. The bark was smooth and grey, not yet weathered. The log had been cut cleanly on both ends. The ends were not fresh, but they were not discolored with age either. No part of the log was embedded in the soil. There was no apparent connection to the ground. It simply was there, free and clear, above the surface. I kneeled and looked underneath. I only saw moss and leaves.

By what effort of will had the old tree managed to grow new life? Where were the new roots? I saw none. Was that vitality the reason why it had grown so powerful in the first place? Was this its last gasp, or was it about to show the saplings around it a thing or two? Did these tiny sprouts really have a future, or was this an exercise in futility, destined to end with their premature death? If I came back the next year, would I see them flourishing, proudly showing off their leaves?

Around my own home is a hardwood forest, and I have always felt awe and admiration at the majesty of the few great oaks and maples that tower over all the others, seemingly invincible. Yet, looking closely at the forest floor, here and there I can find delicate shoots shyly poking through the bushy ground cover. Over many seasons I have seen these young seedlings grow, become strong, put out branches, and start reaching upward. In just a few years, they become graceful saplings, and gradually they reach up to match the height of the great trees that sired them. As they mature, denizens of the forest no doubt revere these beautiful new trees, tell stories about them, and look up to them in admiration as they did to the ancient trees that once shaded whole portions of the forest. Finally, one after another, I have seen the oldest trees fall to the forest floor, and it is as if they never were.

But this tree trunk, stubborn, hopeful, still vital, was fighting back, offering up its own remaining strength in order to give birth to the progeny of its old age.

When I returned to campus the next year, I went searching for the log, but I could not find it. It should have been in a clear area of woods behind the original buildings on the campus. But where was it? And where were those woods? I only found acres and acres that were naked, the trees cut down, the site cordoned off by wire fencing and filled with the harsh sound of bulldozers. Only later I heard that the university needed housing for new students.

This is the way of the world. And my Indian friends accept it with serenity. That may be why we in the west look to India for wisdom, even if our grandmothers might have told us the same thing. Yet, there is something different about hearing that wisdom from the grandparents of India.

Two dear friends, both doctors from India, looked for months, probably over a year, for just the right lot for a new house. Finally, they found the perfect location, and they called us, all excited, to come over and inspect it with them. We did. It was fully forested, and lovely. I called later in the day, to see whether their offer had been accepted, and my friend calmly told me that someone had beaten them out with a higher bid. And the owner had accepted the other bid. I was appalled. I would have been beside myself, raging that I had missed calling in time, but, surprisingly, she did not seem to be upset.

I asked why she was not, and she answered that apparently it was not meant to be. "In India," she said, "We say that on every grain of rice is written the name of the person who will eat it."

In India, things are what they are destined to be.

And they also understand that the Divine is all around us. We just need to recognize it.

Another Indian friend once told me a story. One day, a holy woman was asleep on the ground in front of a Hindu temple that was built around the honored image of a god, when suddenly a passerby awakened her, crying, "How can you sleep like that, with the soles of your feet pointed in the direction of god?" The holy woman smiled apologetically, and said, "Oh, I am so sorry. Please, tell me which way god is *not*, and I will place my feet in that direction."

BIBLIOGRAPHY

Aurobindo, Sri Savitri (Pondicherry: Sri Aurobindo Ashram, 1993).

Adelman, Susan, *After Saturday Comes Sunday*, (New Jersey: Gorgias Press, 2018).

Bashkin, Orit, *Impossible Exodus – Iraqi Jews in Israel* (Stanford: Stanford University Press, 2017) (Kindle).

Bar Ye'or, *The Dhimmi: Jews and Christians under Islam*, rev. ed., trans. David Maisel (London: Associated University Press, 1985).

Bazak, Amnon, *To This Very Day: Fundamental Questions in Bible Study*, (Jerusalem: Koren Publishers, 2020).

Ben-Sasson, H. H., *A History of the Jewish People*, (Cambridge: Harvard University Press, 1969).

Bettany, George T., *The Great Indian Religions* (New York: Cosimo Classics, 2006), first published by Ward, Lock Bowden and Co. in 1892.

Blady, Ken, *Jewish Communities in Exotic Places*, (Northvale: Jason Aronson, Inc., 2000).

Boivin, Michel Ed., *Sindh through History and Representations* (Oxford: Oxford University Press, 2008).

Boorstein, Sylvia, *That's Funny, You Don't Look Buddhist: On Being a Faithful Jew and a Passionate Buddhist*, (San Francisco: HarperCollins, 1997).

Boyce, Mary, Zoroastrians – *Their Religious Beliefs and Practices* (London: Routledge, 1979).

Boyce, Mary and Grenet, Frantz, (Leiden: EJ Brill, 1991) *A History of Zoroastrianism, Vol III: Zoroastrianism under Macedonian and Roman Rule*, pp. 471–6 in the *Handbuch der Orientalistik*, C. van Dijk et al.

Brill, Alan, *Rabbi on the Ganges: A Jewish-Hindu Encounter*, (Lanham: Lexington Books, 2020).

Bromage, Bernard, *Tibetan Yoga*, (London: The Aquarian Press, 1952).

Bryant, Edwin, *The Quest for the Origins of Vedic Culture – The Indo-Aryan Migration Debate* (Oxford: Oxford University Press, 2001).

Buck, William, *Mahabharata* (Berkeley: New American Library, 1973).

Buck, William, *Ramayana* (Berkeley: New American Library, 1976).

Cadge, Wendy, *Heartwood: The First Generation of Theravada Buddhism in America*, (Chicago: The University of Chicago Press, 2004).

Carter, George and Badger, Richard G., *Zoroastrianism and Judaism* (Boston: The Gorham Press, 1918) (kindle).

Carus, Paul, *The History of the Devil and the Idea of Evil*, (1900) (Reprinted 2004 by Kessinger Publisher LLC, Whitefish MT).

Dalrymple, William and Anand, Anita, *Koh-i-nor, The history of the world's most infamous diamond*, (New York and London: Bloomsbury, 2017) p. 81.

Darmestet, James, trans., *The Zend Avesta Part I The Vendidad*, an ancient text republished.

Drescher, Frank, *Jewish Converts to Buddhism and the Phenomenon of "Jewish Buddhists" ("JuBus") in the United States, Germany and Israel*, (GRIN Verlag, Open Publishing 2012).

Durant, Will, *Our Oriental Heritage*, (New York: Simon and Schuster, 1954).

Durant, Will, *Our Oriental Heritage* (Story of Civilization Book 1) (on-line: Fine Communications, 1997).

Eban, Abba, *My People: The story of the Jews*, (New York: Random House and Behrman House, 1968).

Fitzhugh, William W., Rossabi, Morris, Honeychurch, William, *Genghis Khan and the Mongol Empire*, (Washington: Artic Studies Center Smithsonian Institution, 2013).

Foltz, Richard, *Iran in World History* (New York: Oxford University Press, 2016) (kindle).

Foltz, Richard, *Religions of Iran – from prehistory to the present* (London: Oneworld Publications, 2013).

Gaunt, David, *Massacres, Resistance, Protectors: Muslim-Christian Relations in Eastern Anatolia During World War I*, (Piscataway: Gorgias Press, 2008).

Gindin, Thamar E., *The Book of Esther Unmasked*, (Zeresh Books, 2016).

Goldenberg, Gideon, *Semitic Languages*, (Oxford: Oxford University Press, 2013).

Goodman, Hananiya Ed, *Between Jerusalem and Benares – Comparative Studies in Judaism and Hinduism* (Albany: State University of New York Press, (1994).

Goshen-Gottstein, Alon, *The Jewish Encounter with Hinduism: History, Spirituality, Identity*, (London: Palgrave Macmillan, 2016).

Richard Gottheil, and M. Seligsohn, "Helena," *Jewish Encyclopedia*, 1906, accessed in July 2016, http://www.jewishencyclopedia.com/articles/7525-helena

Grayzel, Solomon, *A History of the Jews*, (Markham Ontario: New American Library, 1968).

Hetzron, Robert, *The Semitic Languages*, (New York: Routledge, 1997).

Hobhouse, Penelope, *The Gardens of Persia*, (Carlsbad: Kales Press, 2004).

Hoffman, Adina and Cole, Peter, *Sacred Trash: The lost and found world of the Cairo Geniza*, (New York: Schocken Books, 2011).

Holdrege, Barbara A., *Veda and Torah – Transcending the Textuality of Scripture* (Albany: State University of New York Press, 1996).

Home, Charles F., *"The Kurash Prism: Cyrus the Great; The decree of return for the Jews, 539 BCE,"* Iran Chamber Society, April 7, 2016 accessed July 2016, https://tinyurl.com/ycskksrg

Hornkohl, Aaron, and Geoffrey Khan, eds. *Studies in Semitic Vocalisation and Reading Traditions.* Cambridge Semitic

Languages and Cultures 3. Cambridge: University of Cambridge & Open Book Publishers, 2020, https://www.openbookpublishers.com/product/1167

Ibrahim, Raymond, *Crucified Again: Exposing Islam's New War on Christians*, (Washington D.C.: Regnery Publishing, 2013).

Idel, Moshe, *Kabbalah, New Perspectives*, (New Haven: Yale University Press, 1988).

Israel, Benjamin, *The Bene Israel of India*, (Hyderabad: Orient Black Swan, 1984) (kindle).

Johnson, Clive, *Vedanta* (Toronto: Bantom Books, 1974).

Jung, C. G. *The Archetypes and the Collective Unconscious* (Princeton: Princeton University Press, 1990).

Kalmin, Richard, *Migrating Tales – The Talmud's Narratives and Their Historical Context* (Oakland: University of California Press, 2014).

Kalmin, Richard, *Jewish Babylonia between Persia and Roman Palestine* (Oxford: Oxford University Press, 2006).

Kamenetz, Rodger, *The Jew in the Lotus*, (New York: HarperSan Francisco, 1994).

Kaplan, Aryeh, *The Bahir*, an ancient book republished for Kindle.

Kaplan, Aryeh, *Jewish Meditation*, (New York: Schocken Books, 1985).

Kaplan, Aryeh, *Sefer Yetzirah: The Book of Creation in Theory and Practice* (San Francisco: Weiser Books, 1990).

Katz, Nathan, *Spiritual Journey Home: Eastern Mysticism to the Western Wall*, (Jersey City: KTAV Publishing House, 2009).

Katz, Nathan et al ed, *Indo-Judaic Studies in the Twenty-first Century: A view from the Margin*, (New York: Palgrave MacMillan, 2007).

Koller, Aaron and Tsadik, Daniel, *Iran, Israel and the Jews: Symbiosis and Conflict from the Achaemids to the Islamic Republic*, (Eugene: Wipf and Stock publishers, 2019).

Kumaraswamy, P.R., *India's Israel Policy*, (New York: Columbia University Press, 2010).

Levin, Yigal, *Judea, Samaria and Idumea: Three Models of Ethnicity and Administration in the Persian Period, 2012*, in Johannes Unsok Ro, ed., *From Judah to Judaea: Socio-economic Structures* and Processes in the Persian Period, (Sheffield, Sheffield Phoenix Press, 2012).

Lew, Alan, One God Clapping: The spiritual path of a Zen Rabbi, (New York: Kodansha America, 1999).

Lewis, Bernard, The Jews of Islam, (Princeton: Princeton University Press, 1984).

Lewis, Bernard, The Middle East: A Brief History of the Last 2,000 Years, (New York: Scribner, 1995).

Linzer, Judith, Torah and Dharma – Jewish Seekers in Eastern Religions (North Bergen: Jason Aronson Inc., 1996).

Lord Kinross, The Ottoman Centuries (New York: Morrow Quill Paperbacks, 1977).

Mallory, J.P., In Search of the Indo-Europeans – Language, Archaeology and Myth (London: Thames and Hudson, 1989)

Manasseh, Rachel, Baghdadian Jews of Bombay – Their life and achievements, a personal and historical account (Great Neck: Midrash Ben Ish Hai, 2013).

Margolis, Max L., and Marx, Alexander, History of the Jewish People, (Philadelphia: The Jewish Publication Society, 1967).

Metcalf, Barbara D., and Thomas R. Metcalf, A Concise History of Modern India, (Cambridge: Cambridge University Press, 2001).

Mortimer, Edward, Faith and Power: The Politics of Islam, (New York: Vintage Books, a division of Random House, 1982).

Muller, F. Max, The Sacred Books of the East, Parts I and II, (Delhi, Patna, Varanasi: Motilal Banarsidass, reprinted 1973).

Nagen, Yakov, Be, Become, Bless: Jewish Spirituality between East and West, (Jerusalem: Maggid Books, 2019).

Neusner, Jacob, Judaism and Zoroastrianism at the Dusk of Late Antiquity: How Two Ancient Faiths Wrote Down their Great Traditions, (Atlanta: Scholars Press, 1993).

Padmasambhava, The Tibetan Book of the Dead, (New York: Penguin Books, 2006).

Parpola, Asko, The Roots of Hinduism – The Early Aryans and the Indus Civilization (Oxford: Oxford University Press, 2015).

Prabhavananda, Swami and Manchester, Frederick trans. The Upanishads (Hollywood: New American Library, 1948).

Puhvel, Jaan, *Comparative Mythology* (Baltimore: The Johns Hopkins University Press, 1987).

Raphael, Chaim, *The Road from Babylon – The story of Sephardi and Oriental Jews* (New York: Harper and Row, 1985).

Roaf, Michael, *Cultural Atlas of Mesopotamia and the Ancient Near East*, (New York: Andromeda Book Oxford Ltd., 1996).

Robinson, Andrew, *The Indus – Lost Civilizations* (London: Reaktion Books, 2015).

Rose, Jenny, *Zoroastrianism: An Introduction*, (I.B. Tauris Introductions into Religion, ebook).

Sabar, Yona, *The Folk Literature of the Kurdistani Jews: An Anthology*, (New Haven: Yale University Press, 1982).

Secunda, Shai, *The Iranian Talmud – Reading the Bavli in its Sassanian Context* (Philadelphia: University of Pennsylvania Press, 2014).

Scheindlin, Raymond P., *A Short History of the Jewish People from Legendary Times to Modern Statehood*, (New York: Oxford University Press, 1998).

Shah, Mark, *Zoroastrianism: An introduction to Zoroastrianism*, Amazon, 2016.

Shoshanna, Brenda, *A guide to the practice of Judaism and Zen: Jewish Dharma*, (Philadelphia: Perseus Books Group, 2008).

Shulman, David and Shalva Weil Eds, *Karmic Passages: Israeli Scholarship on India*, (Oxford: Oxford University Press, 2008).

Sher Singh Sher, *Evolution of Sikh Faith and Its Followers*, (Amritsar: Dharam Parchar Committee, 2007).

Singh, Karnail, *Notes Towards the Definition of Sikhism*, (Amritsar: Dharam Parchar Committee, 2002).

Singh Shan, Harnam, *Guru Nanak Dev*, (Amritsar: Dharam Parchar Committee, 2008).

Sigalow, Emily, *American JuBu*, (Princeton: Princeton University Press, 2019).

Stanford, Ann trans. *The Bhagavad Gita* (New York: Herder and Herder, 1970).

Tatz, Akiva and Gottlieb, David, *Letters to a Buddhist Jew*, (Israel: Targum Press, Inc., 2004).

Theodor, Ithamar and Kornberg, Yudit, *Dharma and Halacha: Comparative Studies in Hindu-Jewish Philosophy and Religion*, (Lanham: Lexington Books, 2018).

Thubron, Colin, *Shadow of the Silk Road* (New York: Harper Perennial, 2006).

Toynbee, Arnold, *Mankind and Mother Earth*, (New York: Oxford University Press, 1976).

Wald, Shalom Salomon and Kandell, Arielle, *India, Israel and the Jewish People – Looking Ahead, Looking Back 25 Years after Normalization* (The Jewish People Policy Institute, 2016, online).

Weil, Shalva, *India's Jewish Heritage - Ritual, Art, and Lifecycle* (Mumbai: Marg Publications, 2002).

Weatherford, Jack, *Genghis Khan and the Making of the Modern World*, (New York: Crown Publishers, 2004).

Index